SURVIVING SECRETS

SURVIVING SECRETS

The experience of abuse
for the child, the adult
and the helper

Moira Walker

Open University Press
Buckingham • Philadelphia

Open University Press
Celtic Court
22 Ballmoor
Buckingham
MK18 1XW

and
1900 Frost Road, Suite 101
Bristol, PA 19007, USA

First Published 1992
Reprinted 1993

A catalogue record of this book is available from the
British Library

Library of Congress Cataloging-in-Publication Data

Walker, Moira, 1948–
    Surviving secrets: the experience of abuse for the child, the
adult, and the helper / Moira Walker.
        p.   cm.
    Includes bibliographical references and index.
    ISBN 0–335–09764–2 (hard)   ISBN 0–335–09763–4 (soft)
    1. Adult child abuse victims – England – Case studies.   I. Title.
RC569.5.C55W38   1992
616.85'822–dc20

                                                    92–9376
                                                       CIP

Typeset by Graphicraft Typesetters Ltd., Hong Kong
Printed in Great Britain by St Edmundsbury Press Ltd
Bury St Edmunds, Suffolk

To two of my clients
who shared the same name
who had similar experiences,
one of whom died and
one of whom survived so well

CONTENTS

Preface   ix

1 Introduction   1
2 A web of secrets: Generations of abuse   6
3 Adults reflect: The child's experience   34
4 Childhood abuse: The adult's experience   63
5 Sharing secrets: The child's and the adult's experience   93
6 The development of Multiple Personality Disorder   113
7 Stages in the process of counselling and therapy   143
8 Particular issues in the process of therapy   174
9 Issues for the helper   195

References   206
Index   208

PREFACE

Parting with any completed book feels like separating from an important part of oneself. Parting with this book has felt like parting with other people's most precious and private worlds. I am immensely grateful to all those who have shared so much with me so that this book could be written. In my interviews with abuse survivors it was evident that incorporating their stories into a book was empowering for them and highly significant to them. They were unanimous in wanting others to know their stories: both what had happened to them as children and the effects on them as adults. I cannot thank them enough for the time they gave me – which was considerable – and for entrusting themselves to me. Throughout the book their own words have been extensively used. Minor alterations have been made to ensure clarity, but great care has been taken not to alter the sense of what they said. In order to protect the identity of those I interviewed, all names have been changed.

In this book I have been concerned to explore abuse in all its forms, and consequently the people I have included have experienced a range of abuse – physical, sexual and psychological. I was also concerned to include both men and women. That more women were in fact interviewed than men, and the same is true of the examples drawn from my clinical experience, was in spite of efforts on my part and others to talk with more men. This may suggest that men are more reluctant to talk, or it may reflect the fact that girls and women are abused in greater numbers. Statistical conclusions cannot and should not be drawn from my sample. The stories of these men and women are powerful and meaningful in themselves.

There are many other people I also want to thank. A particular mention and a great thank-you goes to Janet Perry, of the Leicester Family Service Unit. She took considerable interest in this project and was able to put me in touch with a number of those whom I interviewed. Her efforts in support of this book are greatly appreciated. I also want to thank John and Marcia Davis of Warwick University, Rhoda Oppenheimer, John Southgate and his team at the Institute for Self Analysis in London, the National Association for Young People in Care, and David Brandon: they all shared their ideas and experiences with me, which helped me to clarify my own. In the early stages of writing Kay Brutnall greatly helped in the organization and sorting of my material, and my thanks go to her.

However, there is a very special thank-you, and that is to my husband Michael Jacobs. Our marriage began in the midst of writing this book, and has taken over much of my life since. He has been my constant loving support when I was in danger of being overwhelmed by both the quantity and the content of the material. His practical help in assisting with the tedious and lengthy job of organizing and reorganizing data into manageable quantities has been immeasurably helpful. My thanks and love as always go to my daughters Tessa and Sarah, just for being there and always reminding me of other worlds.

Moira Walker
University of Leicester
Counselling Service

ONE

INTRODUCTION

Abuse takes many forms and can involve just one or a combination of these. This book encompasses the whole range of abuse: the individuals who speak through it have been physically, psychologically and sexually abused. Many have suffered more than one form of abuse, and many have been abused by more than one person. This is not an unusual pattern: abuse often comes from more than one source.

Children who have been abused do not have high expectations of others. They do not expect help. They often do not have a sense of indignation when they are ill-treated. They do not feel or impart positive messages about themselves. They cannot easily be self-protective. It is essential to recognize and acknowledge that abuse of a child leads to huge developmental damage which has ongoing implications. The effects do not simply disappear or evaporate as the child reaches adulthood. As later chapters demonstrate, the ripples from abuse spread far and wide into the adult's world, the adult's experience and the adult's relationships. When we talk about a child who has been abused, we are also talking about a person who grows up carrying those experiences inside. We need to recognize that:

> Child abuse is not simply less than optimal child rearing. It is a pattern of behaviour that drastically violates both moral and scientific norms concerning child care.
> (Gabarino and Gilliam 1980:70–1)

Abuse is not a new phenomena: it has a horrifically long history. However, a century ago it would not have been identified as such:

> A book on child abuse could not have been written a hundred years ago. If an investigator were to be transported back to the nineteenth century so that he could survey the family scene with modern eyes, child abuse would be clearly visible to him. In the past, however, it was largely invisible to families and their communities. Before it could be acknowledged as a social ill, changes had to occur in the sensibilities and outlook of our culture.
>
> (Kempe and Kempe 1978:16)

Nowadays the extent and frequency of abuse is being revealed on an almost daily basis. It is a popular misconception that all children, with rare exceptions, are valued and well cared for. This is a comfortable view, but the number of children who are not so positively cared for exist in large numbers. The uncomfortable and threatening reality is that abuse is a widespread problem, permeating all social classes. The Kempes' words remain as valid as when they were written: at any given time society will only believe what is both visible and what is acceptable to society. And what is visible is a more complex phenomenon than is at first apparent. It is closely linked to what is acceptable or unacceptable to the individuals in society at that time.

Denial and resistance are powerful aspects of the psychology both of the individual and, collectively, of society. Both defences come strongly into play if the beliefs and values of either are threatened. Abuse can be, and in effect is, denied, both by those who perpetrate it and by others. The ability of abusers to deny their behaviour, even when presented with incontrovertible evidence, is astounding. And, at another level, society similarly denies abuse. For instance, there was a significant time-lag between the identification of battered children by social work agencies and the police and the wider awareness and acceptance of this by the general public. This is serious and worrying. Similarly, sexual abuse was slow to be recognized. And, although most clinicians and researchers agree that girls are more at risk, boys are also sexually abused, possibly in greater numbers than is generally thought:

Often, when the topic of sexual victimization of boys is raised, it is followed by expressions of disbelief. Many people do not want to admit that boys are 'the other victims' of sex crimes... Boys who are victimized and males who are struggling to survive and heal are confronted by accusations of latent homosexuality.

(Grubman-Black 1990:vii)

Sexual abuse of boys is not widely acknowledged and denial is evident.

Similarly, it was clear from the interviews I conducted in researching this book that mothers abuse, as well as fathers and male relatives. They not only physically abuse, they also sexually abuse, or actively participate in male sexual abuse. Again, the risk of sexual abuse from men is far greater, but helpers and others should be aware of their own possible bias. We come back to the power of resistance and the universality of denial: if the possibility is neither perceived nor accepted, the reality cannot be identified. Evidence is either rejected or is prevented from entering consciousness. Admitting that their mothers have sexually abused them is extremely painful for girls and women. They can face the same difficulty as men do when they attempt to reveal sexual abuse. They experience a disbelieving world that denies their reality.

A similar situation is faced by those who are abused within organized rings, or who have been ritually abused. The debate over the existence or otherwise of 'ritual abuse' and 'satanic abuse' continues. Lynn Eaton (1991:8) comments that:

the profession has moved away from using the terms 'ritual abuse' or 'ritualistic abuse', which have been linked in people's minds with satanism, to 'organised abuse' or 'abuse with bizarre elements'. The two latter terms have been given the official stamp of approval and are now used by the Department of Health.

The descriptions of ritual abuse given by those who have survived it are horrifying in the extreme. In working with abuse survivors, helpers encounter the most intolerable and sickening aspects of human behaviour, in whatever way they are labelled.

As child abuse becomes more widely recognized and identified, and media attention grows, more and more survivors of abuse are coming to therapists and counsellors for help. While it is impossible accurately to quantify the extent of the abuse of children, it appears to many clinicians that this is very considerably greater than was previously believed. Although there are still some who prefer to deny its existence, those of us who work in the caring professions have to face a major problem which causes enormous distress, unhappiness and psychological ill-health. If we are to provide a competent, caring and informed service, we need to question our approach, our attitudes and our feelings. Our practice needs to be informed by knowledge – knowledge that can come only from listening to those who have been abused.

Even if there are some difficulties in distinguishing different child-rearing patterns from abusive practices – and it can be argued that both class and culture need to be taken into account – the question remains: are there some behaviours which are always intrinsically harmful to children? For instance, some societies consider circumcision of female children acceptable, while in other societies this is unacceptable abuse. Whatever the difficulties in defining abuse, and in reaching a consensus on acceptable child-care practices, it is nevertheless essential to recognize as an indisputable fact that abuse of children exists and that it is not a rare occurrence. It can and it does happen anywhere: in the home, in schools, in children's homes and in hospitals. Children in any setting that is isolated from ongoing external observation, for whatever reason, are particularly vulnerable. A child's lack of power and autonomy can be intensified, emphasized and exploited within such settings.

It must be recognized too that child abusers come from all walks of life. They do not look like monsters; they are not generally societal drop-outs or obvious failures in life. They represent a cross-section of society. It can never be safely assumed that a person's position or their job ensures they will not abuse children. They may have sought out that position in order to do so. In many areas of their life the abuser can be successful, talented and popular. As I demonstrate in later chapters, many of those I interviewed were abused by apparently 'respectable' people. I have already indicated that women also abuse children: older children also abuse – both their younger siblings and younger children in schools.

Those of us who work with abuse survivors often hear things we would prefer not to hear and not to believe. That does not make what we hear unbelievable, although it may well be inconceivable. It is hard to believe the tortures that children have to endure. It is hard to believe that any human being could treat a small and powerless person in such terrible ways. It is even harder to believe that they systematically organize with others in order to do so. But they can, and they do – as these accounts will show. Those who have been abused can speak here for themselves. They must be believed, even if belief necessitates facing unpalatable and painful truths. But to face the truth is nowhere near as painful as the experiences that have already been faced by these survivors.

TWO

A WEB OF SECRETS: GENERATIONS OF ABUSE

When I was researching this book, many people who had suffered childhood abuse trusted me with their stories. To retell them in full would have taken more than one book. But their own words demonstrate so powerfully the nature of abuse that I can do justice to them all only by reproducing at least some of them in full. I am concerned to demonstrate that abuse is not a new phenomenon: in their different generations, Allen's, Jane's and Nicki's stories vividly capture both the nature and extent of abuse and the variety of contexts in which it occurs.

ALLEN

When I met him, Allen was in his sixties, living in the community in a local authority flat. It was clearly his pride and joy, representing the home he had been deprived of for so long. He had spent twenty-four years in hospital. His experience both before hospitalization and during it demonstrates powerfully how abuse occurs in many settings and takes many forms. Allen's story speaks for itself:

> As far back as I can remember I was in an orphanage, but those years were good and I really knew love and affection. I was taken from there when I was five years old, and I was

told I was going to have a mother to live with. It seemed a lovely promise to me: I'd never seen or known a mother, so I couldn't wait to go. But when I got there it was a massive boarding-house with lots of adult boarders. It was all right for the first few months, though I went to three different schools in that time and never learned anything.

But it all changed. One day I got home from school, pleased to be home. I went to sit down, only to have the chair pulled from under me and be told to 'Get into the bleeding scullery – that's where you belong.' I wasn't allowed to sleep in what was called the boarders' room any more. I got pushed into the attic. From when I was five and a half to when I was eleven, I slept on the attic floor. I had no bed, and I used to get food from begging on the streets. I used to ask for stale bread, saying it was for the poultry. A lot of people knew the bread was for me, not the chickens, but they never said or did anything.

I've tried to think why she did it to me. I think she fostered for the money. I did find out in later years she was diagnosed as schizophrenic; she'd love you one moment and batter you half to death the next. I got this [pointing to a very badly damaged leg] when I was seven and a half. I was three minutes late from school and she belted me. I fell, and a boiling pan of water fell over me and that was the end of my leg. I was taken into a room, not my attic, and the doctor came. Of course, what really happened was covered up.

When the health people used to come and check up on me, they *never* saw me alone. She'd sit right opposite and made sure I answered as she wanted, and I knew what would happen afterwards if I didn't. So they never got to know about the beatings and what was going on: how *could* I tell them?

When I was eleven, one of the boarders came home when I was being beaten. He'd always been very kind to me and used to feed me. I think he reported it; and one day people came to school and asked me questions. I kept my mouth shut. I didn't think they'd believe me anyway and I thought she'd find out, and it would be even worse if I told on her.

Then they came to the house – just pushed their way into the attic – and I was removed immediately. They told me I was going into a nice big home. It was! It was a mental institution! I was taken into a meal, and it was overwhelm-

ing. The dining-hall could seat about 400 patients, and one of
the first things I saw was someone having an epileptic fit.

I was the only child in the whole place, and I got put on an
assessment ward. We went through locked doors into the
ward. It had bars; and this was where I was to live. Wherever
you went there were keys. They even measured the water in
the bath. Although I tried to talk to the other patients, they
were all twice my age; and so I just sat in a corner and stayed
put. I had to fold my clothes in a certain way, and was told
that I'd get a belting if I didn't. I was put in a little room; the
door was slammed and locked and there were bars at the
windows. The only good thing was that I had a bed. I just
lay there thinking 'What have I done to deserve this?' The
only sin I'd committed was being born.

I was frightened being among all those people. My job
[remember he was still only eleven] was to scrub floors; it
made me feel a bit more secure to be doing something, to be
working. There was an exercise yard, so I'd walk around for
a bit; and then I'd just sit in a corner until mealtimes. And it
was always the same corner. It was barbaric. I lived in a land
of fear. If you broke their rules, the punishment was to scrub
concrete with a brick and cold water; the ration of food
would be cut, and you weren't allowed to speak to anyone. I
did get moved to a second ward, and that was a bit better: it
was locked but not barred. You had to be careful to do what
you were told, or it was back to the first ward.

The attendants weren't qualified – all they needed was to
be good with their fists. They treated me terribly. I got
beaten up on the ward. One day I just asked one of the
attendants a question and he hit me in the mouth because I'd
spoken to him first. They used to throw you in baths of cold
water. They would soak towels and they'd wrap them round
your body and then beat you so you wouldn't bruise –
though it wouldn't have mattered anyway; no one would
have noticed.

The worst thing was the sex that went on. I was sexually
abused by staff and patients. You could walk down the ward
in the day and it was nothing to see an attendant in bed with
a patient. I didn't really understand what was going on at
first: I was only a child. It happened to me a lot. As I got
older I got wiser and better at avoiding it, but not when I
was small. I still get nightmares about all that. I remember

one or two staff who were good to me, but there weren't many like that. There was one who cared in the proper sense of the word, not sexual but loving. I was sent to Rampton for a while for disobedience – I refused to stand up when the superintendent came in. It was the same in there, though at least Rampton was more open about it – they didn't put a show on, they didn't pretend. I often thought I'd die in hospital. There was no hope.

When I was finally released, after twenty-four years, I started getting the wrong sorts of sexual urges. And I thought if I started doing to children what had been done to me, and those children turned out like me, I'd not be fit to walk this earth. It was like crying in the night. Nobody wanted to hear or know. I attempted suicide. The first time I didn't make a very good job of it. The second time I nearly died. Suicide was still a crime. I got put back into hospital and I was prepared to take any treatment; I didn't care what it did as long as it stopped these urges. I was a guinea-pig for a drug. It was very painful, sometimes unbearable, and I had swelling of the breasts. I was very embarrassed – I'd never take my coat off or anything – but it was worth it, and now I don't need it any more. I've been a happy man ever since.

The costs? I am bitter still. Nothing is going to compensate me for all those years. They're gone. Sometimes I'm like a child. I had nothing for so long – like thirty-five years wiped out. I really like parties and things, and birthday cards – there's a lot of catching-up to do. Having my own front door now is marvellous. I can do what I like. If I want to go to bed I can. But there are high costs – living on my own can be very hard, difficult and painful. You see, all those years I didn't have to think for myself: it was done for me – you were always told. So things can be frightening. But things can be exciting – like you coming today. What an excitement – I've really been looking forward to it! And I don't have any money. I've just enough to live. I'm happy, but sometimes when I'm on my own it crowds in on me, closes in on me. And I still can't read and write. I can read print, that's all. I'm dependent entirely on other people.

The most important message I want to get across is that sexual abuse – all abuse – isn't new. It's been going on through the ages. There are so many walking around who have been abused in childhood. Many of them are in prisons and such like; and they need treatment, not punishment. And I want people to know. I want those in training to know what went wrong for me so they don't do it all over again.

The catalogue of abuse is clear: a tragic cocktail of physical and emotional deprivation, of sexual and physical abuse, by many people over a period of years. It is tempting to see Allen's story as ancient history, representing an unfortunate chapter in the delivery of mental health services in Britain. After all, Allen's earliest experiences of residential care were before the watershed of social policy which followed the end of the Second World War. But in the next generation Jane's experience was little different.

JANE

Jane's story similarly shows how abuse takes place in many contexts, and may involve various abusers at different times. When she talked to me, she was in her forties. She had survived much, and was more hopeful for the future. She was living in her own flat. When I visited her it was clear that for her, too, having her own home was a source of both security and tremendous pleasure for her, and a mark of how far forward she had moved. She was then studying part-time in the adult education department of her local university. The quality of Jane's life was improving greatly. But the abuse that had continued for so many years had taken a heavy toll. Again, Jane's words say it all:

My father first sexually abused me. He raped me when I was fourteen. I was living with him after my mother had left us. So I ran away and eventually ended up with her and my stepfather. I did tell my mother, but she totally ignored it. It felt as if she was saying, 'Now you know what a bastard he is, and now you should understand why I left him.' What he had done to me was simply used to justify her position. That was the end of my schooling. I never went to school again. So my education was ruined. I feel as if I stopped growing at that time – like being told just to shut up, ignore it.

It was difficult with my mother when I was younger too. It was for all of us. She emotionally and physically abused all of us. We were all frightened of her violence. I reacted to

her violence at a very early age, but it made things worse.
I couldn't have told anyone, but someone did because the
NSPCC came. They went away again. They only talked to
my mother. They didn't talk to me. My mother was a
powerful figure, a power in the house, and what she said
went. But she never protected me.

My uncle sexually abused me as well, and my stepfather. I
think my uncle thought that, as my father got away with it,
he would too. Nothing was done about my father, so nothing would happen to him either. I think he also realized
I wouldn't say anything, because I was too frightened or too
stupid. And I knew all along that it was a waste of time
telling anyone. No one told me that; they didn't need to say a
word: I just knew. My uncle didn't have intercourse with
me, it was just touching and so on. It even happened when
my mother was around, because it was when we were on
holiday. It was like part of the holiday. I did love him and
I enjoyed it. He was special. I didn't really know what
was happening then, though I think I did know it was
wrong.

My stepfather sexually abused me, as though he took over
where my father left off. That went on for years. I only told
my mother and family when he died. They didn't stand by
me: they blamed me. And I moved away from the area. So I
was the one who was blamed. I was guilty by running away.
To them that proved my guilt. He'd conned them, you see,
but not me. The abuse with him went on right into my adult
years. Except in so many ways I was still the child in the
adult.

I was very relieved when he died. I got summoned to his
death-bed. He came around, and asked God to forgive him.
I was still frightened of him even when he was just like a
skeleton. My sister doesn't understand that I was always
frightened of him and still was then. The feeling didn't go. I
was frightened of him until I moved into my own flat. He
had the ability to allow things in the family to be either OK
for me or not OK. It was that simple. He had enormous
power either to keep it safe for me or to wreck it for me. It's
very hard for me, because I got pushed out of the family. As
far as they're concerned I was the one who was difficult. I
was the one who spoilt things. I did it to them, made them
suffer. That's the hardest thing – that it all gets put on to me.

I did expect better from my sister. She's in the medical profession. She should know better; she's not ignorant like the others. She is more aware than the others, and now my relationship with her is improving.

I had two children. One of them died of cot death when he was small. The other was taken into care when he was nine months old, and finally he was adopted. I just couldn't cope with being with a man, and I'd gone back home to live because there was nowhere else to go. But the abuse from my stepfather went on, and I left. I couldn't take it any more. So the baby went into care, and I got admitted to psychiatric hospital. I was in hospital for the next sixteen years. It became home. No one there ever knew what it was about, although sometimes I'd find myself sitting on the floor screaming, 'I hate him! I hate him!' No one knew who I meant or what I was saying, of course. And nobody asked. I lost a period of my life. At one time I was on a Section [detained against her will under the appropriate section of the then 1959 Mental Health Act] and I was on a locked ward. I used to try to kill myself, and I'd cut myself. I was quite violent towards myself. I'm covered all over in scars. I thought if I changed the way I looked my stepfather wouldn't be interested in me.

One of the male nurses was abusive too. He was a powerful man, and he used his power. He'd let you have a cigarette, and he'd let you go over to the cafeteria, but he had to have a kiss first and he'd touch you up. That's all. So you could have your cigarettes and go out if you were good, but there was a price. At the time I obviously thought it was worth it to get out. He was doing it to others, not just me, and there were others like him. There were two or three of them, and a group of us all the same age that they did it to. I was in and out of hospital; and when I wasn't there I had to go home. There was nowhere else to go, but it meant I went back to the abuse.

Hospital really became home, although not a nice home. The hospital told my mother and sister that I'd never come out, that I'd be there the rest of my life. I just slowly deteriorated as the years went on. I feel as if my soul was slowly murdered. I wasn't very nice to know, anyway – I really wasn't – because one way and another I lost that part of myself. In hospital no one knew anything about me, and nobody ever asked me what I thought it was all about. They never even told me what they thought was wrong with me. The charge-nurse used to make all the reports. I very rarely saw a doctor.

The only time I saw a doctor in the hospital was when he came to give me drugs. Then the heavy mob would come with him. It would take about six of them to hold me down and someone would stick a needle in me. It never occurred to anyone (and I'm not at all convinced that psychiatry is really different today) that all they were doing was treating the symptoms and saying 'Bugger the problem'. All the talking was done by the charge-nurse, but not to you, only about you. They used to have these little meetings among themselves. But you were never included. When I was still on a Section my stepfather would visit, and they let me go out with him. They sent me off with the very person who was abusing me; and so it still carried on.

Being in hospital was a complete waste of time. Nothing about it helped. They put me in hospital and watched my slow deterioration as the years went by, watching the life going out of me. I became a wild animal who periodically fought and needed the heavy mob to get me under control.

I'll tell you about one nurse who was different. I was in a locked ward and she worked nights. When she came on duty she would sing a song, 'Genevieve'. That was our song, and I knew when I heard it that it was all going to be all right. She'd do all the things that night nurses do, and then she'd make a tray of tea for her and her colleague and she'd unlock the door and I'd come out and join her. She'd bring me cakes, and she'd let me sit and talk; and she'd talk to me, not *at* me, *to* me. She never had any trouble with me, because she treated me as a human being. She obviously thought about me. She unlocked that door and let me out and let me in. When she was there it was safe – there were no more dreadful long nights.

Things started to be different when they moved me [to an NHS therapeutic community]. The first thing that happened there was that they saw to my teeth, my dress, my hair – everyday things, very obvious things that no one had bothered about before. I hadn't been to the dentist in years. I came off my medication slowly: I'd been on very heavy doses. They won't have people on drugs there. It was ack-

nowledged that I'd been abused. I went to this interview and
someone said, 'What's been the matter all this time?' And I
thought, '*Me*? Are you really talking to *me*?' So I told them. I
told them all about the abuse when I was little, and the rape
by my father, and my stepfather continuing it.

They realized I was someone with very low self-esteem. I
didn't see myself as having any value. I was there for fourteen months. I'd been in hospital for years by then. It was
very, very helpful, but coming out was hell. The first couple
of years were dreadful. It would have been so much easier to
go back. When I left I think they wondered if I'd survive. I
nearly didn't. I tried to hang myself. It was all so hard. I just
didn't know how to cope with the world.

The last five years have been the best. Each year things get
better. I'm in therapy now, and that's been harder than I
expected, but it's the best thing that's ever happened. I've
found it very difficult to trust, and much more has come out
than I realized. I sometimes get to the stage when I think that
we're almost there, and then I find something else. I have this
great urge at times to run away from it, but I don't. Hospital
was just doing things to me, whereas therapy has been working together on it. It's painful, it hurts, but it's a different
sort of pain. It's hard to explain, but in that hospital, with
all those different people involved, it was private, a secret.
The secret becoming not a secret is hard. You have to trust
the other person, and the trust is ever so fragile. But then it's
like lifting a weight, letting go of that secret, and all the
secrets that go with it. It's not just the one – lots go together.
It's lifting it and discovering you can trust.

I had a bad time recently. I came home and I regressed. I
put it down on paper and sent it to my therapist. And I
regretted it the minute I'd done it. But when I saw her the
next week it hadn't mattered. And I was so moved, because
nobody was ever trustworthy for me before. I realize now,
through therapy, that I can almost set myself up, by expecting perfection from myself and others. I realize it can't be like
that. It's taken me years to get to the point where I'm able to
trust people without them being perfect. Knowing that they
will make mistakes, but that it's all right: that it's not a total
betrayal, that it's just a mistake. The other thing that has
helped enormously has been setting up a support group.
That's been really important.

Looking back on my childhood and all those years in hospital, it was nightmarish, it was hellish, it was all spoilt. Eventually you are all on your own. You've got no friends, no life, nothing of your own. No books, none of the things we take for granted. That's why this place [her flat] is so important. It makes what I've got now sweeter. And I never take anything for granted. My own books, flowers, cuddly toys – just everything is so precious.

It still leaves me with a lot. Things are not easy with my family; it's stormy with them. When my stepfather died, I thought, 'Thank God for that.' He kept on trying to abuse me, although the last time he didn't get away with it. I couldn't say anything, but I was able to storm out; and after that I never went near the place again when he was around. My mother has never taken it seriously and still thinks he was a marvellous man. I've never been allowed to talk about it properly. I hate going to her place because of all these photos of this so-called perfect man. Now he's dead they talk about him: 'Your dad this, your dad that.' I hate it when they do that. It really gets to me deep down, those photos of this 'lovely' man. It was the same when my uncle died: he got the photograph treatment too.

There are positive things from surviving, though I want to do more than survive. I want to live. I really like having different values from my family. I can go my own way, decide things for myself. I'm set free from my family, and that's meant I've been free to have good friends and special friends in a way that they don't have. I'm not like my family, and I'm glad about that.

Relationships with men are very difficult still, and generally I don't put myself in situations where I'll meet men. I did have a boyfriend when I was in hospital. I used to go to his place at weekends. But I got hell-bent on destroying it. I heartily regret not meeting him now. He had the ability to love me in spite of everything. But it was at the wrong time. Eventually he physically abused me. It became so that I wasn't happy unless he was hitting me. I find that very confusing; but it was as if I had to make him like all the others, as if I couldn't take anything nice. I couldn't have sex unless he was hitting me. But none the less he was there, and I never lost the sense of a world outside because of him. I'm very grateful to him for that.

I still find it hard to be around pregnant women and babies, because I can get very powerful feelings about wanting to hurt them, and wanting to smash my head against a wall. Thinking about it, perhaps it's trying to get rid of motherhood and what it stands for. Or trying to get rid of my inability to have any maternal feelings inside me, as if they had all been killed and I was left dead inside.

I do have a strong sense of where I want to go to now. I know where my life is going. I am already involved in working with abuse survivors, and I also run training workshops. The only way that what happened to me is not a waste of time is if I use it now. When I first started to work in this area it was because someone asked me to do it. Now it's because it's essential to me that I do it. And my own studies are very important to me. I missed out on education, so I was almost illiterate. Having to write terrifies me, because I know my standard of English is not good. But I'm working on it. And the satisfactions are enormous.

What I really want to say to people in the workshops I run is: 'This is what it's like. This is what it does to you.' Most people may have an idea what it's like, but they don't really know. Often they don't want to know, because they can't cope: they don't want to think about it, because they can't deal with it. Maybe it's not that they don't want to see, it's just that they can't. It's difficult to explain the sheer terror of abuse. There just aren't the words. They're inappropriate or not enough, and sometimes that can make me feel very helpless. Sometimes people react by feeling very guilty because they've had a good life. That's no help. I don't want to guilt-trip people – they do that quite well by themselves.

Both Jane's and Allen's stories clearly demonstrate the potential for abuse within institutions. This can take more than one form: accepted and formalized practices under the guise of 'treatment' and abuse that occurs through individual or group misuse of power. If we are to take abuse seriously, we have to believe that it occurs in settings other than the home, and that it frequently involves those whom we have entrusted to be carers, not abusers.

NICKI

Even though Jane's story is more recent, the question may still optimistically be asked; haven't things now changed? Allen was the oldest person I interviewed. Nicki, aged sixteen, was the young-est, and her story may help to address that question:

I was first in care from when I was about eighteen months old to when I was five, and those years were the happiest days of my life. I was in care then with foster parents, and it was really good. I was happy and looked after properly.

My mother got me back from care, and I went to live with her and my new stepdad. Even at that age I knew I didn't want to go back to my mum. I wanted to live with my dad, and he did try for custody when I was five. But they thought I should be with my mum, and I don't suppose anyone asked me what I wanted. My mum got what she wanted, I didn't. And once she got me she didn't want me.

She was very cruel. Now I think she must have had a mental illness: her idea of reality wasn't anyone else's. But I didn't understand that when I was five. My stepdad was on the buses and had these heavy jackets and boots. If me or my brothers and sisters did anything wrong my mum would make us stand with our arms outstretched with a boot on each hand and with the jacket on. She'd make us stand for ages, and if our arms dropped she'd beat us and force our arms up again. In the winter she used to stand me outside naked.

She just never cared for us. My brother and I would be made to clean the house at night. She used to go out and come back in the early hours. If anything was out of place she'd beat us. My brother and I used to protect one another as much as we could. We were very close. One day my mother battered my brother and he had two black eyes and a cut along his back. She put make-up on him, and sent him to school with a note to say he'd fallen off his bike. And they believed that. How could they? I did have one teacher who was really nice. She didn't know what was going on, though, but she was kind – I'd like to thank her.

As I got older I used to look after all the younger children, do the shopping, make sure they went to school – every-thing. I was always mum because I was the oldest, but that meant I was the scapegoat too. I got into trouble if anything went wrong. And we were always moving, so I could never settle. In all I've been to fourteen schools and had thirty moves.

When I was younger I used to see my father sometimes. I

don't think he knows the half of what my mother did to me.
And neither of them know that I was sexually abused by a
family friend. That went on between the ages of eight and
ten. I didn't tell anyone. Who was there to tell? My mum
wouldn't have believed me anyway, and I'd have been scared
what she'd do to me. She certainly wouldn't have believed it
wasn't my fault, because everything always was my fault.
I don't know if social workers were visiting. They know
about her now. They know her three eldest children were
physically abused for years. Three of us have been in care.
But nobody is protecting the two youngest. My stepdad gets
drunk and beats my mum up in front of them, and one of
my little sisters got hurt recently. And she's child-minding.
Social services say they can't do anything yet.

I went back into care a couple of years ago and I got sent
to an assessment centre. They said my head was totally
fucked up and they were very supportive to me. But I was
only there two months, and then I was moved to a long-stay
unit and things deteriorated. One thing was that I'd have
a key worker for about two months and then they'd leave. I
had five in all, and the last two I really didn't get on with,
because I was just so sick of what was going on. One man
I found impossible. He was really unfair and used to throw
his weight around. I really didn't like it. He was quite subtle
about how he did it, but he used to get at me. No one did
anything about it – staff didn't support you: even when they
knew someone was in the wrong, they'd stick together.

Being in care is awful. You have no privacy in children's
homes. You can't have your friends to stay or even to come
in. There's no space of your own. You don't have any pos-
sessions; it all belongs to the local authority. It's not your
room, or your bed or your duvet – it's all theirs. Nothing is
yours. When you get moved you just chuck everything into
a black bin-liner – and it all goes in, you've got so little. I got
moved into a semi-independent unit when I was sixteen. I
had nothing. It took them weeks to even get me blankets and
things. It's just a room, and I hate it there. It makes me feel
claustrophobic. I just have to get out all the time.

Where's it all left me? I find it difficult to settle anywhere
now, I'm really restless and unsettled. I can't be still. I think
it's because I've had so many moves, and because it all eats
me up inside. I'm very bitter and resentful, and I know I

need help with all that. They didn't help me with any of that in care, except for the two months at the assessment centre. Then I just got left with it all again. They just didn't want to know.

I desperately need some support for myself, because I've got no one now. I want to try to find a counsellor, but I've got no money. I really want to go to college and get my exams, but I can't go, because I haven't got any money and no one will fund me. So I have to try to get a job. But what I really want to do is to study and get myself trained. I've missed out on my education.

I've lost having a family. I hate my mum and I can't forgive her for what she's done. She won't face up to any of it, and she has a lot of power in the family. I did see her once last year, and she threatened me and screamed abuse at me. I do see one of my brothers, but my two little sisters are with my mother still and she's told them I'm dead, so I can't see them. I did visit one of them at school once, on her birthday, but it was too emotional for her and she burst into tears – and so did I, because I couldn't handle what my mother was doing to them. So I don't see them. There is another brother, and I don't even know how old he is. My father has got three children, and I see them occasionally, but only when my stepmother says I can. Christmas is worst, wondering where I can go.

Something else it's left me with is difficult to explain. It's a trick I learned when my mother was battering me. I learned to turn off my nervous system when she hit me so I couldn't feel it. It protected me then. I'm not sure I could have stood it otherwise, the pain. But it effects me really badly now. Because if anyone threatens me or attacks me, I can't protect myself – I just freeze.

I think what I'd like to say to people who read this is that some of the residential social workers, at least the good ones, really have tried. But others didn't try – they really misused their power. They are abusive, and lots of us would tell you the same. You go from being abused at home to being abused in care. And they have a lot of power, because in the end they're always believed. It's not been good enough, and the ones who try need to work with us against the ones at the top who really make the decisions. Because the system is no good. It does not work. Being in care has not worked. And I really need support, and somewhere that's nice to live, and help to sort my head out, and help practically to live; and I need to know my little sisters are safe. They should not be in that home. But I'd fight to have them kept out of care. I'd look after them, I'd have them live with me, if people would help me to. So you can see that I don't have any of the things I need. What good was being in care? None.

The worst two things about my life are that it's been just soul-destroying and that I've lost my innocence. I've never had a childhood. If I'm ever around kids, whatever they're doing – playing, climbing trees – I want to join in. I never had any of that. My home started to destroy my soul. Being in care finished it.

Nicki's story cannot be rationalized as history. What she spoke of is current practice, and reflects sadly upon the experience of many children and young people who are or who have been in care. The pattern of removal from the home because of abuse followed by abuse within the system is one that is frequently described. It is worth noting that both Allen and Nicki had good early experiences in care. Perhaps for both of them their later history might have been very different if their own wishes had been taken into account, and if someone had acted as an advocate for them.

HANNAH'S STORY

These stories demonstrate that abuse of all types takes place in every generation. It is not just happening now – it has always happened. In some cases abuse occurs in different generations of the same family. Chapter 4 shows that for many survivors their ultimate triumph is in stopping the cycle of abuse, but this was not possible in the two instances that follow. Hannah's own experience of severe physical abuse by her mother in childhood is told in the next chapter. Although she was at times taken into care, this failed to protect her. She was returned, only to suffer further abuse. Here she recounts how she discovered that her own child had been abused by her partner, and she describes the response from the very agencies that had also failed to protect her as a child:

My son and my stepdaughter had been abused by my ex-partner. Unfortunately I didn't recognize the signs. I knew

Lucy was very unhappy, and I used to try to sit with her and talk to her because I knew something was going on. She was desperately unhappy, but she couldn't say what it was. I was very ill, and due to go into hospital for a hysterectomy, but I'd made arrangements for her when I was in hospital, and I'd got people to look after her. It was at that time she told me what her daddy had been doing. She was nine, and Bob was two and a half.

He was prosecuted and found guilty, and got a prison sentence. After he'd got sent down we found out he'd abused my little boy too. I went through hell with social services. It was very hard to believe that this person I'd loved could do this to his children. We'd even watched programmes together and he'd said he didn't know how people could do that. He and my mum, neither of them could face what they could do and had done – they both completely denied it. Investigations started. Because my stepdaughter had been abused for four and a half years, they said I must have known what was going on. If I'd have known, I would have stopped it. As soon as I did know I did something. Then the accusations started. They said, 'Of course, *you* were abused as a child.' Basically it was being said that I had to prove my innocence because of all that.

They wanted a supervision order on my son. He had been very badly abused when he was between three months and two years. He sexually abused him – buggery. I was furious. He had sworn he hadn't touched him. He continued to deny it when he was questioned in prison. My child was re-examined by doctors, and they said the abuse wasn't recent, that he had healed, so I was in the clear. I was going through hell with my little boy; he was showing signs of very severe abuse – smashing toys, smearing, very distressed. He was only just getting to an age where he was talking, so he didn't have the words to tell me. So he was showing it. I was screaming out for help to social services. I just couldn't cope. I was nearly at my wits end. I feel so angry with the system. It let me down when I was a child and it didn't give me any support when I was an adult.

The independent guardian *ad litem* said in her report there was no justification for a supervision order. When the social worker came to my house, he was quite nasty and said they were going to watch me like a hawk. I told him he had no right to treat me like that, but what can you do? The guardian *ad litem* was great. When it got to court it just got thrown out. But it was like I had to account for every scratch on my boy. I was petrified. I was living under all this suspicion. The fear was always there. I was screaming for help, and that's what I got – suspicion. Six months after we found out about Bob's abuse, the social worker asked me if he'd forgotten about it yet: he just didn't know enough, about children or about abuse.

It's so hard that the person you think your child is safest with is the one who has hurt him, and that the person you trust yourself with can do this. He's out of prison now. They won't take him back to court for the abuse of my son. They have all the evidence, but he still denies it and my son is too little to give evidence. The police knew all along they couldn't do anything. So my son and I went all through that awful system, to do it correctly, and still nothing was done.

I feel as if there is no justice in the world. Rob a bank and you'll get fifteen years. He got three years for what he did to his daughter, and served eighteen months – no treatment, on a normal wing. He doesn't think he's done anything wrong; and I think that, until he accepts that, he's a danger to any child.

I've been to hell and back. It nearly broke me completely. I always said I'd never let anything happen to my child. I never wanted him to go through anything that I went through, and I'm only thankful that we seem to have come through this with a close relationship. I hope it stays that way. He doesn't talk so much about it now, but he will tell you straight what his daddy did to him. He doesn't want anything to do with him, although I had decided that as he was his father I would do my best not to turn him against him.

But he's decided for himself. My son is very much aware of what has happened to him. We have both been let down so badly. You really never think your own partner will do that to his own children, especially when they're just babies. For the first year after I found out, I was just existing; I didn't think there was any way our lives could or would get any better. It was in the papers. People's attitude – that I must have known – hurt so much. It makes you look at yourself, too: I felt really guilty. What had I done wrong?

Wasn't I giving him something? There were so many questions I was asking. I was trying to understand why. I still just don't understand it, how he could do it. It's so hard for me to trust anyone; and I did trust him. And now, to be honest, I don't trust anyone, except my son, and that's it. I certainly couldn't trust my mum, and my dad just did anything for a quiet life.

It's really difficult to describe how I feel, and how I felt at the time. For a while I buried how I felt, just existing, getting through one day at a time, knowing I had to keep going because I had Bob to look after. There wasn't any choice, but I was just going through the motions. When I did start feeling, I felt anger. But not just at what *he* did. When it all first came out with Lucy, I'd had this major operation and was very weak; and only two days after the operation the police came to get a statement off me. They wouldn't wait. They were really callous. At first I couldn't believe my partner was the same person who had done these things. As time went on I started feeling so angry and asking him 'Why?'; saying 'How could you have been doing this all along, treating me in one way and then doing this to your daughter?'

Awful as it sounds, I started to hate him so much I was thinking of ways of killing him – different ways. That was before I knew he'd done it to my son too. I was so angry I was living in a sort of fantasy land. I only knew about my son when he said something one day. I let it drop at first, I think I didn't want to believe it. Then Bob said to my brother-in-law and his wife, when there was a couple in bed on the television, 'Me and daddy do that.' They were baby-sitting, and told me when I got back. He was very insistent about it. I wanted to find a way of explaining it away. On the third occasion I was with my friend, who's a nurse, and Bob said 'Daddy hurt my bottom.' He wanted to tell me. I should have listened to him before. I knew I had to find out and couldn't ignore it any longer. But my stomach just fell. I was petrified someone would take him away. I got in touch with the authorities, and he was examined, and it all started all over again.

I'd just started to pick up at that time, and then it all fell apart again for a second time. The shock was awful. I've had no more relationships since: I can't trust a man again. It made me not trust my own judgement. Even with friends I'd

known for years and years, if they went out of the room to
go to the toilet I'd have to go into Bob's room. I'd make any
excuse. I just had to be sure they weren't going into his
bedroom. I was too scared to bath Bob or do anything for
him. I wouldn't let him in the garden. If I went to friends, I
wouldn't let him out of my sight. That all went on for ages.
I really felt as if it was me against the system. I think the
system stinks. It's done nothing to help. People imagine child-
molesters are dirty old men in macs, but they can be anyone
– including mothers.

LINDA'S STORY

My second example of abuse occurring from generation to generation comes from Linda. Again, some of her childhood experiences are included in the next chapter: she was physically abused
by her mother, and sexually abused by her brother and her uncle.
She married very young, and had four children in four years. She
then physically abused one of her daughters. This was part of her
story:

> I married at sixteen, and it was awful. I couldn't bear anyone
> near me. He was twenty-one, and very violent. My husband
> was the oldest of twenty-four children. All his family had
> huge families. By the time I was twenty I had already buried
> one of my sons and was expecting another. I honestly don't
> remember the conception of those children. He would get
> angry and knock me half-senseless, and that's how they came
> about. Our marriage broke up about eighteen months later. I
> just couldn't take what he was dishing out to me.
>
> He told me I'd married him under false pretences, that
> he thought I was a virgin, and, as I wasn't, what was all the
> performance about? He wanted to know why I'd let the
> abuse happen, and what had I done to encourage it. He didn't
> believe me: it was something filthy and evil I'd dreamed
> up. My mother had always told him what a liar I was, what a
> filthy slut I was; and he believed all that, because now I'd
> proved it true.
>
> I met another man and we had a child, and I adopted his
> children from a previous marriage – his wife had died. I
> really did have tender feelings for him, but when we'd been
> married about five years I felt really bad about pretending

sexually. I'd told him about the abuse when I'd known him a couple of months. I told him everything. He spent weeks and months just talking to me. He didn't have the reaction I expected. I really thought he'd understood.

With my second husband, the fact that I didn't have to live with violence tempered down the violence inside me. I gradually loosened up on the children in those years. He helped a lot with the sexual problems. We talked about them, and I didn't feel he would hurt me or force me, beat me half-senseless; and I did start to enjoy sexual contact. But he couldn't cope when I told him I pretended sexually, and that's what ended the relationship. After a while he went off with someone else.

But he turned my life around in another way, and I rarely discuss this with anyone. I used to be extremely physically abusive to my two eldest daughters, especially the oldest one. To my undying shame I was terribly abusive to her. One day I was really laying into her. She was only five. And as usual I was crying, and he came into the bedroom and he took hold of my hand. I waited. I thought he was going to hit me. But he just picked me up, and put his arms around me and just held me. He took no notice of her screaming. He just took me out, and held me and stroked my hair. I couldn't believe what I'd got. I haven't got much to be thankful to him for, but I know that on that day something in me began to slowly turn around. It was so unexpected. It started to heal. I just howled and howled, and he kept on holding me and stroking me, and telling me it would all be all right. It didn't happen overnight that I stopped being violent to my children, but it began to turn me around.

I got the hitting under control and I never abused either my last child or my son. My last one was just joy. I did abuse the eldest one even as a small baby, but it's the second one that I know I have damaged. She's now anorexic, had a couple of disastrous relationships, and has precious little self-esteem. I do try not to beat myself with the hammer of guilt unnecessarily, but I am realistic and I know what I have done. I have learned that I was part of a cycle of abuse that I also perpetuated.

That's partly why I don't continue to beat myself with guilt, because I understand where it came from in me. Almost as if it could have been me I was beating. I used to cry so bitterly while I was doing it to her. What was inside me was so enormous. I did stop hitting her, but I did go on scapegoating her. I knocked her confidence from under her whenever I could. I didn't want to do it to the older one or my son or the younger one. Now we're very close. I have talked with her long and hard. I've been as honest with her as I can be. I've cried with her. I've told her that I hope one day she'll forgive me for the way I was with her.

She tells me she has precious few memories, and I believe that. She remembers being friendless at school, because not only did I scapegoat her but so did the other children in the family. It was the example I set. She has suffered very badly as a result. She is the one left at home now. I actually didn't like her, though I don't know why. I didn't like her until she was about fifteen or sixteen. I feel I owe her her childhood. Perhaps somewhere she reminds me of me.

My son now has a daughter, and that's wonderful. I'd have liked another. I was so fascinated by my last one and loved her so much because I didn't have all the other awful stuff in me that had been there before. She was pure joy and I'd have liked another chance. I've been so ashamed of abusing my children. My abuse wasn't my responsibility, but I did what I did, and as an adult you have to take responsibility for your actions. I felt if I told anyone they would throw me in prison and throw away the key, and I wouldn't be allowed a life at all. And then everyone would know me for the terrible person I was portrayed to be. I felt that I was a terrible person.

Also, my daughter was sexually abused when she was ten by a man with a mental age of fourteen. She was systematically sexually abused by him for more than a year. I couldn't believe it. I had made silent promises to my children when they were born that it wouldn't happen to them. I failed in that. I have all sorts of thoughts: that I didn't see it, and who should know better than me? I knew there was something wrong – I'd been to the school in case she was being bullied – but I just couldn't figure it out.

My oldest one is settled. The next one needs a lot of help. She is anorexic, and I suffer from bulimia. But she has some lovely qualities, and I hope things work out for her. My son is happy now, but he hasn't been at times. They've got the baby they dote on. He's got his own shop now.

Things seem to be going OK. The youngest one is eighteen and is going to go back to college, but she has a very bad eating problem.

I haven't married again, but a few years ago I did meet a wonderful man who was sympathetic, but not shocked, and let me talk honestly with him. We were able to talk about our sexual lives together; and he was satisfied with me, and for the first time I experienced sexual gratification. It was a new dimension, and I actually welcomed intercourse and a man inside me. It makes me now really loath to be without it, though I'm not in a relationship now. I lost the shame. I lost the reactions that I used to have inside me to certain phrases or actions. Slowly, and I don't know how, they just started to dissolve. I actually started to have a bit of fun with sex, and to find and express some power through sex. It was a very important relationship, and after two years I loved him so much. My family were having such horrendous problems, especially my son, who was sent away to a residential school; it seemed all I had to offer him was worry and problems, although I believed he loved me as much as he said he did. He was the genuine article. And I found myself running away.

What I felt for him frightened me; how I might ruin his life frightened me. In the beginning we talked about getting married, and we got engaged. It was like something beautiful was happening in my life, that this was really going to be it. I was so happy with that idea, but I couldn't handle being that happy. I was so happy that I couldn't cope, and so I finished that relationship. I felt that my entire being, my problems, my children's problems, were a threat to him. He'd say, 'You're not going to have the children for ever; they'll grow up, and you and I must look to the future together.' But I couldn't see that future.

ABUSE IN CONTEXT

Many of the issues raised in these accounts are discussed in later chapters – the effects of abuse on the growing child, the effects in adult life, the relative helpfulness of interventions by different professional agencies, and the implications of all this for counselling and therapy with abuse survivors. For the present, I wish to

examine the question of what we mean when we use the term
'abuse'? It is now widely used, but many readers will recall the
days when it was not part of everyday vocabulary. Baby-
battering was not widely recognized in the UK until the 1960s
and 1970s, and child sexual abuse was not on the agenda for
another decade. Clearly, such late recognition that the abuse of
children is a major problem should alert us to the fact that many
adults are living with the long-term consequences.

But recent acknowledgement of abuse does not mean that it is
a recent phenomenon – as I have already shown, the abuse of
children has a long history. It simply indicates greater awareness
of the extent of the problem. How much this has led to more
effective methods of intervention, either with the child or with
the adult survivor, is clearly an important question. What is
certain is that the extent of abuse is on a larger scale than anyone
would like to believe, and that it is unlikely that our knowledge
of its extent is anywhere near complete.

Allen's and Jane's stories show that the violation of a child's self
and body is not always limited to childhood years. It can continue
into adult life, and can take place in the very institutions that
supposedly exist to care. Nicki was removed from home because
of abuse, but entered a system that failed to meet even her most
basic needs for support and accommodation. What is clear from
these accounts is that abuse is not limited to a particular form:
children who are sexually abused are frequently also physically
abused. This was true of Allen, Jane and Nicki, and they are not
unusual. All forms of abuse are emotionally damaging, although
emotional abuse can take place on its own. It can include constant criticism, contempt, rejection, convincing children they are
unlovable, refusing attachment and dependency, being invasive,
using derogatory names and inducing fear. David's words illustrate the point:

My parents continually put me down. When I was very
small, if I ever woke up and cried at night they would
ridicule me and tell me horror stories about children who
woke up being carried off by monsters. They'd tell me real
boys don't cry. I was terrified of spiders, and my father
would pretend he'd hidden lots of them in my room and that
they would come out when I was asleep. As I got older,
everything I did was wrong: I was called the disruptive one,
a liar, and they criticized just about everything I said, did or

was. I was bullied a lot at school, and they told me it was my fault – that they weren't surprised nobody liked me.

Neglect, as distinct from emotional abuse, can be understood as a passive form of abuse: a failure to provide basic nurture and to meet a child's basic needs for love, care, food, clothes and a safe environment. Neglect is often linked to poor social conditions; but this does not explain the level of neglect sometimes seen in institutional care, or in well-off families. My interviews indicated that neglect in these families is rarely identified. The following words are those of Anna, a woman in her mid-twenties, describing some of her childhood experience. As well as the neglect she describes here, she was physically abused by her brother, an abuse that continued into adulthood, frequently in the presence of her well-known and very wealthy father. A large part of her childhood was spent with her mother and stepfather. The family was visited regularly by social workers, since they were registered as foster parents, caring for up to four children:

> I tell no one this. I realize it sounds like something out of Dickens, and that's what it *was* like. We lived in this big house, and my stepfather was very well known and respected. He was on charity committees and, being a doctor in a small town, he had a lot of status. So you can see why I never told anyone. I used to sleep in an attic room. It was very cold in winter. It was the only room without heating. I wasn't allowed to use any electricity, so I couldn't have a fire and only a very dim light-bulb. If he was angry with me he'd take that out. They didn't feed me. I wasn't allowed to eat with the rest of the family. I was hardly allowed into any other rooms. I used to go for days without being spoken to. He used to forbid my mother and the other children to speak to me. And they wouldn't give me bus fares, so I often used to have to walk to school; and it was a long way. My friend at school was the head-teacher's daughter and they'd often feed me. So I think they must have guessed some of it. I've only recently wondered why they didn't do something, but I expect it was because of who my stepfather was, and who my father was.

Not surprisingly, Anna found her story difficult to tell. She lived for years with an unbelievable and intolerable situation; but for her it was her reality. Although unbelievable, it happened. And even when it felt intolerable she had somehow to survive.

Sexual abuse is currently given widespread attention and pub-
licity. Most of those who are now presenting as adult survivors
suffered abuse at a time when sexuality was unlikely to be discussed openly. The term 'sexual abuse' encompasses a wide range of
sexual interference, but common features are the betrayal of trust
and responsibility, the abuse of power, the fact that a child cannot
consent (that is an irrelevant concept) and that force, threats or
coercion are used. Sexual abusers may be thought to come only
from a child's immediate family. Whether it is boys or girls who
have been abused, and in whatever context, the vast majority of
abusers are men: fathers, stepfathers, uncles, and brothers. It
is not unusual for assaults to be carefully planned. In cases of
physical or emotional abuse, the abuser is nearly always from a
child's immediate environment (whether home, boarding-school,
children's home or any other institution). But the perpetrators of
sexual abuse can also come from a child's wider world: teachers,
doctors, policemen, vicars, neighbours, family friends, strangers,
youth-club leaders – all have been mentioned by those who spoke
to me. It is not infrequent that they were highly respected leading
lights in the local community, often apparently greatly concerned
for the well-being of young people. Beth told me of her abuse by
a local vicar, who was giving her organ lessons:

He would ring my parents and check very carefully about
offering me a later lesson time. He explained that he would
be alone with me and if they wanted to come with me, or if
they couldn't agree to the time, he'd quite understand. He
said he did realize you had to be so careful with adolescent
girls, because he realized some of them could make up
stories, although he was sure I wasn't like that. But he must
protect himself by being quite sure they knew I was there.
My parents were very impressed, thought he was so careful
and were very shocked at the idea of these dreadful girls.
They were very shy themselves, and sex was never mentioned. I was only just fifteen, and I ended up having sex
with him. He had children only a bit younger than me. It
was horrible. He'd planned it and I couldn't stop him,
although afterwards he blamed me for wanting it so much,
saying I was a wicked girl. I had to keep on going to the
lessons because my parents wouldn't let me not go; and I
knew I couldn't tell them the real reason why I didn't want
to. It would have killed them. And, anyway, they'd never

have believed my word against his. And yes, it happened more than once.

In contrast, physical abuse rarely arises in settings other than those where a child is directly cared for. It can result in very serious injury or death, although much physical abuse continues unrecognized for years. Whereas sexual abusers are predominantly men, a different picture emerges in physical abuse. Women are frequently named as the physical abusers of their children or stepchildren. Although much of the research suggests otherwise, my own work does not suggest any particular class bias in this. It does suggest that considerable physical abuse goes on both in middle and upper class family homes where it would not be easily suspected.

In such homes, a variety of factors help to hide the abuse. Houses are often larger and neighbours are less likely to hear. Generally the perception of 'battered children' does not include children in middle- or upper-class families. The schools these children attend share this perception. Only recently a head-teacher of a private school told me firmly they did not have children from 'those' families in the school, despite contrary evidence. Affluent and professional families are simply better at covering up the abuse and presenting a convincing image.

It is clear to me that this presentation covers a variety of abuse, both physical, sexual and emotional. Interestingly, the image is highly consistent with the 'ideal' family beloved of recent government: two parents, often with above-average earnings, apparently solid citizens bringing up their children in the desired mode. There is a lesson to be learned: it is dangerous to assume that respectability is any more than a façade, especially when the ideal image deflects serious enquiry.

It is not an unusual pattern for children to be physically abused by a female relative while being sexually abused by a male relative. This was Carol's experience:

> I was sexually abused by my father from when I was about four. It started with touching-up, and progressed to intercourse when I was eleven. And my mother physically abused me very badly. I had fractured arms, concussion, extensive bruising and continual vaginal infections. They both knew. My mother encouraged my father because if I allowed my father to do what he wanted he'd be happy around the house. On my mother's side my father never said anything – he just

totally ignored it. His abuse became very violent if he was
angry or bad-tempered. If he was being loving it was vaginal
intercourse; if he was angry it would be anal. My mother
would come in afterwards and sort me out.

Carol's family was just as I have described above: respectable,
hard-working and well respected, and seen by outsiders as having
happy relationships and a normal lifestyle. However, this was a
veneer that covered a totally converse reality.

It is now more widely accepted that abuse in children's homes
and hospitals is not unusual, although there is less awareness of
abuse in schools. It is obvious that boarding-schools have greater
potential for abuse. Children are there for long periods of time,
and may have little contact outside the school. Parents who send
their children to such schools would be advised to examine their
structures carefully and critically.

There is an assumption that large fees ensure a high and responsible standard of care. This cannot be assumed. I include
some of our better-known schools in this warning. In my own
clinical practice I have heard of a public school where older boys
regularly supervised younger boys during after-school study – not
in itself unusual. In this instance the older boys systematically beat
the younger boys on a regular basis. They would have com-
petitions as to who would be the first to make a child cry. If
a particular child resisted, they would burn him with cigarettes.
Only certain children were singled out, identified as significant in
some way, as potential or actual leaders. In this way the pain
inflicted was also associated with peer-group credibility and status. In due course those boys who had been subjected to this
violence went on to inflict it on others.

Any discussion of the extent and meaning of abuse is inevitably
complex. We may not know its extent, although we do know
that it is a major social problem. As the following chapters show,
we now know that the costs to the child and then to the adult are
horrifying. It is a difficult subject to consider. It is hard to contemplate how many lives may be damaged in this way. It is hard
to look around and realize that some of those we know, or have
known, are abusers. It is hard to look back at our own childhood
and wonder which of our friends were abused, or to look at our
children's friends and wonder the same. Inevitably some readers
will find what I write difficult – facing the facts of abuse is a harsh
and painful reality.

In reading these accounts, individual readers will have their own various responses. If even a small part of my reader's mind resists accepting these accounts as true, this in itself provides a clue to the denial and resistance still so widespread in society. The truth is uncomfortable. The impossible is possible. And it happens not just in 'those sorts of families, not like ours' – it happens everywhere.

THREE

ADULTS REFLECT:
THE CHILD'S EXPERIENCE

To understand the impact of abuse on the adult, it is essential to know about the experience of the child. The people I interviewed for this book were able to recall vividly many incidents and feelings associated with those earlier events. Some felt their pictures of childhood were complete and ordered; for others their memories were disjointed, as if they possessed assorted photographs from different times, with the blank spaces being as noticeable as the recalled memories. For some, memories were still returning; others felt the jigsaw of their lives was as near complete as it could be. Their recollections of childhood were, of course, coloured at times by an adult perspective.

THE EXPERIENCE OF ABUSE

For most of those who talked of their childhood, abuse had been a major part of their lives for years. It was not an isolated incident; it was rather an ongoing way of life. For Tina, the abuse began when she was eight, following her mother's death. She was removed from the family home to be cared for by her older sister and brother-in-law. Her father, although still alive, had a 'drink problem' and was incapable of looking after her. Tina, bereft of her mother and her home, had to cope with moving to a household where crying and grief were not allowed, and where subsequently her brother-in-law abused her:

It went on until I was about fifteen. He sexually abused me
for years. I don't know what happened to him at that later
stage, but there were less opportunities to touch me and
abuse me. He just used to bully me instead. Perhaps as I got
older I just got less vulnerable, but it gradually tailed off.

Tina was abused by a family member living in the same house,
but Amy's experience was a little different. She too was sexually
abused by a family member from when she was little until she left
home. Her uncle was the perpetrator. Although he did not live
with the family, he was adept throughout that time at creating
situations where he could abuse her:

It started when I was very little – well before my fourth
birthday, because I remember it happening before my sister
was born. I've got very angry feelings of my parents going
out and he babysat me. He only did once, apparently, and I
would have been just three. Certainly he was touching me
when I was in little dresses that only very little ones wore. I
can earmark events when it was happening that I now know
were when I was younger than three. There are so many
things, so many memories. Eventually touching my shoulder
became worse than being touched in more private parts because it was the start and I froze. My mother was physically
very vicious too, although only to me, not to my sisters.
And as far as I know my uncle only abused me. Family
picnics were a nightmare, because he always managed to get
me alone.

Jill's story is similar: she was abused from a very young age.
Her abuser was her father. As with Tina, the abuse finally stopped in adolescence – not an unusual pattern, although it can continue into adulthood. Jill recollected:

It started as early as I can remember. The earliest memories
are really etched on my brain – and on my being. It didn't
finish until I made a great big fuss about it, somewhere
between the ages of thirteen and fifteen. I remember he
would touch me in the bath, and if I knocked his hand away
he'd bash me, and I'd hit my head really hard against the
wall. No one else knew or cared about our reality. It was
living in an awful secret world. The worst thing was if others
homed in on you too. I knew it was wrong even when I was
very tiny and I used to try to stay awake to stop him doing

it. I couldn't stay awake. I was so young and he was doing it as I was falling asleep. I knew he was a perpetrator without knowing the word. I would have loved a nice, kind, safe father. I wanted him removed out of my life. There were times I wanted him dead. I remember being very small and desperately wanting him to fall out of a window he was clean-ing. He knew I was hating back, and what I was wishing. Children are better off without fathers.

The ongoing nightmare quality of Jill's childhood and her clear memory of wanting the perpetrator removed need to be noted. She was not alone in saying this. Some children may be anxious to avoid family disruption, but for others the disruption can be settled only by the removal of the perpetrator.

Louise was also abused by her father. Her memories were very fragmented. She described some of what she remembered, illus-trating through her story why she and many others also forget, because such memories are simply too painful:

There are a lot of very dark and angry memories, but only in snatches. One is of being hungry and asking for a sandwich. My father said to me 'If you ask again I'm going to put you in the bath.' I did. I was hungry. And he picked me up and put me in the bath. I think he put my head under the water, but I can't remember now. I remember screaming and hold-ing on to him, shouting 'I love you! I love you! Please stop!' and him pushing my arms away and pushing me in again.

It is not only what is done directly to children that is abusive: it is also what they see done to others, especially those they love or depend upon. Louise witnessed considerable violence towards her siblings and her mother:

I remember being put in the same bedroom as my parents and my father beating my mother very badly. One night they had an argument, and I woke up. I heard my father go out and come in, and my mother say, 'If you hit me with that you'll kill me.' I was petrified. The next thing was my father hitting my mother's head against the wall – just constantly. And I screamed and screamed and screamed, remembering what she'd said, that 'you're going to kill me.' And I remember my father coming up to me, and putting his huge hand over my face, and smothering me, and trying to stop me. Another time, I remember hearing noises – my mother moaning – and feeling sick in my stomach, not knowing what he was doing to her. As an older child I thought he'd raped her. It was like abusing my mind, letting a little child see and hear those things.

Louise's story is an example of the pervasiveness of abuse in some families: a combination of physical assault, psychological pain and sexual behaviour that is damaging and entirely inappropriate:

When I was thirteen my mother was on night duty, and my father asked my mother to ask me if I'd go into bed with him because he was lonely at night. She asked me to, so I did. One night he snuggled right up to me, put his arms round me, put his head right against my breasts and rubbed his head to and fro, making cooing noises saying, 'I love you. I love you: you're so nice and warm.' Me lying there thinking, 'I can't stand this, I'm going to be sick. This isn't right. My dad shouldn't be doing this to me.'

Her mother's collusion in this confused and worried Louise greatly: she knew the situation was not acceptable, yet could not understand why her mother had asked her to 'keep her father company'.

When Peter spoke to me, his knowledge of his childhood was very clear. It had, however, been completely repressed from his consciousness until a few years ago, when he was suddenly flooded with memories:

I was completely gone. I was seeing me as an eight-year-old being very, very badly beaten by my father; and then being thrown naked on the bed, as he was, and him raping me. My earliest memory is of abuse when I was two years old right up to my teens. I was very violently beaten. He would use his fists, his feet, leather belts, bamboo sticks, anything which came to hand. The physical abuse went on right up to when I was seventeen, until I hit him back and he knew I was stronger.

Like Louise, Peter witnessed violence towards his brothers and sisters. They were all abused physically and sexually, and developed strategies to try to cope with the most horrific levels of abuse:

One of my sisters used to go completely still like a statue –
no emotional response – and he would get angrier and
angrier. We would recognize that each of us were in trouble,
and I would recognize that it was her turn next. So I would
divert him by breaking something, stealing something, so I
would be beaten and abused. But she'd do the same for me,
and my other sister did it for both of us, and we did it for
her. She would sit on his knee, stroke him, get him going
that way.

In Peter's family, where all the children were abused, the siblings tried to protect one another. In other families siblings can
collude with an abuser so that they escape and attention is focused
on a brother or a sister. Sometimes only one child is selected, like
Amy, or in this case Mark, who was physically abused by his
father although his brother was not:

It's difficult to remember, but I don't think the battering
bothered me. I had no reason to suppose that it was unusual:
in fact every reason to believe it was quite usual. The fact
that I'd get beaten hell out of, and not my brother, was a bit
confusing.

Mark lived in a community in which he saw male violence as
the norm. However, the contradiction was evident to him, even
as a child, that for some reason only he had been chosen to receive
such abuse.

Caroline, like Nicki in the last chapter, was a young woman
who had been abused at home and then taken into care. She told
me:

They kept taking me in and out of care. They'd take 'place of
safety' orders and get me out; and then send me back, and
so on. I got told to try to cope with my parents and talk to
them, but I don't think they acknowledged the fact that I was
abused. I was sexually abused by my dad. They didn't deal
with a lot of things, including that. And for years my brother
and I got battered – my head was put through a kitchen
window. I used to just cut off when I was being battered,
and just not feel or cry or anything; but it didn't work,
because I just got hit more because they wanted an effect.
And then they'd say, 'What are you crying for?' When I was
in care, nobody helped me sort out what was going on in my
head.

This sequence, of abuse at home followed by entry into care where the experience is unsatisfactory or blatantly abusive, is one that is frequently reported. Abuse does not take place solely within family units. The care system may be portrayed as a safety net, but it is one that is full of holes that the most vulnerable can fall through. It is not adequately resourced. Neither is it adequately monitored. Anne, removed from home because of sexual abuse, described one incident:

> The first night I was in that assessment centre I was lying in bed with my headphones on, and this bloody man [a member of staff] was on top of me, and he was trying to fuck me. I got him off me; and in the end I had to bargain with him to get him out.

Hannah was a victim of severe abuse, whose story runs through these chapters. As a child she went from one abusive situation to another:

> It started when I was two years old. She [my mother] didn't sexually abuse me, she physically abused me. She used to beat me severely, and lock me up. It just went on and on. It was a daily occurrence, not an isolated incident. Some of the things she did to me I'll never ever forget. I don't remember when my brother started sexually abusing me, but I was very young. More damaging than the sexual abuse from my brother was the physical abuse my mother put me through, to the point where, when I was twelve, the welfare authorities were called in and I was sent to live with an uncle and an aunt. It was decided all round that it would be best if I didn't live with that family any more. I wasn't told it was going to happen. I remember I came home from school one night, and there was a suitcase in the hall; I don't know how, but I knew it was mine. I had to get changed, sit on a chair, and wait. It was unusual, because what normally happened when I got home from school was that I had a couple of slices of bread and I went to bed. But I sat on this chair with my clothes on, and I knew I was going to this home.
>
> But I went to my uncle and aunt. I loved my aunt, except when I went there I had my uncle to contend with. And it was like going from the frying-pan into the fire. At least my brother (although he'd hold me and I couldn't get away from him) wasn't rough and he didn't physically abuse me. That

didn't feel as bad as my uncle, who was a foreman ganger on the railway and was very strong – twenty-five years older than my brother. And in the two years I was there he raped me several times. One day he hit me hard and made me fall when I wouldn't cooperate. My head was bleeding, and I was on the floor, and everything was very fuzzy. He got worried and went to get a cloth. I managed to escape to my room on that occasion.

For some children there is no escape. They go from one awful set of circumstances to another. Nicki and Caroline expected their move into care to provide respite. It did not. Hannah expected similar respite when she was moved to live with her aunt, whom she loved. Instead she was faced with yet more horrors. And yet this was a situation where clearly there had been some official concern. Yet again intervention proved ineffective.

Rachel's history appears more unusual. She was sexually abused by her mother:

I know that before my mother started to abuse me I'd told her about my grandfather exposing himself to me, and she hadn't believed me. Then I was evacuated, and I thought I'd been sent away because of what had happened. When I came back from being evacuated, she started abusing me. I don't know how long my mother abused me for, but I know it happened a lot.

As I have already indicated, mothers and girls are frequently mentioned as physical abusers but rarely as sexual abusers. Where they are involved, it is often in the context of colluding either actively or passively with a male partner. So it appears that Rachel's experience was unusual, although it is by no means unique.

John was neither physically nor sexually abused, but he vividly described to me the psychological abuse he was subjected to:

It was my father and not my mother; but she was so scared of him that she was no help. It's quite difficult to describe, but he constantly ridiculed me. It was like ongoing verbal assault. He wasn't so bad to my sister, but only because he didn't think girls were worth bothering about. He always criticized just everything, and if you tried to do what he wanted that was not right either. Everything about me was wrong – just the whole of me. When I was small he forbade my mother to pick me up, hug me, anything like that. There was no escape, because you couldn't keep out of his way – he'd follow you, he'd find you out, and it would all start over again. There is nothing positive I remember about him. He turned my childhood into a sort of hell. He systematically dissected my whole being: an utterly joyless existence, never anything more.

John did not find it easy talking about his childhood. He knew how consistently awful it had been, and yet explaining this to anyone else felt difficult. He showed how abuse of this nature gradually and systematically erodes the victim, so that those who have suffered often feel they should not complain. They make out that the abuse was not so serious. Their reticence and apparent acceptance must not be taken at face value: psychological abuse, especially when it is so tenaciously applied, is an appallingly effective way of demolishing any coherent sense of self.

THE ABUSERS

Recalling the experience of abuse evoked memories of the characteristics and tactics of the abuser. Some of those who spoke to me obviously experienced the abuse itself as deeply traumatic, but their knowledge that manipulative power had replaced trust was particularly painful. Tina described it so:

It wasn't the physical abuse that's had the most major impact on me: it was the manipulation, the power, the extremes he would go to so that he could abuse me, and the pressures that he put on me not to tell. My sister used to go to evening classes, and he'd wait and he'd make sure that I wasn't able to go out those evenings to friends. It was very devious, and that's the sort of behaviour I find it very hard to believe people would do. I'd wait in the back yard for my sister to come in; he'd know I was waiting: it was a game we were playing. I'd dash through the house pretending I'd been there all along, and he'd say, 'I'll get you next time.' It was a dreadful game he was playing.

Living with this degree of careful planning and pure ruthlessness was also Amy's experience:

I used to bite him and kick him, but it didn't stop. He had so
many ways – lying, playing tickling games. He used to come
after work on a Friday, and was always careful to be there
before my father got home, and always played these games.
Occasionally it was fun and I'd relax; and then I'd realize it
was silly to relax. He'd play these games with me and get the
others to join in. It would hurt me and I'd lash out. Then I'd
get blamed, because he'd tell my mum that it was my fault,
and then I got it. And she was very, very rough with me
anyway. He would call me the troublemaker. He'd say [to
my mother], 'You'll have to do something with her.' He
induced a lot of punishment from my mother. He persuaded
everyone it was my fault. He was a great charmer, utterly
convincing and always believed; and, because he had me
labelled as such an exaggerator, if I had tried to say anything
I would never have been believed.

He never did or said anything except when we were alone.
He was very crafty and very calculating, and he knew that. I
bought a tape recorder. I saved for it. It cost me £33. I was
about twelve, and I had a plan that I'd catch him out on this.
I hid it under the dressing-table and he came in. He found
it and said, 'We've been clever haven't we? but you're not
going to catch me out on that.' After that, everything really
collapsed. It felt as if he could even read my thoughts. It was
very frightening. The only time I found I could think without him somehow inviting himself in was in the middle of
the night. He was into pornographic photos, too, with two
highly respected men in the community.

The degree of scheming, planning and manipulation in the
stories I heard is outrageous in its cold determination. It is reminiscent of Beth's story of her vicar in Chapter 2. Such accounts
demonstrate the impossibility for children of gauging the inten-
tions of adults. They are rendered helpless and powerless. Those
who might help them are caught up in the same system of power
and game-playing. The child cannot move: it is as if all avenues of
potential escape have been spotted by the abuser and blocked.
Other children did not experience this same degree of planning
but, like Mark, they were caught in a web of contradictions:

My father was the archetypal example of the incoherence
between the public life and the private life of males. He
would make tears come in Quaker meetings on a Sunday

morning, talking about 'caring matters most' and the need
not to allow violent and aggressive means, and then beat hell
out of his family in the afternoon. Although I don't like
words like 'schizoid' it was almost like the guy in the morning was not the same person in the afternoon. You wouldn't
dare to bring up the inconsistency, because the idea that you
should be consistent wasn't part of our understanding of
what life was about. It was all fragmented.

John also had a very violent father, and his stepmother did not
initiate abuse but would join in. His family appeared to be the
ultimate in respectability and responsibility. They cleverly hid
what amounted to torture of their children. John, however, was
concerned that his father's behaviour occurred elsewhere, even if
in a more muted form:

He was very clever at covering up what he did to me. He'd
do things that wouldn't show, and he'd be very careful that
neighbours didn't see or hear anything. They thought the
world of him, and he used to drop hints about me being a bit
difficult and not very trustworthy. He was a teacher, and I
think he was awful to the kids there, too, though I bet he had
a good sense of whom to leave alone and how far to go and
who wouldn't be believed anyway. It makes me sound as if
I'm paranoid, but I'm not. It *was* like that, and he was like
that.

This subtlety in planning abuse was also Carol's experience.
There was a system of signs:

If I was playing outside and they wanted me in, they'd stand
by the window and my dad would have his arm round my
mother; and that would be a sign that I had to rush in and go
in between them and say, 'No, he's my daddy, not your
daddy.' That's how I was called in. It was a signal; and that
was one of the times I'd be abused.

The examples of careful planning that I quote above all relate to
abuse within a family. However, the most careful planning, and
most meticulous systems of signals, take place within organized
rings of abuse (e.g. using different locations, passwords, telephone and other signals, and having carefully planned escape
routes and alibis). Clearly, the more people that are involved, the
greater the care that has to be exercised to avoid discovery. Judy's
experience gives some idea of the extent of these rings:

It was quite a big ring. When I took an overdose, I got
referred to the child psychiatrist and he was also part of the
abuse ring. There was no hope then. The last door closed.
I'm still not sure how far out the web went. I'd allow all
forms of abuse. I was totally subjugated. The more my
memory returns, the more I'm aware of how many men and
women in responsible positions I was sold to. Like police,
social workers, psychiatrists, psychologists – these were the
people who sexually abused me. It was a child-prostitution
racket, and there were films and photographs of me too. I
saw part of one of them once and I couldn't cope. And to see
it wasn't the dirty-mac brigade watching it, but this complete
mix of people. A lot of the films used to be made in a dental
surgery.

For others their abuse is not part of an organized ring, nor is it
organized at all, but it is still totally incomprehensible. This is
particularly true of physical abuse. Samantha never knew what to
expect:

You'd go in some days and she'd be fine. Just sort of ordin-
ary. Other days she'd just set eyes on me and explode, and
I'd find myself kicked and thrown around. It just happened.
I never knew from one day to the next how she would be.
There was no pattern, no predictability.

And, for Annette, a close and trusting relationship with her
father ended abruptly in one incident which was never repeated:

It only happened once. He forced himself into the bathroom
when I was thirteen. He exposed himself to me and touched
me. It seemed as if it went on for ages. It never happened
again. I don't understand how he could let himself do that to
me.

When Jill's father finally stopped sexually abusing her, life
remained extremely difficult:

The sexual abuse was the thing I wanted out of, and that did
stop. But I was still living in the same house, and ostracized
by my father. He told me he would never speak to me again
and he would disown me as his daughter. So it was a bit
difficult then. There were never any signs of sorrow, and the
abuse had always been thought out so he did it when my
mother wasn't there. Quite calculated.

Peter was clear in his view of his father:

> He was an evil man...I think he'd have killed us eventually. The pattern of abuse was the same: it came from one to another right the way through – always one of us being sexually abused.

And Anne, who was taken into care, recognized the impossibility of remaining with her father:

> I had to leave. The only other solution would be to have imprisoned my father. Then my life would have been brilliant. If he had been jailed, everything would have been much better.

This did not happen. It was Anne and her siblings who left, while their father remained. Anne gave evidence in court against her father, but the case was not proved.

Hannah, abused by her mother, described the following:

> She always told me it was my fault: I had an evil streak, I was jealous, I was the Devil's daughter. She took me to see a psychiatrist when I was thirteen years old, and at the end of the session he said, 'There's nothing wrong with her – she's a normal girl.' After that she beat the living daylights out of me, saying it was just an act I'd put on. And how dare I? She even took me to church and tried to get me de-possessed by the priest. She thought I was possessed by the Devil.

These comments on abusers, their behaviour and their tactics illustrate some of the dilemmas faced by abused children. Children are intrinsically less powerful than adults. They have as much or as little power and control over their lives as adults care to give. These examples show how children are at the mercy of adults. Exploitation by adults renders children helpless, and creates traps they cannot avoid.

Those who still insist that children need to look at their own responsibility for abuse would do well to listen to these accounts. Writers such as Lamb (1986) need to be careful when they suggest that children in abusive situations can exercise choice: 'Teaching children that some of their choices showed poor judgement is not to label them as "bad", but to point out that children have merely not yet learnt enough about the world to make the best choice in certain situations.' Fortunately, few writers share a view which

shows remarkably little understanding either of the true nature of
choice or of the predicaments faced by abused children.

THE EFFECT ON EVERYDAY LIFE

With abuse such a dominant feature of a child's experience, it is
easy to forget how ordinary daily living might be effected. Those
who can observe children at home, whether their own or others',
know just how significant everyday activities are for a child:
visiting friends, playing games, simply wandering around with
others, watching television, or doing nothing at all but lazing
around the house. For young children particularly, their whole
life revolves around home and school. Even teenagers moving
into the wider world need the secure base of home from which to
launch themselves. Tina described for me some of the important,
ordinary parts of life that were spoiled for her:

> I had to have permission to do anything – even stopping at
> school to do netball practice. I had to formally ask for per-
> mission even if it was just half an hour. I had to be back by
> nine o'clock if I was allowed to visit friends. There were lots
> of arguments all the time about anything I wanted to do,
> however reasonable. And I was a very quiet child really. He
> would not allow me to do it.

Power was exercised over her simply for the sake of it. It was not
a question of setting age-appropriate boundaries: it was unnecessary, callous repression, involving the placing of unreasonable
restrictions.

Amy found her whole life affected either by the possibility of
her abuser's appearance or by the reality of his invasiveness:

> I couldn't relax when he was around, or when he wasn't
> around in case he'd turn up. He used to kerb-crawl me, too.
> I had to fail at tennis when I just started playing at school.
> I longed to play tennis, but the courts could be seen from
> the road. There were lots of vantage places, and he used to
> watch. I hadn't realized he would be around during school.
> He did the same sort of thing at netball when I was younger.
> Everything I became interested in, he became interested in;
> and so I had to give it up, because he got involved and took
> it away from me.

Even helping to wash up became a problem area. She would try to avoid this, but was unable to explain that if she was at the sink her uncle had opportunities to assault her:

> Washing-up was an issue he could pull my mother into, too. He could incite so much trouble. It was like injections: the effect of one would start to wear off and he'd be there with another. I tried to get my sister to wash up so that I could dry up. That gave me free movement around the kitchen, you see. When I washed up when I was quite small, he'd come up behind me and I was trapped. I couldn't move away from the washing-up without being branded lazy.

She could not escape safely at school either; and even being ill did not offer sanctuary:

> I was on barbiturates very young because of a fit I'd had. I often felt unwell anyway. One day at school I felt less safe because a lot of the girls were away on a trip and there was no one to go home with. I looked down the steps of the school and saw his car. I just fainted. I was taken home and came round at home and had a fit. I was taken to hospital and was in a coma. It wasn't safe being in hospital either, because he came. His wife was a nurse and, because he was known and liked and respected, he could come and go as he wished.

Amy, like many others in her position, could not enjoy the ordinariness of life. Her only solution was to grow up fast, leave home and become independent. For the abused, childhood is not a safe place to be:

> I was planning all the time to be old enough to leave home. I got a job as soon as I could in the evenings. I was away more and I was safe. I was very competent because in many ways I was very grown-up. I was never a little girl. I really wanted to get right away and get my own mortgage and so on. I wanted to escape from being little.

This desire to leave home, or at least be out as much as possible, and to earn money was echoed by Mark:

> The only way you could deal with my father was by not being around. If you were, you got beaten up. I had a bicycle and I was into earning money very early on. I was financially self-sufficient remarkably early, buying my own clothes and

so on. And I used to get the hell out of it. I'd walk and
bird-watch and cycle.

Hannah also went out to work young, but her mother wanted
to control that too:

> When I was twelve I went out and got a job. I was too
> young, but my mother had told me to get out and earn. She
> wanted me to save all the money, but one day I went out to
> buy some new clothes. When I got back, first she beat me,
> for stealing my own money, although I'd earned it; and then
> she told me to burn them, which I did. She literally tore
> them off my back.

Hannah had no chance to do or to be anything, the restrictions
on her were so great:

> Most of the time I was scared to move. I just sat in a chair
> very, very quietly. I never asked my mother if I could go
> out, because I wasn't allowed to. Looking back, it was like
> being a prisoner. I just didn't have a normal childhood. I
> didn't really have one at all.

Peter left home when he was very young:

> I was about fifteen. I literally ran away to sea. I got a job on
> a boat with my brother. Another brother left when he
> was fifteen; my sisters both left at seventeen. One of them
> got married very quickly. We all left as soon as we could.
> We couldn't have any normal childhood; we couldn't enjoy
> ordinary things. It wasn't a possibility. I was a consistent
> runner-away from home when I was younger, too.

The book *Young Runaways* (Newman 1989) illustrates that
Peter's response was not unusual. It shows that 18 per cent of
young people entering a 'safe house' over a two-year period said
that they had been sexually abused at some time in their life. This
figure does not include those who may have been physically or
psychologically abused, so the total number in all categories is
likely to be significantly higher. Gabarino and Gilliam make a
similar point: 'The denial of a home endangers adolescents physically, emotionally and sexually. Many of these teenagers are
called runaways, but they are really throwaways' (1980:13).
Linda was one of those who was forced to leave home early to
escape from abuse. She had left her aunt's home and returned to

live with her parents and brother. Her brother attempted to abuse
her again:

> By this time I had had sex lessons at school, and I knew what
> was and what wasn't appropriate in families. I knew what I
> was going back to. I knew I couldn't get back into that.
> Within a few days he wanted to carry on as things had been.
> I couldn't cooperate with that any more. So, five weeks after
> I'd gone back home with nothing but the clothes I stood up
> in, I left my job, took my money and just didn't go back.
> There didn't seem to be any other choice. I was fifteen.

Louise found it difficult to say how the abuse had affected her
everyday life:

> I don't know what it did to me, because I lived all my time in
> a dream world. That's what it did to me. I removed myself
> from reality. I just fantasized, and it was lovely – I loved
> those worlds. I went somewhere safer and nicer. Because I
> wasn't there, I don't remember.

Children who enter care find restrictions on very ordinary activities irksome. Anne told me:

> There are a lot of petty things, like wanting to borrow a
> broom so I could sweep up the room I was going to move
> into. I asked and was told I could have it. I took it and
> returned it; and then other members of staff kept going on
> and on at me because they thought I hadn't asked. And then
> there was another member of staff who I didn't like. One day
> I was really upset, and because I wouldn't talk to him – I
> wanted my key worker to talk to – he said that if I didn't talk
> to him I would have my privileges taken away. And when I
> needed my bus fare for work I had to ask him, and he took a
> long time. There was no encouragement, no real interest.
> They set me back. A lot of opportunities I've missed out on –
> like I've never had a proper holiday.

We have to remember that this girl was in care because of sexual
abuse. Instead of life in the children's home compensating her for
some of her losses, another layer of deprivation was added.

Karen's experience was similar:

> If you live with parents, you've got someone to go back to.
> If you're in care you've got no one; you don't feel you've

got a relationship with anyone. I wanted my social worker
to come to an open day at a college I wanted to go to. I
expected her to want to come, but she wouldn't because it
was a Sunday and she doesn't work then. I wanted her to
come as a friend or a person. But it's just a job. It turns me
into a number – nothing more. I'm not an object.

The pain in these words is obvious. The real essence of parenting,
is that it goes on seven days a week, fifty-two weeks a year, and
cannot be replaced by a social worker, even one who really cares.
There is a huge gap, which no one can fill. And Anne added:

If you're in care you may be a real enthusiast over some
activity but you may not be able to carry it on, because you
can end up miles from home and lose everything familiar.
You lose your social network.

It is clear that the loss of everyday experiences is considerable,
although it frequently goes unrecognized. The impact of such
losses must not be underestimated. The child's world becomes
limited, limiting and unfriendly. 'Children who are abused or
neglected see the world as dangerous and inconsistent, and human
interactions as unrewarding. These children believe that they
must protect themselves from others, and limit contact in order to
survive' (Gil 1988:23).

THE EFFECT ON FRIENDSHIPS

Losses in childhood are bound to have considerable effect. Another
important area is that of friendships and social relationships,
which are essential for a growing, developing child. Many of
those whom have been abused can say little about friendships in
childhood, which in itself says much. As children, they frequently
found themselves socially isolated.

Finkelhor sees isolation as an effect rather than a cause of abuse:
'Children who are being abused by family members are often
prohibited from having friends. Children who are feeling shame
and stigma as a result of having suffered victimisation often iso-
late themselves from others' (1986:72). Although he writes about
sexual abuse, his comments are valid for other forms of abuse.
Certainly the people I interviewed remembered friends as not
being welcome at home, or themselves having been uneasy about
initiating invitations.

Additionally, abused children have difficulty in dealing appropriately with conflicts, and these inevitably arise when children are learning the rules of friendship and social interaction. Amy's experience was not quite so negative. She had a few friends, although she never took them home:

> I had a friend at school but I couldn't have told her any of this, and I got very used to being by myself as a child. It wasn't a house to have friends in. But I did like walking to school with the other girls. It just couldn't develop more than that.

Mark was very isolated as a child, and his behaviour precluded friendships:

> I had no friends. I was too violent and too difficult to have any. I didn't know the meaning of the word 'friend'. I didn't know the meaning of social occasions. No birthday parties. I was never even part of the family. An extraordinarily lonely existence, except that's retrospective – it's only when you're not lonely that you realize how lonely you have been. I never knew anyone well enough to talk about it, and so my assumption was that this was life.

Like Amy, Jill had some friends but was similarly restricted in developing these relationships:

> I used to like walking home with friends. I couldn't take friends home. It was unthinkable.

However, she had some experience of how relationships could be different. Abused children who have contact with other families (although many do not) can catch a glimpse of a better life, together with a hope that there may be more:

> I was looked after by another family after school when I was between the ages of five and seven, and that taught me a bit about other families: how to behave at table, to talk; that there were such things as outings and treats and going out and routines. Lots of gaps were filled. They had fish in a fish-tank. I learned not to steal. They were a caring family. There was no punishment, no recrimination, so it wasn't what they said but what they did and how they were. I'd pinched all sorts of things, but one day I had the chance to steal and decided not to. And I didn't again. I think they must have carefully handled their own children's annoyance

at what I was doing. Transplanted anywhere else I would have thrived. Children want to be happy.

But Samantha was entirely alone:

To say I had no friends is an understatement. At one time I used to steal money so that I could buy sweets. I was literally trying to buy friends.

Anne not only lost out on friendships by going in and out of care: she also lost all social contact with her siblings:

I didn't see my brother either. He just cut himself off. My other brother was fostered out by the time he was three or four – they weren't feeding him, and things like that. I didn't know where he was.

Hannah had an idea that there was more to life. She caught glimpses of another world from behind her curtains, but she was not allowed any contact with it:

Although I didn't know different, I could see that other kids were allowed to play out on the street. I was never allowed out to play. I could never have friends round. I had to be in bed by half past seven, even in summer when all the others were out. I used to peep around the curtains, but I'd get beaten if I got caught.

And John remembered:

Friendships were a mystery to me. I could see other people had them, but I didn't know how to. I was always uneasy with people, always waiting to be attacked, and I usually was. I think I was a bit like a wounded animal, just cringing. I had no idea at all about relating to anyone else.

Peer relationships are very important to all children, although they become particularly significant at adolescence. It is easy for adults to dismiss childhood friendships and relationships, and any resulting conflicts and squabbles, as trivial. But of course they are not: they are essential to the child's whole being, as well as being a preparation and testing-ground for adult relationships.

THE EFFECT OF ABUSE ON SELF-PERCEPTION

Relationships with others are deeply significant to childrens developing views, and sense of, self. If feedback is primarily negative the experience of self becomes sadly distorted. Tina's lack of belief in herself as a child is one that is shared by many of those who have been abused:

> I found no way of dealing with it directly. I was told so often it must all have been my fault that in the end I believed it. I had no good messages about myself. I also learned to avoid conflict if I could. It was easier that way. People were usually bigger than you were and they'd win in the end. And I was teased such a lot as well. I just retreated into myself.

Amy had to struggle to hold on to reality, and her remarks are reminiscent of many who as children felt they were going mad:

> I used to have to be so certain that I wasn't imagining things that I'd dig my nails into myself, and hours later I'd still have the marks. There were so many contradictions, and my experience was a million miles away from what I was being told. That made me feel I must be imagining things, because these things were not mentioned, didn't exist. I was told I was the ugly duckling, and that had its effect on me. I'd always be blamed, always be called the troublemaker, always be told I was a liar. It got so that I didn't know what was real and what wasn't.

For children to maintain their sense of self in these circumstances is a serious difficulty: it is as if their whole being is under attack. Mark expressed it this way:

> The violence was only part of something else; and what really makes me angry about people who say the real problem is about psychological violence, not physical violence, is how on earth you can separate the two from one another. Not only was my father beating hell out of me, he was trying to assassinate my whole character and personality – the most enormous flow of sarcasm and verbal aggression I've ever actually heard. He was not capable of remaining silent. You could never get away from it if you were in the house. The actual battering for most of us is a very small part of what actually is happening. Your psyche is being battered. There was no escape. The message coming across was that you were no good and that you had it all wrong.

Jill pointed out that, although good things may be happening amid the horrors, they become crowded out by the impact of the abuse:

The good things were cancelled out because I was null and void. Everything I did was criticized. It wasn't just the sexual abuse, it was actually a systematic. . . I get a sense of what the Holocaust was like. My father was like Klaus Barbie. It was a systematic breakdown of personality – the mind, the person and the physical side. It was torture.

Anne, who was in care, felt as if she had ceased to exist:

I feel like a non-person who has disappeared off the face of the earth. They never thought whether I had got all the things I needed to leave care. They didn't deal with anything that had happened or give me what I needed. It's as if me as a person simply isn't there.

Hannah finally bowed to her mother's opinion:

I believed what she said about me in the end. I thought I must be totally bad, I'd heard it so often. I really believed it must be me, especially as my brother wasn't treated like that. I didn't know any different. Just what she told me.

Linda faced the threat that she was so bad she would be sent away:

I was told I was going to be put in a home. That was a threat that had been held over me since I remember: that naughty, evil people like me went away into a home. In my imagination it was like something out of *Oliver Twist*, because that was how it was portrayed to me: that you got up at five o'clock, and you only had porridge, and you scrubbed floors, and only had cold water. And that I would deserve it. I believed it, that I must be bad and useless. Why else would they want to send me away?

John remembered constant verbal assaults:

I can't even say if I believed it or not. It didn't get as far as me asking that question. It was just how I was. Bad, useless, lazy, pathetic. You name it, he said it: that was me, and no questions.

Louise simply said:

I was convinced I was useless, thick and stupid.

Samantha was entirely convinced of how bad she was:

It got to the point where if my mother wasn't hurting me, or other children weren't hurting me, then I'd hurt myself. I used to imagine myself as a child as being full of nasty green pus. Other people had blood. I would just ooze mess and badness. It was a very clear image. I was just rotten through and through.

Mark had used the phrase 'assassinate my whole...personality'. That sentiment expresses the totality of destructive intent that many people felt as children. Even those who felt some respite from the abuse remember seeing themselves very negatively, with little to balance such a view of themselves.

THE EFFECT ON EDUCATION

I have already referred to education, and how bullying in boarding schools is much more extensive than is often recognized. But abuse has other effects on schooling. The need to escape from home and enter employment as soon as they are able, which some people have described above, has the obvious effect of ending education sooner rather than later. This happened in Tina's case:

I deliberately left school as soon as I could, thinking – wrongly – that I'd be able to earn enough money to leave. That backfired because, of course, it wasn't that simple.

There were some positive features about school:

It was the time I wanted to leave school at fifteen. One teacher didn't want me to. He wanted to do something, but wasn't sure how. He tried to give me the opportunity, but I couldn't take it. He was the sort of teacher who would want to help. He didn't know how, and I didn't know the words. When I left his house one evening, it was a clear starry night and he said to me that I was capable of reaching for the stars. No one else had ever made me feel I could possibly do anything worthwhile. I'd had no encouragement at all, and I couldn't quite even grasp what he meant. But it gave me a bit of hope.

Amy's hope was to go to university, but her ambition was thwarted:

I so much wanted to be like my cousins and go away to university, to get a good job and move away from him. I did

so well at school, and I got through to the grammar school.
But he fed my mother terrible stories about the things that
went on there – like girls getting pregnant but everyone
keeping quiet about it, and so on – so he even made that
difficult for me. The abuse has so got in the way of things I
wanted to do, and could have done – particularly education.
I wanted to go to university, but it wasn't possible.

Peter's education was interrupted even more directly. There
were times when his injuries precluded his going to school:

There were many, many occasions when I couldn't go to
school for a week or two afterwards, because of the beating I
got. It's true to say that I was robbed of my education.

Jill found she was labelled as having particular difficulties, so
school became yet another nightmare for her:

They thought I couldn't read. But I haven't got a reading
problem. I always thought I was stupid and inept, because
that was implied at school. I had a teacher who always had to
make me cry. He would do it systematically. And another
teacher humiliated me in front of all the others because I
couldn't read or write properly – two more men in power
who humiliated me. If you set yourself up like that, you
should know better. But my worst fear is that they *did* know.
That it wasn't ignorance makes it worse. It was a nightmare
at home, and sometimes at school too.

Sadly, many children who are abused are also bullied at school.
Others simply become isolated, unable to mix with their peer
group. They can get ignored. What Jill said indicates that children
are bullied not just by other pupils – the popular picture of
bullying – but by teachers too. What is particularly worrying in
Jill's case is her sense that the teachers mentioned were not ignorant but had somehow picked her out as an abused child. Teachers
are very powerful figures who sometimes use their power negatively, either by failing to stop bullying or by being directly
abusive themselves. I do not forget that others, as Tina described,
can be much more positive in their response.

When abused children are teased or bullied at school, this adds
yet further abuse to their experience and increases their uncertainty about social contact. Additionally, they are perceived
as being 'different' by other children and are thereby more likely
to become the peer group's scapegoat. Another vicious circle is

created. Such children are less likely to have parents who will intervene with the school or help the child to deal with such occurrences. Furthermore, children who have experienced pain, and who have learned to tolerate it, find it impossible to act convincingly in their own defence. Bullying is therefore likely to intensify. Bullying at school must be acknowledged as a serious problem: it is not a 'little bit of teasing' or 'just harmless fun'. It constitutes abuse in its own right, and must not be let pass as within the acceptable limits of behaviour. Bullying can turn school into a living nightmare for children, and when they are already suffering abuse elsewhere it is even more horrific. Schools should be a place of safety and relief, but they sometimes become another trap.

Samantha was abused by her mother at home, and was bullied to such an extent at school that she was physically injured. The police were involved in escorting her to and from school. Looking back at those times, she remembered feeling that the teachers did nothing to protect her. They turned a blind eye:

> I stood out like a sore thumb. I was oddly dressed, living in a perpetual state of fear. And I'm sure they could tell. The bully-ing was dreadful. I was always bruised, either from school or home. It's more difficult to understand the teachers, though, because they did know.

Rosalind Miles observes that, like child abuse, bullying is a 'victimless crime', with the victim rather then the perpetrator being made to feel 'bad', guilty and ashamed (1991:69). School author-ities everywhere have been culpably slow to acknowledge the existence of bullying, let alone its routine occurrence, especially in economically deprived or inner-city areas. Yet a 1989 Home Office enquiry chaired by Lord Elton, a former Home Office Minister, found that bullying was both widespread in schools and as widely denied by teachers and head teachers.

Louise was aware that she must have lost much, although her recollections of her education were few:

> I have few memories of school. It's a huge gap. I've looked at photos and it doesn't mean anything: it could be a picture of a child not known to me. It's very odd. I have snatches of school incidents, but I remember no details of names or people. I only remember bad things. I remember a general feeling of victimization at school and a feeling of rage and powerlessness. I couldn't do anything about it. I was often

accused of doing things I hadn't done and it was like being utterly powerless. It was really very blank that time in my life. I lost a lot in terms of education. My parents told me I was a lazy child, because my reports got worse and worse. They used to ask me why I was doing so badly. It was all my fault, all my responsibility. Educationally there were great losses, and I failed all my exams. My father was just furious because I had failed him.

Children in care found the move from familiar schools very disruptive, and their education suffered accordingly:

At least we would have been educated by now, because we were at good schools and doing well. It ruined that for all of us. There was no encouragement at all when we were in care. She loved education and would have really encouraged us. She loved books, but he wouldn't let her read them.

Hannah showed considerable talent, but had to leave school at fifteen:

I had won a scholarship to an academy of music and drama, but my mother wouldn't allow me to go. I had to go back home and start paying them back for all the years they had cared for me. There was nothing I could do or my aunties could do. I had to go back.

The irony of her words is obvious. It was Hannah who had been abused by both her mother and her brother during the years she was then supposed to 'pay' for.

Rachel was disruptive at school, although this was never recognized as anything more than extreme naughtiness:

I was a very, very naughty child. I realize now I was disturbed, and nowadays I would have been diagnosed as such. So when I was fourteen they sent me away to a convent in Belgium, and it was terrible. I learned to be a nice girl, to conform, to push it all away, to repress; whereas before I'd been trying to tell them something was wrong. I had always been in trouble at school, but nobody wondered why.

The vicious circle of abuse becomes horribly clear when experiences such as these are described. Not only do children lose the hope of a safe home, but their schooling is also affected. Because children spend much of their day at school it offers the possibility of being a positive and compensating environment. It can offer both a safe retreat and some hope for the future, but it appears that for many of those whom I interviewed, their abuse coloured their school life as well.

WHY DID THEY DO IT?

In talking with those who had been abused, I soon realized how important it was for some of them to consider in retrospect why they had been abused. Although some had no wish to know, others explored this question with me. Tina, for example, thought her brother-in-law's family background was significant:

> He felt very powerful. He came from a very complex family where there were three sets of step-sibs all living together at various times. And they were all different ages. In fact for most of his childhood he was brought up by an older sister, and her husband was a bullying bloke. I think somehow he thought that was the way a chap should behave. And I was eight years old and desperate for affection. I don't know, but maybe he distorted my need for affection as being a way of gaining sexual satisfaction and also being powerful. At around the same time my sister had a stillborn baby, and she had desperately wanted it and was devastated. And when I was twelve she had a handicapped baby, which lived only a short while. Looking back, although I had none of these thoughts at the time, I wondered if they were having major sexual difficulties. And I was there. And in that sense it's not forgiveness I feel but more of an understanding that it wasn't acceptable, it shouldn't have happened, that he's only human after all. I think that's why I feel a bit protective towards my sister as well. It was a very difficult time for her, and she was very hurt, and I needed to protect her.

Mark felt that his own personality as a child played a part:

> In some ways I feel I have to take some responsibility for the violence, because another child would not have had the determination and strength as a very young child to threaten my father. I knew what it was about. I knew how to get at him in a way my brother didn't. My father was very insecure and didn't have a very well-formed sense of himself. And he saw me as a miniature and very threatening adult; and he

tried to make me do various things, and usually he couldn't.
I would find a way to be defiant. He had the constant experience of battering me not working. In a way I was the
successful one, the competent one, and the more successful
I became the more of a threat to my father I became.
My father thought that he was a failure. He'd been a public
schoolboy – lots of opportunities – but he failed in work and
in marriage. The relationship I was in with my father was an
extraordinarily powerful one. In an old book I have of my
father's he had written, 'The son should never be cleverer
than the father.' That was really very important, and of
course I was doing very well.

Jill felt that in her father's eyes she somehow did not exist:

I don't think he counted me as a human being. I don't know
whether he had such bad feelings about himself that I was an
extension of him, so he treated me badly because neither of
us was worth anything; but I just did not count.

Louise thought her father's own experiences might explain his
violence:

He was tortured in the prison camps. It doesn't take away
the anger, but makes me think, 'Oh God, abuse multiplies
abuse.' I realize now that, at that time, it was impossible for
my mother to leave. Divorce was the pits where she lived.
The stories spread about a divorced woman were just incredible. She would have been better off by herself, but she had no
choice. I know we would have been better off too. We were
just piggies in the middle of their horrible marriage. We were
fodder for them, used by one or the other as it suited them.

Her feeling that the abuse could only have been stopped by
her mother leaving the marriage was echoed by Peter, who also
thought the family history was important:

The only thing that would have stopped the abuse was for
him not to have been there. But what could she do with five
children? My father was abused by his father, so was his
mother by his father. One of his brothers is a compulsive
tidier, like me, and the other one is very violent. On my
mother's side, her mother was a prostitute and my mother
had a long succession of 'uncles'; her brother is completely

mad; her half-sister is totally screwed up with no children. It's a bleak picture.

Rachel discovered a similarly difficult family history:

When my sister died last year, my mother told me that she had been abused by her father when she was very small. When she was six she used to get up in the mornings and wash the sheets, because she didn't want her mother to know. And his brother abused her. Then she was sent away to school and came back when she was twelve. She told my son that then he used to pay her, from the age of twelve to seventeen. But she never told my father; so when I told her about grandpa I suppose she just panicked in case my father found out.

A CATALOGUE OF LOSS

The losses to any child who has been abused are enormous. They are certainly not quantifiable, and sometimes feel indescribable. They are so great that words alone do not adequately convey the awfulness. For this book I have only been able to select some extracts from many more experiences and perspectives that have been told me. The thread that runs throughout is that of children who have never had a childhood. Many have lived a nightmare existence from which there was no escape and little respite. There were few opportunities to form trusting and secure attachments with adults. Peer relationships at school and at home were equally damaged.

Although I find it hard to find the right words, coming away from many of the interviews I have drawn upon in this book I was left feeling that what I had heard described must have been sheer torture, reminiscent of both concentration camp and of methods of persuasion and punishment still used by many regimes today. Jacqueline Spring (1987:49–50) vividly echoes my feeling:

And when I read about those camps, survivors' accounts of what they were like, I realize with a shock that, on some level that is not physical, I have been there. I know about being there. I know about the colour and the cold. I know about the tall barbed-wire fences, the searchlights, the dogs ...I know about the self-effacement, the secret fantasies of what it would be like not to be small, trivial, powerless, hungry for love. I know how vital, but how dangerous these fantasies were. I know about trying to hide tiny treasures in dark places, so that they can't be taken away. I know about trying to hide myself in a crowded classroom, in a crowded family, so that I won't be seen and brought forward for interrogation, ridicule, punishment, disgrace.

Her words convey how abused children live in an atmosphere of fear and distrust. Their capacity for play and spontaneity is destroyed. They are alone, with no one to rescue them. The very people who should protect them are their persecutors. There is nobody to turn to.

In Chapter 5 I show how for the majority of those whom I interviewed either they told someone of the abuse or there was someone who already knew. Often this was a person close to the child. Others were certainly in a position to know but, either consciously or unconsciously, refused to acknowledge what was before them. For whatever reason, many people chose to deny or collude. Others actively joined in the abuse. It is perhaps hard for the reader who has not experienced abuse in childhood to imagine fully the impact of this level of betrayal. The horror is too painful to permeate fully into consciousness. But if we are to take child abuse seriously, and to work with adults who carry these memories within them, we have to hear these stories and to acknowledge the real agony. That may be painful for us, but our pain gives us only a hint of the magnitude of the suffering of those who have experienced abuse directly.

FOUR

CHILDHOOD ABUSE:
THE ADULT'S EXPERIENCE

The previous chapter highlighted the devastating effects of abuse
on a child. As I have already made clear, such appalling treatment
does not simply evaporate when children grow into adults. In this
chapter I record how adult survivors view themselves. If they had
much to say when talking about their early life, the men and
women I interviewed had even more to say about life as an adult,
and their current experience. Whereas childhood memories were
sometimes hazy or even lost in the unconscious, most of them
vividly recalled and described more recent times. Their descriptions were often powerful, and so extensive that inevitably they
cannot be recounted in full. But the impact of their words is so
considerable and powerful that in this chapter they again speak for
themselves.

COPING WITH THE EFFECTS OF THE PAST

Different people have various styles of coping with and of re-
sponding to abuse, although similarities can be detected in their
stories. Tina distinguished her adult self from the child who was
abused, although she recognized that earlier events could resurface:

Something in the family happened recently which made
me realize that it's dead but not buried. It's still there, and

catches you unawares. It seems a long time ago now. It happened to the child I was, not the woman I am. To regurgitate it does not seem worthwhile. It's important to hold on to my adult self now. I don't exactly split it off and say it didn't happen to me, but I do say that it happened to me then. And that feels safe. It's only on rare occasions now that I think about it. I think, 'that poor child'; but it's that poor child then, not me now, which seems a very healthy and comfortable way of dealing with it.

I recognize that I had been a sort of an adult child, and yet when I became an adult there was still a lot of child in me. It all got turned on its head – I didn't feel grown-up until I was in my late twenties. I didn't feel in charge of myself somehow. Until then I had always done what others wanted. Until I got rid of the baggage, I couldn't ask 'What do I want?' and not feel pressured by anyone.

I still feel often less than adequate. I mentally judge people when I meet them, how much better they are than me. I very easily downrate myself. That's what I call my inferiority complex. But I'm working on it, and I'm much better than I was.

I sense I have a sort of inner strength, but I don't know where that inner strength has come from. I suppose I dealt with it my way. I've seen people who have dealt with it very differently, and I don't think there is one way. There is no magic solution. There has to be a right time to talk.

In Amy the effects lingered on in many ways:

The summer has always been easier and still is, because he wasn't around so much in the summer and the abuse was less. It was a safer time of year. But I still get depressed in the winter, and that's always been the case.

It's affected me not just with the big things in life but in little things too that may not sound important: it was years before I'd wear short-sleeved dresses, because he used to go on about the dirty black hairs on my arms. And there were some colours that had awful associations for me. Some of that I've overcome, but not all.

How I see myself has been tremendously affected: I felt people didn't believe me because I'd been in mental hospital. And even now I still feel that if something goes wrong I must have deserved it. Almost all of it is still with me one way or another.

Mark's presentation of himself to the wider world, and his self-perception, had been greatly affected. Deep down he saw himself as remaining as unacceptable as he felt when he was a child. There were some gains in being an adult, but the losses were also evident:

> As a young adult I saw myself as basically unattractive. The reality was that I felt I was a bad person and that I didn't have much. I really still believe that I'm not very lovable as a human being, and there are many layers of that which remain untouched. I still feel that the only quality I have is hard work, industry: that at the end of the day I can work harder than other people, and that I don't have any talents apart from that.
>
> I know I come over as being on the aggressive side. I communicate a sense of power to people. In many ways that's not really me but the sort of twistedness that comes from abuse. I know I can still rage, and usually when I do it's nothing to do with the thing I'm apparently angry about: it's about what happened *then*. I can get very angry with things I can't do. But in a way I wouldn't have it any other way. So many people are half-dead and don't have the capacity to feel deeply that kind of rage, that kind of love, that kind of energy. So the strength of feeling is there – enormous strength and confidence in survival, knowing I will cope. Of course, other people have to cope with the strength of feeling.
>
> You have to live with the damage that is done to you: it's not possible to repair it. That sounds pessimistic, although it's not meant to be; but you have to accept that is the life some people have. And that you have a problem. And that you come over to people as aggressive. I don't feel that I'm an aggressive person at all, although I can well see that is people's first perception.
>
> The abuse has left me knowing that at the end of the day you know you are not, and cannot be, a thoroughbred – a very English but important belief. You know that however many books you write, programmes you appear on, meetings you address, you know that you cannot make it. There is no way in England.

Some of Mark's sense of unacceptability and the long-lasting effects on the whole person was echoed by Jill. The abuse did not give her an aura of aggressiveness and power, but one of uncertainty and lack of confidence. Like Mark, she found young adulthood a hard time. Although she managed to leave home to undertake professional training, the transition was a difficult one, with no escape route. Life was no easier later on, although she too felt there had been gains:

> After I'd left home it was really hard. There was no respite if you needed a break: nowhere to run back to; no retreat. It was like camping on an open plain without even a cave to go back to. And it's canvas, so you've got nothing firm. And I was still suffering under the delusion that it was my fault: that a lot of what happened had been to do with me. I carried that one for ages and ages: like, 'What do you expect? It's you.' And the sense of difference that I had all the time through my childhood, that just carried on and coloured lots of other things all the way through.
>
> It leaves you accepting the unacceptable and never being surprised at anything. It took me ten years into the marriage to think, 'Perhaps this isn't how it should be.' There is a resignation that comes from abuse that lasts into adulthood, and it took me a long time to wake up. It made me ignorant of myself and everything else. I'm beginning to learn to be nice to myself. I felt I didn't deserve nice things. It's also made me shy in earning money.
>
> It affected me in so many ways. Up until a few years ago I starved myself because I thought I mustn't be more than eight stone or I'll get desperately fat like my mother. It was quite irrational. In so many ways I was chained down. I was shackled. But I began to think, 'What do other people do?' And I realized they ate three times a day, and sometimes in between if they wanted to.
>
> Being a woman was a real difficulty. Now I just experience the same difficulties just walking around the world as other women do. And I'm actually writing poems. I don't always need my husband's approval now. I'm actually a person. I can walk down town just feeling no more and no less than any other person. Me. I can just walk about. It was the feelings before that were so awful. No one else would have known. Now I know I'm important to myself. I also know I'm no more important than anyone else. It's not gone over the top. I went around in black trousers for years, and

now I wear skirts. I've literally blossomed. I've got a bosom now – I wouldn't let myself have one before. It was responsible, literally, for some of the pain.

It's not that I don't have problems now, but I can cope with them. It's like that awful old thing has been cauterized. I can be happy in myself, I want to join in things. I know who I am. I know I've got a certain amount of rights. I know I can still be put down very, very easily; but nevertheless I can now enjoy things. I'm beginning to wake up. And that's lovely.

But I really do think it was a waste, all those years – a long time to be asleep. It does make me so angry with myself and with others. When I look back I feel anger, a sense of loss, a feeling that I won't be able to live life to the full; that I've been wasted; that I've missed chances and opportunities. But it's deeper than that, because anybody could say that. I'm not talking about extraordinary things, but the ordinary low-key level of life. Just missing those things. And a sense of not being *bona fide*. And sadness. Those are the negatives. On the other hand, I'm more aware. I'm starting to live now. I'm sensitive to things, and very aware of hurt. In some ways that's very painful and I hate it. It's not selective. I feel I shall never be a good person.

Louise also had anxieties about her self, and was aware that her enjoyment of sexuality could be affected. As a child, the abuse caused her to lose aspects of herself, and the losses were repeated in a different way in adulthood:

It's left me with a very, very deep need to be approved of. And a dreadful fear of disapproval. If I do something someone doesn't like, I think, 'That's it, finished – destroyed with no possibility of it being mended ever.' And it will all be my fault. I am aware of that now, and I try to stop myself being sucked into that. I am able to challenge it. I still have a sense of guilt, a very deep-seated sense of lack of worth, and a low self-esteem that gets knocked very easily. But I am much stronger now than I was.

When I'm down I hate myself because I lose my sexuality. I lose a part of myself. But I know that it comes back. As a child I always had to be terribly good and sweet, and people were very cross if I got angry. It's left a problem of being angry, although I'm not very aware of that side of myself.

Peter attempted suicide on many occasions when he was younger. In his thirties, he did not feel suicidal, but there were other difficulties:

> I've tried to kill myself on many occasions as well as having a lot of suicidal fantasies. Fortunately when I was younger I didn't know how to do it properly as I do now; and now I don't have the same feelings. Things have improved.
>
> Being out is difficult. For instance, if I'm out in a pub I have to go with a group, and I have to have my back to the wall and be able to see the door. It's fear of being hurt, with all those men around. When you're outside, who protects you? Only yourself. I still find it difficult to walk through town. Waiting outside a shop in town, I'll walk round and round the tree to see who is coming at me. I know it's repeating a pattern, but it makes me more comfortable. It's all to do with control. I have to control the situations I'm in. Some I can let go in. It's getting less of a problem. And certainty my sexuality is all over the place. I've had relationships with men and women. But it is all over the place, and I think that's a direct consequence of the abuse.
>
> But for three of us [he and his siblings] it's ended, and we have made a very definite choice about how we stop it. We said, 'That is it. No more. It stops here. We can do something about it. We will not propagate what has happened. We will not become abusers. Or allow it to happen.' But it doesn't take away what's been done to me, or its effects. It's left me scarred.

Hannah was still piecing together her childhood, but she recognized how deeply she still felt the effects of the abuse. Like Peter, she had contemplated, and attempted, suicide:

> She was very vicious. It started to change my life dramatically once I realized it wasn't my fault. I was slowly starting to build my confidence up, because it wore my confidence away. Before, if anything went wrong it was my fault, whether it was or not. I allowed people to treat me like dirt. There are still bits of my childhood I don't remember – some of it's just so bad. Even now I still get memories coming back – it's like fitting a jigsaw together. When I do remember things, none of them are nice.
>
> It does affect your whole life, just all of it. I'm only just

finding me, and there is a long way to go yet. I haven't had the foundations, and sometimes I feel very lost because I haven't memories to look back on. I haven't had the closeness of a mother and a child. But now I think I've learned to listen to myself about what's right. And I listen to other people's children and other mothers. There was a time I couldn't cope with it any longer. I just wanted out. I was nearly seventeen. I took a massive overdose.

Linda was virtually brainwashed by her mother into thinking herself evil, and was still struggling to let the world see her as she is:

A lot of my life I'd felt I was one big con. I believed what I'd been brought up to believe: that I had evil in my veins. I will never forget feeling like that. And even now it's ever so easy for me to slip into feeling like that. The world did, and does, see me as confident, because it's what I like to portray. But I am learning I don't have to portray that. That has been a huge step, and I am still taking it.

Rachel saw her abuse as having ruined her life, with little to compensate for the enormous losses, damage and destruction that had been wreaked. She frequently considered death, and had a major breakdown in the past when she was hospitalized. Her marriage had finally ended. She vividly recaptured as an adult the dreadful dilemmas created by her childhood experiences:

It has totally ruined my life. I'm now in my fifties, and I can see the end of therapy in sight. But abuse ruined my life; and the only thing I can be thankful for is that I haven't done it to my kids.

It spoiled sex for me for years. I was terrified. I think I must have had orgasms when I was abused, and when I had one as an adult it was like experiencing the depths of depravity – it brought back such awful feelings. It took away the pleasure of my body, and my ownership of it, and my choice to give it or keep it as I chose. I could not bear being touched either.

And when I started having my breakdown I had these terrible fantasies. I couldn't see a knife without seeing penises being cut off, or my breasts being cut off. I could not go in a shop with a bacon-slicer. I still get these fantasies sometimes.

But I do feel that if somehow the boys will be all right one day it won't be so bad. Although it's so painful that even knowing I've stopped the abuse doesn't always help. And it has been such a struggle to live at all. I have felt suicidal all along, for many, many years. Even when I was a little girl I can remember wishing I had never been born. Really, that's all I remember – this longing, this wish, that I had never ever been; and then I would have avoided all this pain. I veer between fear of being alone whilst not wanting to be back in the marriage how it was. But I am very frightened. My home is for sale, and recently my job ended.

I think I've reached a stage when I want to be all in one piece myself. I realize I'm two people, and I'm only just beginning to be one person. And when I'm one person it won't matter. I think I'm nearly there, but it's very, very painful, trying to let my true self, who I've tried to push away, come into me, because she's very, very frightened. It's really a battle inside me between two bits of myself.

It is hard, because you feel so terribly, terribly dirty. I remember saying in a session with my therapist that I just want to be washed clean. But you have to do it yourself. And I still get this feeling that both my mother and grandpa must have known something terrible about me that would have allowed them to do what they did. I'm only just, after all these years, accepting that I'm not wicked: I had always known that I was wicked and so dirty, because I thought that they must have seen something inside me that allowed them to do those things, otherwise they wouldn't have done it. We're all brought up to believe that families are good to us and for us – particularly that mothers are. And the alternative, that it must be them who are wicked and dirty, is too frightening for a child. Who will look after you then? Who will be responsible for you then? It's as if there are no boundaries if you possibly dare think they could be that wrong.

For those who have been in care as children there are even greater difficulties. Not only have they experienced abuse at home (the precipitating factor for their entry into care); they have often encountered a 'care' system that dismally fails them. Karen felt

really chock-a-block in my head with so much to do. Not even knowing where to start or what to do about it. I cope, but put on a front, and the next minute I can be very angry or very depressed or very upset. If anyone lets me down over any little thing, I refer to the past all the time. And everything gets out of proportion. I was told I had a bad temper, but that it came from what my dad had done.

There are other things, too – practical things, but they really matter. I really struggle with my housing. I've only got one heater and it's freezing, and it takes ages and money to sort it out. They can make you feel awful by the way they speak to you on the phone, as though you've no rights. I started with disadvantages and it's got worse. It's easy to get into debt, and no one helps. In care, you don't know about money. It's all the policies that cause problems: it's people, not objects, they're dealing with. I know that when anything goes wrong I get too despondent. I start thinking this is how its always going to be for the rest of my life. I just think about my past and everything that's happened and I can't look forward at all.

Anne felt she had gained in strength, and she was working with huge determination to change the system. But she clearly still carried a considerable burden. At a young age she experienced abuse at home, followed by abuse in the system. Her attempts to deal with the latter brought her into contact with the most vicious forms of abuse. Small wonder that at the age of twenty-one she spent her weekends sleeping:

In many ways it's made me stronger. It's had to. I want to constructively change it. My life revolves around that. We've been dealing with some horrific cases of organized abuse, sexual abuse rings. It is actually dangerous and threatening. We had a boy involved in making snuff movies, which is the killing of children. And we know about the Amsterdam connection. And lots of pornography. I think in the last few years of Thatcher it's got worse. You can't be hopeless in this work, because you can't afford to be. But you can only go on so long, and you get so stressed and exhausted. I spend all weekend in my bed trying to recover.

I set out Nicki's story at length in Chapter 2. After a childhood spent in and out of care, she felt

very bitter and revengeful towards my mum; and I'll get back at her if I can. It eats me up. They didn't help me with any of that in care, except the first two months in the assessment centre. I carry memories around with me all the time. I need help and hope for the future.

It is also worth noting that abuse survivors report a high level of illness. As children, their bodies and minds faced ongoing onslaught. It is hardly surprising that the body also continues to respond later in life. Among the illnesses and symptoms mentioned there were migraines, asthma, eczema, epilepsy and pseudo-epilepsy, back pains, throat problems, stomach pains, severe mouth ulcers and gynaecological problems. Eating disorders were also commonly reported.

CAREER, EMPLOYMENT AND EDUCATION

The accounts of childhood experience in Chapter 3 showed how schooling was adversely affected by abuse. This has obvious ongoing implications for employment potential, particularly when the job market becomes increasingly competitive and qualifications become more significant. When the low self-esteem and lack of self-confidence already described above are added, adult abuse survivors are inevitably disadvantaged further. Tina described her struggles in this area of her life:

I left school as soon as I could and got a very low-paid job. It was useless. I couldn't be independent, which was what I longed for: my earnings were far too low. So it didn't even achieve that. And I do feel resentment (although that's not quite the right word) that I wasn't able to continue my education, which has left me at a disadvantage in many, many ways.

I've caught up a bit now, and I really needed to prove myself to myself. There is still that throwback sometimes of 'I'll never be good enough.' I was recently made redundant after ten years in the same job, and that was tough. And it was quite illogical. I think it's because I wasn't good enough. I find myself now in a job that's quite challenging, and I have to gear myself up to thinking I can do it and tell myself that I am good enough. I still have to push myself a bit.

Amy did well at school, but she left early to take up employment. As a result, she missed the chance of going to university, and her job prospects were also disrupted:

I lost one good job because of breaking down and being admitted to psychiatric hospital. They wouldn't have me back, so I lost a lot at that time. Then you get labelled as a dreadful, vicious deranged person. It doesn't help you find work.

Mark's choice of work (he is a therapist) was influenced by his abuse:

I think it is one of the reasons I've come into this work. I worked with a couple recently who had both been abused as children, and it was like there was an immediate recognition. And also I've never learned to work in a team – I just don't know how to do it. I've undersocialized, and I don't have the skills you need.

Jill trained as a nurse, but when she became a mother she was unable to work. When *her* mother worked, her father had abused her:

The last thing I ever wanted to do was to go out to work. To me, that was what my mother had done, and look what happened to us. I could not possibly have done that. Of course, I had no other example of a mother going out and of a father taking over responsibility in a reliable way, so for me it was a direct correlation between working mums and abused children. As a result, the levels of my ambition are much lower than the average. When I was older, I stopped my university course. I found that difficult, but my daughter was having a baby and I knew she'd need help.

Louise was in her thirties when she undertook professional training. As a young adult she had underachieved:

I left school at sixteen and spent a year housekeeping at home, because my mother was studying at university. When I went to an interview I was the most nervous and anxious seventeen-year-old they'd met. I went into nursing, but at a very low grade. I had no confidence at all.

Peter's choices were similarly limited:

It stopped me going further because of the inability to concentrate, because of fear. And I lost so much time from school. It's also greatly affected my choice of jobs. I know it's why I chose the army and the prison system. No matter

who I am, these people will look after me, because that's
the way it works. The structure makes me feel safe and
protected.

Nicki was 'semi-independent' at sixteen, but she saw little hope
of employment. She desperately wished to continue education,
but at her young age there was no financial support available. Yet
another door had closed. Hannah and Judy both felt the possibility of education and employment had been taken from them.
Now, in their forties, they were both studying. It had been an
enormous struggle, but a great achievement to have come so far.
They both hoped for a career in a caring profession. But Rachel
felt her career as well as her whole life had been wrecked by the
abuse:

> There is no doubt I would have been a successful singer but,
> you see, when success was there I couldn't let myself have it.
> I ruined it. I had to spoil it. So now I'm back typing, where I
> started from. So it never ends.

RELATIONSHIPS WITH CHILDREN

Most of those I met had their own children. There are some who
have been abused who cannot have children: their bodies have
been too severely damaged. Others decide not to have their own
family, because they cannot risk the possibility of perpetuating
the abusive cycle. One woman, abused by her mother, told me,
'The history of mother–daughter relationships in our family is so
bad, I would not risk having a child. That is the only way to be
sure I will stop it.' So the losses can be compounded.

Relationships with children are wide and various. Some experience delight in their children in a way they could not have
predicted. Others have less positive feelings. Some veer between
the two reactions. Tina had always felt very protective towards
her daughter, determined that as a parent she would be entirely
different from her own experience. She left her first husband
because of his violence, fearing he would hurt her baby. She
entered a second marriage with her daughter as her priority:

> I was very protective of my daughter in choosing a man who
> would be a good parent to her too. That's worked out ex-
> tremely well. They relate very well together. I had a sticky

patch when she was eight. It was months and months before I realized what was happening. It wasn't just because I was eight when the abuse began: it was because of losing my mum at that age. I had no maternal pattern to follow, and I was acutely aware of that; and she was growing and changing quite rapidly at that point, from being a quite pliable youngster to someone who obviously had a mind of her own. I didn't want to squash that, and I felt quite vulnerable in myself. I realized I had to find my own path and I had to allow her to be herself too. I try to be very open and enable her to talk about anything with me, so she can always talk if she needs to.

Amy had found being a parent constantly overshadowed by her own abuse. Her sense of constant danger was overwhelming:

Where the children are concerned, I feel I've brainwashed everyone into accepting how things have been done for years. Things I've been doing for the wrong reasons I now question. On a daily basis it affects everything, although I try very hard. I've always turned up at times I'm not expected – completely unpredictable: bath times and other danger times when my husband was alone with them – making sure. I creep up on them – just to be sure nothing is happening. It sounds horrible, but I can't be quite safe. I actually feel I have to do it.

There is a danger of my abuse making my children as isolated as I was because of it. A couple of years ago I'd have squashed all ideas of my daughter wanting to go on a school trip. It wouldn't have felt safe. Now I will think about it, though my first response is 'No. Never.' It's so hard to trust them with somebody you don't even know. I find it agonizing taking them to school, collecting them from school – it's dreadful. Dancing shows are dreadful because of the memories they bring back. The feeling of threat is huge. Children's birthday parties – I just don't know what to do. So they have a very isolated life too.

Mark's son reminded him of his father:

In some ways my older son reminds me of my father, although it's not a serious problem. But there are a lot of parallels. There can be a danger of reproducing a child who is in some ways like the abuser out of anxiety to make it different. I've never abused my children. If I've found myself getting really angry I've gone and broken the Olympic record, walking so fast. But I know I'd never hurt them.

Jill, who felt unable to leave her children to go to work, found her protectiveness extending to her grandchildren:

With my granddaughter it was an absolute priority, like my protectiveness extended right through. My daughter broke down at times, and we had the baby here. The baby went to a child-minder. I felt I was fighting for her. I knew when that child wasn't being real, when she was putting on layers to protect herself, to survive. I could see her doing it and I recognized it. But I felt she was at risk, and I was the only one who would protect her. I was desperate. I could almost think it was me. She looks like me. It stirred up so much.

I always thought I was an absolutely abominable mother. But I now allow myself to be a reasonable mother. I'm not saying any more I'm a hopeless woman and a hopeless mother. That's been liberating, and I'm actually quite pleased at some of the things my children are. My own abuse did get in the way when the children were young. I didn't take enough notice of the little things that would make life nicer. They had expectations without the props. I should have fought more for them and demanded more from their father. I didn't get much beyond the nurturing and that sort of thing. There were lots of times when I wasn't calm. My fears came out in lots of ways.

My oldest daughter is understanding about the abuse. My middle daughter doesn't want to know. She blames me for a lot. She wanted me to bring up her daughter. I've stopped myself being hurt by her. My son has been very understanding.

Louise was very positive about being a mother, but recognized the effects of her own abuse:

I can be over-protective and have a huge need to protect her from her father's anger even when it's quite unnecessary. I can get very anxious and frightened and tense. They can be battling quite happily and I feel awful. She isn't at all intimidated, but it touches terrible things in me. I realize now that jumping in to protect her could get in the way of their relationship, and that sometimes worries me. I do feel a huge sense of achievement that the pattern has stopped, that my father's abusive childhood, my mother's abusive childhood, our abusive childhood have stopped here. I am just so pleased. I just feel really good that we have such a good relationship.

Peter had a young baby and a daughter by an early marriage:

I have a thirteen-year-old daughter whom I don't see because I'm frightened by how I perceive I could feel towards her. I was so disgusted with myself when I first acknowledged why I didn't see her, and then so disgusted with him [his father] for having made me feel that way. I've pretty much dealt with that – although I still don't see her, because I don't want to ruin her life. She has a family. I don't want to bounce her back and forwards. It is a big loss. I see in her the child I could have been. She reminds me of me.

I have a new baby now. It felt like a weight had gone the day I realized I wanted children. I know I'm not going to be like my father. I have an absolute certainty about that. When our baby was born it was a hard labour for both of us. I looked at him, and it was like this little voice inside saying 'It's OK, it's going to be all right.' It was very significant for me. I knew nothing was going to happen to him like it had happened to me. It's the chance to make it all better. I'm going to have so much fun growing up with him. We shall play together. I know my sister does that. One has a little boy. The other can't have children because of what my father did to her. That really makes me angry and sad, because she'd be a lovely mother. He did so much damage.

Rachel had two sons. Motherhood was not easy:

I wonder what I've done to my kids but, thank God, since I've had therapy I can talk to them and I can say I'm sorry; and we do have a good relationship. But I wonder if they're all right. With the elder one I was hopeless, absolutely hopeless. I didn't want him near me. I did all the right things, but I can remember I desperately needed to be alone and I used to put him in one room and leave him all morning. Anybody being near me was a tremendous threat, although I loved him and I worried about him.

When the oldest one was born, I was absolutely convinced there was something wrong with him: that he wasn't formed properly. It was different with my younger son: we were

very close. But I sometimes wonder about that and his homosexuality. With the older one I could never make contact,
although now he knows what happened to me – he asked
me – and it has made us so much closer. I'd never told anyone else apart from my therapist. And I was able to say
sorry. I was so blind and made so many mistakes. And now
I'd give anything to have those years back. Now I'd be good
at it. It's one of the great unfairnesses: you don't get a second
chance at these things in life. But at least I can talk to my
children.

FRIENDSHIP

The social world of children is greatly restricted by abuse, and
this pattern continues in some adults, although others branch out
into friendships. Tina was one of those who still sensed some
restrictiveness:

I find it quite difficult to make small talk; a lot of my feelings
are quite serious ones. It can be difficult socially. I think
that's a bit of an offshoot. I can function quite well if there is
a subject – it's safer – but I find it quite difficult to be trivial
and social. I have to think, and make an effort – it's not
spontaneous. We don't socialize a lot. I find it quite hard
to make relationships, to get the trust right. The friendships
I have are quite long-standing, very much made with care. I
have a small circle of close friends, but once I make that jump
from acquaintance to friendship it's quite strong. It's as if I
test people out to make it safe, and then it's OK.

Amy remained in the isolation imposed on her during childhood:

We don't have any life with other people at all. We don't go out.
I never use babysitters: in a circle, you never know whether the
husband or the wife will turn up. And I don't want people in
the house. I do, but I don't. I don't want people seeing a mess or
poking around. It's hard to let other people in. I grieve for a
close friend. I can't say I pine, because it's so long since I had
one.

Mark was in a similar position:

I keep strangers at a distance. The hard thing is meeting people
for the first time, especially in a small group. It makes me take a

very pro-active, brick-in-a-sock approach until I know they're OK, and then I can do something else. I can see myself doing it. The trick is to stop doing it.

But I'm still fairly isolated. I don't think things have changed that much. I don't think I have a close male friend, and to have one would be an enormous hill to climb. And that certainly comes from the damage. I have enormous difficulty in trusting a man, and I don't really like being around men. Most of the close relationships I have are with women.

And Peter found friendships a problem:

I have very few friends. I find it very difficult to trust people. And why would these people like me? A feeling of being unlikeable. If I don't like me, how could anyone else? When I did find people who weren't judging me, who were accepting me, that screwed me up a bit. That's difficult – it's almost easier to perpetuate it. But to believe they like me – I can't handle that. I almost deny crossly when people like me.

It was a major step for Jill to have a close woman friend:

I met my friend, and something I'd never had before started to happen: I made a contact outside. We meet once a week, always, but we write reams to one another, and tell dreams. It's a very special friendship, with a history there: we've brought up children together. And it doesn't matter that there have been times when we haven't been able to meet – we can shelve that. She has given me a lot of strength. It's a real dialogue. We can admit the things we find difficult and aren't so good at.

Louise had also found friendships very supportive:

A few friends have been very significant, very supportive. I tend to have a few close friends rather than a large circle. But they're very important, very validating.

And Rachel valued her friendships with women:

I do have good friends. I've always tried to be honest. It's been a deep longing in me – not to have secrets and to be safely honest. It hasn't spoilt my friendships with women. That is so important. There are one or two who are extremely close: they are essential to me.

RELATIONSHIPS WITH PARTNERS

These often opposite responses to closeness are reflected in what those who have been abused say about intimate partnerships: some have found in them a life-saver; others have experienced closeness as deeply threatening and even unthinkable. Some, such as Tina, have been able to leave a bad relationship and make a more satisfactory one:

> I deliberately sought out someone to marry in order to leave home, and it didn't work out. I didn't tell my husband what had happened to me. My first husband was an appalling choice, and everyone said so. I so badly wanted it to work. I wanted someone fond of me, someone to be with. Looking back, I think I went and found someone who was also damaged. He'd had lots of stays in psychiatric hospital, and also poor physical health. He was violent. We were divorced when my daughter was fifteen months old.
>
> I met my present husband quite soon after that and, looking back, that could have been a major disaster, because it would have been healthier at that time to have had longer alone. I was extremely fortunate, rather by luck and accident than by design. He's older than I am, and we look as if there is an age difference, and people notice it. But it doesn't feel like that, except I am very frightened of losing him. He's quite a rock for me, and he's the first person I ever told about the abuse. He prompted me to grow in all sorts of ways. He saw I had potential and encouraged me, and gave me the strength to value myself a bit more, to have more confidence. I dread to think what would have happened if I had not met him. He was terribly important.

Jill had also married twice. Her first husband knew about her childhood, but did not fully understand:

> I think I told him from the beginning, and he reassured me and said, 'You'll be all right with me.' I thought, 'What a lovely relief,' but I think that's the last we heard of it. I don't think he understood. In my second marriage he knew and was sympathetic and careful about it. It wasn't until a couple of years ago that I wrote something and showed it to him. It stunned him. He hadn't quite realized until then the implications and how I felt about it.

My first marriage was almost like a utilitarian marriage, just like the furniture you bought after the war. I wasn't enough of myself to make it better, and there were things I could have stopped but didn't. On the sexual side I did finally say 'No' to something. And he did stop doing it and I was amazed. That's the other thing I didn't realize: that I had any power. I gradually realized, and in my second marriage I slowly found out more about myself. He has to take credit for some of that. He would like to take it all, but that isn't right. I think this is the last frontier, which is – to put it too simply – his dominance. He is a very, very, controlling person, and has his own problems as well. Sometimes that clashes.

Amy's husband was an important stabilizing influence early in her marriage, although ultimately this broke down because of his violence. Violence was so familiar to her that it was some while before she was able fully to acknowledge it and its effects on both her and her children:

It has finished now and it's been very difficult and I should have recognized sooner what was happening. But it was an important relationship. It was all too much for him. We did really need help together. There were so many things he couldn't say and do. He didn't always realize that things change, and that some things he couldn't do are now accept-able. He couldn't cope, and has said that he's really been quite suicidal on several occasions. It got really bad during therapy, because things started coming out rather than being pushed away. The abuse made things too interwined: at one time he was everything – my confidante, work partner, lover, everything. I'm so isolated – there was no one else. It affected my marriage in all sorts of weird ways.

Nor had Rachel much positive experience in her marriage:

I think if we'd been able to talk about it it might have been different. But it had been so terrible for both of us that we couldn't. I was twenty-five when I married, and I'd known him since I was fourteen. I always knew it was really him I wanted, but I think now I had to marry a man who was deceitful. He was and is a very deceitful man.

I now see I had to marry someone like that. I think it was because the three important people in my life were not what they seemed. There were all these secrets in our house, and I think I had to marry someone who had secrets. I knew he was that way inclined before I married him, but at twenty-five my conscious mind thought that once you got married that was it – he'd just change his behaviour.

My experience of abuse didn't come out until I was much, much older. I had pushed it down totally. When I got married, I realized I was totally frigid. We went to Paris for a honeymoon, and I just wanted to kill myself. We were terribly fond of one another, and I had no idea why but I couldn't bear to be touched. I'd had boyfriends and put up with it, because I wanted to be liked; but when it came to marriage the whole thing came back, although I didn't know what it was.

My marriage is now over. It finally ended a year ago. It's taken all that time to get out of it and face the fact that it hasn't worked. I know I have to prove to myself that I can manage and can live alone.

On the other hand, Louise placed enormous value on her marriage:

My relationship with my husband leaves me in constant wonderment that I've had the good fortune to meet a man as gentle as he is, and as understanding. When I have very low and black times, he will just leave me be, or sit down and listen to me for hours and hours. It's left an area sexually that at times becomes very difficult, but I don't think that's unusual with women when they're unhappy – they don't want to be invaded.

Mark had been married for many years:

Meeting her was a turning-point. Realizing that I wasn't quite so unattractive, that I could be liked for myself. And that I could do things. It has always been vital to me. We've been through a lot together.

And Peter's partner was similarly important to him:

She knows all of this and she's still here. She's had my baby. She hasn't fulfilled my expectation of what I think people should do. It makes me justified in being what I am. It frequently amazes me.

It is clear that the quality and meaning of adult survivors' relationships vary. Some have reported anxieties about how demanding they can be in their relationships. For example, a young woman, aged nineteen, had been physically abused by her mother and sexually abused by her father. Not surprisingly, her boyfriend

> became everything I've never had: mother, father, best friend, lover. He was all I had. All my needs went into him. It was too much – I utterly swamped him. No wonder he couldn't cope. He's only young himself, and his family were so normal. I thrust him into another world. Now I'm completely alone again. I feel like an orphan, because in any real sense I have no parents. I despair of other relationships. Who could cope with all this lot? I'm just a bundle of needs.

A woman in her thirties, again abused by both her parents, was criss-crossed with scars all over her body from where she had constantly cut herself:

> I'm lesbian, and I feel that is a result of the abuse. All my relationships with women have failed. When I get close, my possessiveness is indescribably great. A relationship with a man is unthinkable. Being in the same room as a man is only just tolerable.

Others are frightened of the damage they may do to anyone they get close to. A young woman who had been sexually abused by her two brothers spoke of her terror of close relationships

> because of how I feel if I get close. I know I can hurt people, and it's when I get close the risk is greatest.

A young man physically abused by his father, and his body also scarred both by the abuse and by self-mutilation, told me:

> I did have a girlfriend, but she couldn't cope; she got frightened. I have very strange moods, and she wouldn't know what was happening. And my body scared her because of the scars. Another girlfriend had been abused too. That was a disaster. I don't know which of us was a bigger mess.

There is a little more hope, tinged with anxiety, in the following, spoken by a young woman who had been physically abused by her mother and sexually abused by a male teacher:

Everything is so much better now, but the big test will come when I feel able to enter a relationship. So far it hasn't felt safe enough – if I sense a man is interested, I'll run a mile. But I don't want it always to be like that.

CURRENT RELATIONSHIPS WITH THE ABUSER

Many of those I interviewed were still in contact with their family of origin and in some cases, therefore, with the person or persons who had abused them. Even those who were not shared similar strong feelings about their family. One of the important issues that arises in counselling the abused is how to deal with the abuser, both practically and psychologically.

Tina was in contact with her sister, who was married to her abuser and knew about the abuse:

She has always been dominating – always there, not letting me be. I feel quite sorry for her now. There's no way that the type of husband she's got feels very worthwhile. It surprises me that they've stayed together. I can't begin to understand how they have in the circumstances. Trust would have absolutely gone if it had been me. I barely talk to my brother-in-law. When we do talk it's terribly stilted. If I can avoid being in the same room with him I will. We don't have a conversation. I think now, in their eyes, they've decided on the picture they're going to paint, and the memory they are going to have is that it was all OK. So it's all been brushed under the carpet. And that's how it goes on.

There's a link that makes it important enough to maintain contact with the family. Even if I feel that what we've got is only second best, it's better than nothing. I think for me a lot has been resolved with a degree of peace. Accepting it is the way I feel about it. There doesn't seem any other way to be.

It was important to me to make sense of the abuse: it means I no longer feel I caused it – it comes from something in the other person.

Amy's family, however, had never been told the extent of the abuse by her uncle:

My sisters know bits about what happened, but still no one in my family knows all of it. My younger sister knows something now, and I've been able to talk to her on the phone recently – I can't manage face to face. I think I blame my mother most. I realize that most of the time I still hate her for not asking the right questions, and for not listening when I did try to talk to her. She reckons she loves me to death. I don't see my uncle now.

Linda also struggled to understand why in her case her father did not stop her mother's abuse:

In the last few years, as I've read and thought and understood more, I've learned what a pathetic man he was. He sacrificed me. He knew what she was doing to me, but for the sake of peace and quiet he did precious little: rather like being the sacrificial lamb. I was certainly the family scapegoat, although that's a term I've only come across in the last few years when I've been studying.

It's made me challenge my image of my father, and be more realistic about him. I see him now more clearly and can acknowledge that he didn't protect me, that he sacrificed me, that he failed. In doing that I've had to sacrifice some of the respect I had for him. That was awfully difficult – almost as difficult as finding out he wasn't my father. All those years I'd hoped she wasn't my mother. And she wasn't: I was adopted by them both. I'd been convinced that she couldn't have been my mother but that he was my father. That was very difficult.

Some of what I have learned has tempered down the terrible feelings I had towards her. I don't feel those any more. I think I can view my older brother realistically now. I've had to understand and accept (because memories have become clearer over the years) that my mother knew what was happening when she sent my brother to my bedroom, because she would be outside my door. And I also have to accept that my younger brother was paid for his silence.

Mark wished his parents had never married. They were both dead, although their influence remained:

Whoever brought my father and mother together had a black sense of comedy. They should never have been married. It was ridiculous. Their marriage was a disaster from the start, and they never had enough money to separate. In a middle-class family in a modern climate they wouldn't have stayed together.

I recognize that my father's contribution to me is immense. There was more than the violence: he gave me access to other worlds. He was important in the Labour Party, and that was hugely influential to a working-class boy as I was.

Peter's father was also dead, but his mother was still alive. His relationship with his two sisters was very precious:

My mum is very much in the background. I've had to spend a great deal of time looking at that. I eventually worked out that she knew what was going on but didn't do anything about it, was powerless to do anything about it. I remember when I hadn't spoken to her for a couple of months, and then I called her and went to visit her. She asked me how work was. I said I didn't know, that I hadn't been for weeks because my father fucked me. What a way to drop it! It felt so powerful. And her response proved to me that she knew it was happening, but she refused to acknowledge it even then. It's too much for her to deal with. She's always been in a fairly fragile mental state. But I was getting vengeance in a way for what had happened. Telling my mother was very important, although my sisters didn't want me to. It was still about keeping secrets. I wouldn't play the game any more. I had to break the rules. I had to tell.

I find it very difficult to talk about my father. I refuse to acknowledge him. The only positive thing I can say is that he's dead. I wished he'd been buried, not cremated, so that I could dig him up and jump on him. I wish there was more I could do to him. I couldn't have remembered the abuse when he was alive. It only came back when he was dead. I escaped from him because my hatred of him outweighed my fear of him. I know that. But the fear was still there, and I'd had to acknowledge his presence because he was with my mum and I was in touch with her.

My sister and I are closer since my father died, and I've learned a great deal about her abuse. And knowing it was her as well, not being on my own, was a relief. The feeling of isolation was incredible – it was so frightening. It's left both of us very confused about our sexuality. She really understands, and we talk and talk – all those shared experiences of what we can do and what we can't do, and how we've reacted to things. We have talked to my other sister, though she and I don't talk about it specifically now.

Jill regretted the absence of a family in the background:

You can't refer back to your history, but it's still there. On one occasion, as a young adult, I tried to pretend I was a normal person with a normal family and wanted to take friends home for the night. I spoke to my mother on the phone, and then my father came on and just screamed down the phone. It was terrible, and I was absolutely devastated in front of everybody. It was a case of what not to expect. I could expect nothing. When I had the children, there was no one to refer to at all.

The contact with him had got less and less as the years went by, but it was still there and still something we did. He had remarried. I felt some sense of responsibility towards him. My sister had decided to sever all links. For me there was still the chance that something might have been salvaged. And the children had a grandparent. He obviously wasn't allowed to play a part, but nevertheless he was there. There was a sort of truce. I couldn't go very far with it; I couldn't be deeply sympathetic.

And when he was genuinely ill it was terrible. When we were young he was a dreadful hypochondriac and he'd be off work, ill or convalescing, and that's when we'd be abused. So when it was genuine I felt no sympathy whatsoever. When he was in fact dying and we were going to the hospital, I couldn't touch him. I could just about manage to sort his pillows out. I didn't feel anything at this funeral. It was a quite joyous occasion. We were all there together. People made it nice for his widow, and she was free of him. He was an awful person to live with.

Hannah's abusing mother refused to have contact with her:

She totally disowned me, and the last time I spoke to her on the phone she said to me, 'You never were like a daughter to us.' It was the first time I'd ever spoken back to her. I said I'd always tried to keep in contact, to ring, to write, and I got doors slammed in my face. She was very abusive even after I'd left home, but not to anyone else. From what I've now read in reports, from when I was a baby until when I was two it was all right; but from then on everything went drastically wrong. But I don't know what or why.

But Rachel maintained contact with her mother, then in her eighties:

Recently she and I have been having terrible rows, and I asked her if she realized why I sometimes go berserk. She said, 'No,' and I said, 'It's because you won't believe what I say.' What I can't understand is how she let her own father, who abused her, anywhere near my sister and me. I couldn't bear to let my own mother near my children. I was absolutely petrified. I think she must have been so afraid of him.

My sister wasn't abused by my mother, but when I told my sister she did say she wasn't surprised. She felt the relationship between us was very peculiar. I had to talk to my sister because my mother couldn't live alone any more, and I couldn't have her living with me.

One of the hardest things to accept is that you came out of the body of someone who could do that to you, because it's even more intimate than your father. I can't bear to think she ever breast-fed me. I would never ask her. I don't want to know. I feel such revulsion to think that I came from that body.

How I feel about my mother now is very split. I admire her tremendously. She's got tremendous guts. I can't love her. I'm sorry for her. I feel responsible for her. But ever since my husband left I haven't had her in the house. I can't bear to. I never take her out – I visit her once a week – and I don't even reproach myself with it. If she dies, I don't think I'll feel guilty because it's something I cannot do. For years and years I had her for lunch every Sunday. Having my husband there, although he couldn't stand her, made it tolerable. I cannot have her in the house alone with me. I can't bear her to see my unhappiness. It's as though she's invaded my privacy. I have to keep her out so she can't get in. There is still something that I haven't worked out yet.

MESSAGES

I asked all those I interviewed if there was any particular message they wanted to convey through my book. Some felt they had already said all they could, but others welcomed the chance to make a final statement. Their conclusions must take precedent over mine.

I want to say I think there is a general fear around, looking back to teachers and so on who perhaps thought something was amiss: a fear of imposing on people by wanting to find out. And I wish that fear could be reduced. I really want to encourage people, to enable them to feel that they can en-quire more deeply, and that they can handle it. (Tina)

For parents *not* to stay together supposedly for the sake of the children. It's hell for children to be caught up in hellish relationships. (Mark)

Really listen. That's most important. And awareness. When a woman is saying 'I was abused' it's too late – it needs to be picked up sooner. Always look under the surface of the supposedly happy, nuclear family. Be sensitive and aware. Some families can be salvaged; others can't. I'm very pleased you're doing this, because I want people to know the damage that is done. I also want to say I think there is something missing in men, and I want them to know what they do. The very thing that makes them successful as a species makes them very bad as people. They lack a moral awareness at a different level. They cut things off and go straight for it. (Jill)

Never stay together supposedly for the sake of the children. If a marriage isn't working, then get out of it. Leave. It's hell for children to be caught in the middle. I was just piggy in the middle: pulled this way and that in the middle of an appalling marriage which never worked and which they never sorted out. We all suffered horribly as a result. I was like the sacrificial lamb on the altar of their unhappy relationship. I get very angry when people talk about the sanctity of the family and how children will suffer without two parents. They have no idea what can go on, and the suffering there is *with two parents* and the scars it can leave. (Louise)

It is partly wanting the world to know, that I've been so happy to talk to you: so much is hidden and people don't know. The more we can bring it out, the easier it gets for people who are down the line from us. I get so angry about people not wanting to talk about this. I don't like the secretiveness. So I want to say: you can't keep this secret any more. If you do, you destroy yourself. Tell. Don't keep the secret anymore. Let people know. We've kept it quiet too long. (Peter)

I want people to wake up and listen to kids. I wish more people would really care, and really take notice, because what is happening to kids in care is just the sharp end of what's happening to kids everywhere. And kids in care ought to be looking out for one another, just keeping an eye on the person next to you. And I want those in the system not to label you psychologically disturbed or dangerous just because you're trying to speak. (Anne)

Residential social workers – at least the good ones – have tried, but it's not good enough. They must work with us against the ones at the top. And I need support and somewhere nice to live; help to sort my head out; and help practically to live; and knowing my little sisters will be protected. They should not be in that home. (Nicki)

I need to pick up all the pieces and put them back together. I need help, but I don't want it or trust it – it's too late. Nothing has happened in the past when I've tried to get help. I don't believe it will be different. But we need help. We need to know where to get it. We need to be able to trust it. I can't pay. It should be free. That's what I want to say: help! (Karen)

Listen to children and treat them as individuals. Children should be given a lot more rights, and if they want to get out of the home they should be able to do so. There needs to be a whole network to help children. But also for us now, as adults, because it can be buried but it never goes away. Once it has happened, abuse is part of you – you can't just ignore it. A lot of textbooks should be thrown out: they don't understand abuse well enough. Social workers should be much better trained. People too easily lose touch with what it's really like to be abused. To work in that area, they should know. I hope so much that your book makes it clear to people. Really spell it out. (Hannah)

For God's sake, stop doing to children what is still happening. Don't take the child away, take away the offending parent and treat them – offer them therapy. And work with the child and the other parent to help them. There's something wrong with the abuser, not the child. And try to leave them with as many loving, familiar people as you can. It is not their fault. I think it's evil to remove the child as they do. The parents of my friends were so important to me, and I lost them as well when I was sent off to school. How you make it different I don't know. But dawn raids – really! – it's terrible. I can't make sense of how professionals act sometimes. So many should be better trained, because they're powerful and that can be abused. (Rachel)

CONCLUSION

While it is not possible to cover adequately the numerous and extensive effects of abuse on the adult, those who spoke to me gave graphic and disturbing accounts of their present life. Many of them felt that by sharing themselves with me they had been given a voice that had previously been denied them. I hope that they can be heard. What they say is often distressing but it is enormously enlightening, with implications for professionals concerned with abuse at different points in a child's or an adult's life. What they make clear is that even better training and even greater awareness is needed.

Anyone who works with abuse survivors should be aware of the issues outlined in these accounts. Goodwill is not enough: it needs to be solidly backed by knowledge, awareness and recognition of the complexity of abuse and its effects. Those who have been abused should be heard and taken seriously. They have an absolute right to be involved in their treatment plan in whatever context this takes place. They did not have a voice as children. Their rights were systematically demolished. This must not be repeated in adulthood, especially in the guise of 'treatment' or 'help' that in reality is imposed rather than negotiated.

These accounts also begin to raise questions about the effective use of resources: whether, for instance, the use of drugs is really appropriate. As the accounts in the next chapter clearly demonstrate many of those who have been prescribed them think not. Challenging the caring professions is not easy, and the lay person might wish they took more obvious responsibility for challenging themselves – for example by actively seeking the patient or client's opinion. The first line of help, as we shall see, and often the only one that is obviously accessible, is the medical services. Because of their position, they have a particular responsibility.

Similarly, we need to ask whether psychiatric care is the best use of resources? How do patients experience the care they received? Is it what they want? What do they find helpful? As the next chapter shows we have to ask whether some systems of care are being perpetuated that are outdated and inappropriate.

FIVE

SHARING SECRETS: THE CHILD'S AND THE ADULT'S EXPERIENCE

THE WORLD OF A CHILD

A frequent response to the horror felt when abuse is revealed is, in effect, to put the responsibility on the abused: 'Why didn't they tell someone?' In fact many children do tell someone, only to find another betrayal awaiting them. However, there are many reasons not to say anything, as the accounts that follow vividly illustrate. But a more apposite question might be why so many adults have for so long denied and avoided the truth. And why the adult world makes it so hard to speak. Society appears to have a blind spot about abuse and its effects, and a disregard for children's needs. One example is the continuing practice of expecting children to testify in open court. This can only be explained as either an extraordinary insensitivity to the effects of abuse on a child, or as a lack of knowledge, perhaps combined with resistance to changing an outmoded and inappropriate system. Either explanation is equally inexcusable. If justice for children is to have any meaning, the system must be changed. Children cannot speak out in an atmosphere that is bewildering and intimidating.

In order to begin to understand a child's difficulties in speaking out and in being heard, it is essential to comprehend a child's world, since it is one that is all too easily forgotten in adult life. If adults find it hard to deal with bad and painful experiences, especially when caused by trusted friends or partners, how much harder it is for a child, who lacks the adult ability to reason, conceptualize, consider and challenge. Not surprisingly, memories are often erased or muddled, as the only way to cope; and it must be difficult to find the right words. Two effects of abuse that I have already made clear are its interference with a child's normal course of development and its destruction of a sense of well-being: these combined effects make it all the more difficult to stand up and speak about what is happening.

A child's world is a small world. It expands very gradually in the early years, encompassing just a few people and a limited number of situations. Understanding the world takes place within that limited context. At that early stage there is no other yardstick with which to measure experience. A child does not know and therefore cannot understand that children and parents in other families may live, think and act differently. A child cannot make comparisons. They only know what is happening in one place, at one time. Their particular existence, their lifestyle, their treatment is their norm. There is no other. In the early years, their world-view is based on how their immediate environment responds and behaves. And, since a child is in one sense so self-oriented, it is easy to believe that anything that happens is in some way self-caused. When other people behave responsibly that is not a problem; but if they do not, the burden of anxiety, confusion and unhappiness that a child carries is heavy.

Children are almost completely dependent on adults for love, care, food and all their wants. Options that may be open to an adult do not exist: they cannot leave home; they cannot resign, retire early, or emigrate; they cannot divorce their parents, or even imagine being able to live without them. There are no escape routes, except perhaps to retreat into an inner fantasy world or to become difficult and hope someone notices. Even then, basically there is no way out. Hiding either in a fantasy world or by keeping a low profile may provide temporary relief, but it is not a permanent solution. There are few choices open to the child. Life has to be as it is, for good or ill.

A child's world is confined to a small area, and of course children are themselves physically tiny. Adults literally loom large. Adults have real power and control – physically, psychologically, economically and legally. They can hurt or they can love; they can empower or they can abuse; they can facilitate development or stop it in its tracks. Yet to some children it feels as if love and hurt are much the same. They are told that their parents and family love and care for them, and they accept that message. They are increasingly aware as they get older that their whole culture also extols the virtues of family life. We live in a climate of opinion which has blind faith in the family and is virtually unassailable in its insistence on this as the only context in which to bring up children. This is reflected in story-books, schools and the wider media. It is very difficult for a child to comprehend that the treatment they are receiving in their particular family is not acceptable. And to imagine that they need help and assistance is a huge conceptual and practical leap.

An essential element in a child's world, central to our understanding of the child, is trust: learning to trust or learning not to trust. The capacity to trust forms a cornerstone for personal development, and is essential to the ability to form relationships as a child and in later life. Try to get inside a child's experience: the essence of trusting, and knowing that you matter, is the belief that when someone throws you up in the air they will also catch you; that when you are frightened someone will comfort you; that those who matter most will not go away and leave you. What then, if instead you find yourself hitting the wall, or falling to the floor; or if the person who should provide comfort is the one who frightens you most; or if you find yourself abandoned? When that happens, your small world becomes senseless; there is no one to tell: your potential protector has become your actual abuser. As a child you have no way of understanding any of that. You are left struggling to make sense of the senseless, when you are already hurt and utterly betrayed. Additionally your abuser probably blames you or threatens you. You are left feeling insignificant, bad, frightened and alone, with precious little self-esteem. Life is dangerous. There is no comfort. Fears are intensified, and anxieties justified. The inconsistency is often so great that everything and everyone becomes unpredictable. The world as the child knows it becomes unsafe, while any world that is perceived beyond the immediate one is distant and unattainable. In these circumstances the question 'Why didn't they tell someone?' is shown up as naïve and devoid of understanding. How can abused children tell or trust anyone else? What else can they believe, other than that they deserve what they get? Why should other adults be any different?

Children need to feel important. More than that: they *are* important. To say that may seem like stating the obvious. Children, as well as having intrinsic value of their own, matter also as the citizens and parents of the future. The question that needs to be asked is whether in our society children really are valued, validated, listened to and believed. The experiences which I now retell suggest that many of them are not.

WHEN CHILDREN SPEAK

Many of the adults I interviewed could not as children tell anyone, because they did not know: their abuse was so horrifying that even at the time it was obliterated from consciousness or was confused and interwoven with an adult's version of events, or an adult's denial. Others could not recall clearly or accurately: their trauma was such that details became blurred and different incidents were confused. Inability to describe abuse clearly and concisely does not mean it did not happen, only that recollections are fragmented and cannot be presented as a neat, precise and sequential account. Earlier chapters have already shown how repressed memories may return only in adult life. In such cases there was, in one sense, nothing to tell as children.

When Tina's sister discovered that her husband was sexually abusing Tina,

> the impression I got was that I was absolutely to blame. I was devastated by that. I hadn't told anyone before: I hadn't felt able to. He had told me I'd be put away, and that no one else wants you. And I felt unwanted. Mum had deserted me (that's how I felt); Dad didn't want me: I didn't know what other possibilities there were. I didn't know what was on offer. There was just no one. So the prospect of being sent away was quite horrific. My sister found out and she was just so angry, and I thought the anger was for me. She said, 'It isn't true, is it?' It all felt as if it was on my shoulders. I was sent out of the house when he came home from work, and told not to come back until I was fetched. I just went and stood in the street. And then I was brought back in and I was told that that was it: that it was finished and that we were never to talk of it again. But it didn't finish at all, and he had this lever on me that I wasn't to tell or else I'd be sent away somewhere. And I believed it.

When she was older, Tina tried to tell her doctor that all was not well, but he failed to hear:

I went to my doctor when I was fifteen, just before I started
work, and said to him, 'There's something wrong with me
down below.' He just took it as needing to reassure me. He
examined me and basically said 'No...Bye-bye.' Later on I
thought he might just have said, 'Why? Is anything troubling
you?' or anything like that. It would have helped me say.

For many years Amy told no one of the abuse she had suffered
since she was very young. As a teenager, she attempted to tell her
mother about one incident:

I told my mum about the one incident, and she told my dad.
If she had asked the right questions I'd have told her more.
But she didn't. The next time my uncle came round I was
called in, and he denied it. My mum wanted me to reaffirm
what had happened, and that made me feel I didn't have her
backing. My dad went and hit him. I was sent off and I could
hear raised voices, but he denied it. It was difficult to pin him
down, he was so sly. It had all been a silent happening. He
had only said anything a couple of times and there was so
much talk about my imagination. I had to be really sure.
That 'imagining' thing followed me along. He was a pre-
dator. When I told my parents, they diluted it a little. They
didn't stop it. My dad hung around more, and my uncle was
more aware.
   I tried to waylay my father several times. I would have
preferred to have told him more, but I never could. You see,
I was always branded as lazy as well as exaggerating – a sort
of down-market view of me that helped him along. He
threatened me indirectly: he used to read things from the
paper about girls who said things had been done to them and
as a result families were split up. He used to say. 'Little bitch,
lying like that – she should be sent to the asylum.' There was
one up the road and it had always been used as a threat. And
I was worried the wrong person would be blamed, and I
couldn't have let anything happen to my dad. I had to protect
my dad: they might say it was him. I was worried he'd be
put in prison.

I have already shown how abusers can be systematic in their
planning, and so thwart discovery. It is clear that they can also
systematically manipulate their victims and others around them
to minimize the risk of disclosure. Amy had regular hospital

appointments, but, even when suspicions were aroused, conditions did not facilitate her saying anything:

> Somebody almost picked it up at Great Ormond Street. But
> they interviewed me in a room like a toilet with a gap under
> the door, and my mother was outside and so I couldn't say;
> because afterwards I would have had to deal with her and
> why I hadn't told her.

By that stage, Amy's level of trust was minimal: she could not
believe that adults would protect her. Neither the circumstances
nor the approach induced sufficient feeling of safety. There were
other reasons why she could not tell:

> The health visitor thought the world of my mother. We were
> so beautifully looked after. I saw a side no one else saw. And
> everyone who could have acted saw her as a paragon of
> virtue.

Jill told her mother of her father's abuse when she was thirteen.
She thought others might have suspected but did not act. She had
her own explanation for their failure to intervene:

> I think a doctor might have wondered. I was being examined
> once by the family doctor, and he always used to look at me
> in a worried way. When he put the stethoscope on my chest
> my pulse rate went up an alarming amount. Had he asked a
> few more questions I would have told him. He didn't. He
> just looked worried. And what could he have done with the
> answer? The family is sacrosanct. The family has a real hard
> circle around it, like a metal compound you can't break into,
> especially when it's a man. A man would never encroach on
> another man's territory.
>   By the time it was coming to an end I did tell a teacher
> when I was late for school. The sexual abuse had stopped
> then, but the trauma wasn't over. There were lots of argu-
> ments and fights. When I told the teacher why I was late that
> day, she just didn't take it on board, she just excused me.
> That was the end of it. There was no response. I don't know
> what she thought. Whether she thought I was just hysterical,
> or 'This is just too much; this isn't my job.' I just don't
> know.

Jill finally told her mother, but her response left her with an
unanswered question:

I don't know how much she already knew, how much she was in thrall to him. Even when she had the chance and when it had all come out and she was asked why she didn't leave, she just said she loved him. She could have been independent: she was earning more money than he was. But it did stop when I told her exactly what was going on.

When Louise screamed at night after witnessing her father attack her mother, her brothers came in; but she was explicitly told not to tell them:

My brothers were told I'd had a nightmare. And that was it. The next day my mother told me not to say a word to anyone. And I didn't. It was very lonely and I felt I was dishonest. And it was awful to see what my father could do.

She found it particularly painful to recognize that there was no question about telling her mother, because her mother already knew:

The thing that was really bad was that my mother saw and heard, and didn't do anything to help me. That was awful: she colluded and didn't defend me. I was very, very badly let down by both of them simultaneously. It may be misplaced, but in some ways I'm angrier with my mother for not defending me.

Louise, like many others, was under considerable pressure to say nothing. The family had to be protected at all costs:

Nobody thought about what was going on: the family was sacrosanct; the family was perfect. There was a pretence about the family: we were built up to be so superior to everyone else. It was ludicrous – a huge difference between the image and the reality. And being told from early on to 'never ever say anything bad about the family to anyone else. If you do, you don't love us.'

Peter also believed that the image of his family would protect his father against any accusation:

Now I think I should have gone to the police, but who would have believed me? We were a highly respectable family; my father had his own business, a member of the Lodge and all that sort of thing. Who would believe this young lad? And also because so much of the time I was trying to shut it out myself. I couldn't even tell myself it was really happening half the time.

When Anne was abused in residential care by a member of staff, it felt too much to go through it yet again:

> I didn't want to tell anyone, because I didn't want to go again through what I'd been through about my dad. I had fourteen court cases, and nothing happened to my dad – we all went into care. A few weeks later another girl was so upset because the member of staff had raped her. But there was nobody there as a witness. I went to the staff then, because it had happened to other girls too. In the end they just told him to go somewhere else. And other members of staff were still talking to him – even the women. It made me feel gutted, because at the end of the day they stick by their staff, so you know not to trust them.
>
> Social services are very powerful, and if they're not helpful it's really difficult. And without parents you've got no one to go back to. I don't think most people realize that: how we depend on social services if we're in care. It's their job, but our lives.

Karen's school actually witnessed the violence towards her and yet did nothing to help. Even when social services were involved, which they were on many occasions, they were ineffective:

> One day my mum and dad battered me in front of teachers at school in the office. They didn't say or do anything. Social services should have taken us into care earlier, because they knew my brother and I were being battered. Then my father wouldn't have been able to go on to sexually abuse me when I was older. I was thirteen then, and I was in and out of care from the age of nine. I was on and off the 'At Risk' register.
>
> They didn't do anything to help me when I was sexually abused. I was asked if I wanted to prosecute, but I couldn't go through all that as well. It would have been more torment. I just wanted to forget it all, and I thought I could. It's only now I know I can't.

Anne felt that the 'care' system was grossly inadequate for children and young people in need, and that radical changes were needed:

> Young people in care should be treated as customers; and those who make policies should talk with them about what

they need. They are the consumers. I'd like to see much better training, with young people in care involved so they actually talk to the people concerned. It's not the answer to get rid of children's homes: foster homes are getting overcrowded, and they're being used as a cheaper form of children's home.

Young people who have been abused within a family may just not be ready simply to join another family. Fostering isn't an ideal situation. There should be a range of provision available, taking into account individual needs. It should be to do with children's needs, not to save money or because it's fashionable. Children's homes need better staff, not to be abolished. Attitudes should be changed. Young social workers are really too idealistic, and then they just get demoralized and give up and leave. I think anyone who has been in care has been abused by definition: the care system is abusive.

Hannah's father clearly knew how her mother was treating her. He would not intervene directly, but he tried to prevent the abuse in other ways:

In his own way he tried to be kind. I was a chronic bedwetter, and that got me into a hell of a lot of trouble. It was one of the times she'd beat me, and he knew that. Sometimes on a Saturday morning, when she was out, he would help me strip the bed, wash the sheets, put the electric fire on, dry them and get them back on the bed. But he didn't do anything else to stop it: an utterly weak man really.

She tried telling other relatives, but once more too much was ranged against her, and she was not believed:

I had tried telling aunties, but they'd talk to my mother and it would just cause more trouble. I was never believed, and I'd end up being called a liar and all sorts. You see, materially I had everything. The home was nice and my clothes always beautiful; and at the time, until I was a teenager, I didn't question anything. I just thought that's how life is.

Rachel's father was also aware of her mother sexually abusing her:

My father came in once and found us, and said, 'What are you doing? This girl will never be normal.' And I lived that out – I never was. He said to me, 'We'll forget all about it,' and I worshipped him. I thought he was my knight in shin-

ing armour, and that when he found out he'd do something.
I did what he said: I forgot it.

Marie quite simply felt that there was no one to tell:

I couldn't have told anyone anyway: there was no one to tell.
I was too scared that it would backfire on to me. It might
have got worse. I was afraid of my mother. She was a
terrifying person.

Many of these adults made an attempt as children to communicate what was happening to someone. Others were so threatened
that they dared not try. Some had been betrayed previously, and
so had no reason to believe that further attempts at eliciting help
would be any more successful. In fact they had every reason to
believe that worse would happen, already knowing how very bad
life could be. Adult powers had been ranged against them, and
they had no belief that it could be different. They lived in a
dangerous world in which their abusers were the very people who
should be protecting them. In this situation, remembering they
were children at the time, who could they turn to? No one. The
adult world seemed to conspire against them.

In my own clinical work I have heard many more instances of
children who attempted to tell someone, and of agencies being
alerted but failing to recognize the abuse. I know of many children abused in professional families whose very status seemed a
protection against discovery. Abusers in these situations are members of the very professions children are often advised to talk to:
teachers, vicars, social workers, foster parents, police and doctors.
Children in care are particularly vulnerable. Their abuse has
already been identified: that they can then be abused within the
care system is outrageous.

WHEN ADULTS SPEAK

Adult experiences of telling others and of receiving help are more
immediate and easily recalled. They include the positive and the
negative, the helpful and the unhelpful. Those who work in the
caring professions need to be consumer-oriented, although sadly
they seldom are. Some professions seem to forget they exist to
provide effective services, and make no attempt to monitor their
effectiveness as perceived by the consumer. The stories in Chapter
2 illustrated how individuals who had already suffered terrible

blows suffered still more at the hands of so-called caring professionals. Pockets of excellence do exist, and many individual workers are doubtless committed and caring, but the whole picture is not yet good enough.

Tina had not received professional help: it was her second husband who had helped most. His ability to accept and to absorb was crucial:

> I was twenty-five, and I realized this was like a stone hanging round my neck and I wanted to give it away. I wanted to give it away to someone who could bear it. We weren't having a relationship at the time. I'd just met him, and I thought, 'Here's someone who can bear it.' I had a long chat with him one day, and cried a lot, and shared it with him. I'm not sure how important it was that it was a man, but I think it was very important. He just listened and absorbed it, and said that it wasn't my fault. I needed to hear that. It wasn't very easy to accept. Within a few weeks I felt able to talk to my friend about it, and I think she didn't quite know what to do, although she was very hurt for me. I needed her to know because she'd known my family.
>
> I then spoke to the rector of our local church, and he didn't know what to do with the information. It was just at the time of the break-up of the marriage, and he was more concerned with trying to save that. He really didn't handle it well. He was quite judgemental, so he wasn't helpful. I shared it with him to release the burden a bit more, and he didn't acknowledge what I said at all. So that was no release.
>
> I haven't had any professional help, but my husband has worked with a lot of very vulnerable people and so has a depth of awareness and really just accepted me when I needed to be accepted – the dirty bits as well.

Amy had received help from many agencies:

> Psychiatric hospital was a very bad experience. They drugged me up so I didn't feel in control. And that is awful for me. And it would have helped if they had even listened to me, but they didn't. They thought I was imagining things when they were actually real. A monastery would have been more helpful – a place of escape would have helped, with no telephones, no children, just some real peace and quiet without the drugs. Like a real asylum.

It was all wrong. I wouldn't recommend a soul to the psychiatrist: there just didn't seem to be anyone there. It's difficult to explain it. He must have had a lot of training, but he just wasn't aware. He wouldn't even talk about what was happening now; and if I'd had someone with the sense to talk about that it might have been someone sensible enough to see that was happening now had been caused by what had happened before. And ongoing treatment, the working-back, was what I needed – and what others in there needed too, because many were in there for the same sorts of reasons, I discovered. That just never happened.

I was desperate to talk. I actually managed to tell a bit of what had happened with my uncle. I waylaid this person, and talked to her for an hour and a half. And then she said, 'I'm not really the person you should be talking to.' It was so difficult to say, and then she said that: that she couldn't do anything to help me, and I must see a doctor. I remember feeling so let down. I can still feel that feeling now.

When a doctor did attempt to speak to me, I was so worked up, I was so cross because this other person hadn't stopped me talking to her – she'd even asked me some questions – but she'd done nothing. No one took any notice, and no one was doing anything except give me lots of pills. Everything I said they ignored. They didn't even believe I'd started my period, and I had nothing with me. In the end I took my knickers down and showed them, and said, 'Look, I can't stay like this.' Then I got hauled off for exhibitionism. And I was labelled an exhibitionist. They didn't treat the abuse; they didn't listen. And it was no help being in hospital – no help whatsoever. Absolutely no help.

Nobody did anything constructive in psychiatric hospital. And that is only a few years ago – really quite recently. They should have done more. Don't let people convince you it's all different now. Nobody with my history should have been ignored like that. I really felt nobody wanted me to talk about it: they wanted me to have my head in the clouds the whole time. It was just drugs, and a lot of them. I had tried hard to get other help, but I didn't know what there was or what was available. I spoke to Childline a lot, and generally they were very nice. She talked to me, but there seemed nothing for adults.

I'd like time away: quiet and peace. And definitely more

counselling. You see I have had some, but I didn't know the
words. I didn't make use of the counselling as I could have
done. She asked me what happened, and I froze and I'd chat
about anything other than that. I desperately need it now. I
now know it won't go away quickly, and that I need two or
three years' help. That acceptance is a step forward. I really
need that. Hospital was quite useless. Counselling would be
my own special time. I need continuity with one person. I
need to know they'll stay there, that they won't go away,
that they can take it and won't stick me on drugs. I've always
been depressed, but I don't want antidepressants. I want
help. I've also been in an incest survivors' group, and it was
helpful; but I need someone to myself, too.

Jill also met with a variety of responses, helpful and unhelpful:

I was absolutely amazed at the amount of ignorance. The
first interview with a doctor I had was when I was at my
wits' end with young children. I mentioned it, and he
thought it was better if I didn't discuss it again. Just leave it
as it was. I don't want to be damning of doctors – after all
what do they get in their seven years? All that knowledge to
cram in. And they're young, and they're often men. And
the majority have had success, and done the normal things at
the normal times, and made the best use of their education.
They've gone from one block of education to another, and
then they're just launched with little idea of other worlds.

I mentioned it to another doctor later, why I was so upset,
and he was gravely concerned. He wasn't an empty-headed
bloke. But it got lost because so much else was going on.
There was no real response or suggestion as to where to go
for help. It might be different now as he has developed. And
at least now I could take it up as an issue if he hadn't. I was
put on a course of antidepressants, which was the last thing I
wanted. They made me feel terrible. I still knew something
was wrong, but I was even less able to do anything about it.
I went around in a haze, but it wasn't a pleasant haze. I knew
it was getting in the way.

Before the break-up of my first marriage I went to a
marriage guidance counsellor, and she was an elderly lady doctor and I told her what had happened. I was very, very upset
and she was very, very quiet. Eventually she said, 'Well, at
least your father chose you.' I didn't go back to her.

I read about the counsellor I saw. It was the first person I'd heard of who might help. First I started going to a group and realized that wasn't quite right. So I then saw my counsellor by myself for over a year. It was helpful. It was at the right time. I found out some of the things I could expect. And that made me allow things [to come out]. I found out what was normal for my circumstances. The recognition was important. I needed someone to know, and since the people in white coats had been so useless – I'm afraid their track record for me was absolutely appalling – that was very good.

It was like being given time – time out – and that time was very important: the attention and her ability just to sit and take it. She wasn't astonished, which was useful, and she said some very crucial things to me. That was very helpful. I could find my own answers and direction, but the prompt was essential. It helped me realize that some of the things happening in my relationship with my husband weren't just me. He could say, 'That's just because of your attitude,' and it was like it was all my fault. I didn't want that, and it's helped me sort that one through. It was like writing me off: like saying you're only complaining because you're premenstrual. It gave me more confidence and trust in myself, and I could be more constructively critical about the way he was behaving. She suggested strategies but didn't tell me what to do.

It took me right back. All the hurt and the pain and the sore. It brought it all back. Part of me didn't want to know, but the things that were said made sense. Some I spoke about; some things I couldn't say. Now I feel there is a lot of work I need to do myself. I'm at that point now where I can take responsibility. I don't know whether I'll ever live a life: you hear people say this isn't a rehearsal, this is it. What I've learned is that the journey towards something is possibly a lot of it. The bits on the way are important.

Peter's experience was also mixed. Memories of his abuse had only surfaced recently:

I'm involved in HIV work, and I went to work in the London Lighthouse. I got involved with a chap there, and for the first time in years I could be me and no one was judging me. It was very freeing. That and being involved with a local voluntary organization – being able to be me and being supported – allowed me to remember. They were genuine friends – something I've never had before. And my partner was important too. There was all this support, and I think I recognized deep within myself that the time was right to let these memories resurface.

When it all came back it was horrendous. I went to our local doctor. I explained what had happened. I got nothing from him. All I got was a sick certificate. He looked all the time at his clock on the wall, at his notes, telling me he only had ten minutes, that he was already behind. He did what my father had done: he was abusing me, not listening, not caring. He wrote on the sick certificate 'nervous disorder' and I could have killed him. Anybody could have made a better response than that, and he was a fucking doctor! He wanted to send me to a psychiatrist and I didn't want to: I am not mentally ill. I needed somebody to help, and he wasn't hearing. The next week I went back, and it was the same. My GP was a prat, useless.

An AIDS support group put me in touch with a counsellor, and I saw him for three months. What helped most was that I believed myself, and he believed me. I needed his acceptance, and it was important that he was a man. I was frightened of him – he's a powerful man, and I'm frightened of powerful men – although he was helpful. I saw another woman GP at that time, and she was extremely good – gave me all the time I needed, and just sat back and let me say it all and let me get upset. Some are good and some aren't. They're a mixed bunch.

I've seen another counsellor since, for longer. I had to admit I needed more help. It's helped a great deal. It's enabled me to help myself, and recognize myself. I knew psychiatry wouldn't help, especially those who adhere rigidly to certain ways of thinking. It wouldn't have enabled me to move myself. This has allowed me to be me. I was very introverted and frightened, and could be frightening to others. I'm much more free now to look at myself and to be happy with what I see. Before, I had this incredible guilt at being happy, as if I wasn't allowed to, didn't deserve to be, and didn't deserve help. Guilt is a huge legacy. Dumping that guilt has been so useful. Now I'll feel guilty for an appropriate amount of time if I've cocked something up.

It's helped me be more assertive about what I want for

myself, allowing myself things, to do things I've wanted to do for years – like a whole new life has begun and I want to be free to enjoy it. Before there were just the trappings, but underneath was still this little boy who didn't really know what he was doing and was intimidated by everybody. It feels as if I've been enabled and empowered to release that. I've had to grow up very rapidly. I needed time off work to work through the process.

Now I can admit that I see someone, and that has given me more strength. It's been important to acknowledge that I do need help. It has been so good. She is a woman, and because of my fear of men that was good. Now it wouldn't make much difference, but then it did. A lot of things have fallen into place. I can sit back and think, 'Hang on. Why is that affecting me so much?' I've been given back the power through counselling so now I can take it for myself. She hasn't made the decisions for me but has told me I have the right to take them myself, and helped me to see why I wasn't able to take them. And acting as a mirror for me – I can't do that for myself. And it's been a big jump of trust. And so has been talking to you.

Linda, whose story I reported fully in Chapter 2, was afraid of trusting and confiding. When she finally decided to talk about her childhood of abuse, and her violent marriage, her trust was betrayed and her difficulties escalated:

Just before the marriage broke up, my oldest child, who was five, was pilfering from school. It was decided she should see an educational psychologist, and she asked to see me. She told me she thought there were problems at home. She felt I wasn't able to open up to her, that perhaps I didn't trust her, and that she wanted to see me in my own right and build up that trust. So I did see her, and managed to tell her about the marriage and the violence. Eventually, for the first time ever, I told her about my brother and my uncle, and how my mother had hated me. I do remember I couldn't look her in the eyes when I told her, because I was scared how she'd react. I didn't want to see what I thought I was going to see there.

One time when I went to see her I'd cried off the previous appointment because my face was pretty bad after my hus-band had beaten me, and I didn't go out when I looked like that. The next week I went and we talked about what had happened, and – I don't know why she did it, but I know it wasn't ethical – she wrote a letter to my husband. He didn't tell me about it, but she asked to see him and she told him everything. When he came back, he gave me the worst hiding I've ever had in my life. He knocked me from wall to wall and back again.

I think if she hadn't done that I would have continued to trust her and told her what was happening, because I needed to. After that I had no access to help, and I'm not sure if I'd have risked it again. And I would have been very frightened to acknowledge that anything was wrong.

Later on I did an Open University course on abuse, which did help enormously in putting pieces together; and I talked to lots of people, especially at the NSPCC. It left me sitting alone at home trying to work it out by myself. No one else helped. I would like counselling, but I don't know where to get it. The course taught me about family dynamics and why children aren't always protected.

Shortly after Rachel married, she sought help:

I went to the family-planning clinic and they asked me how I was getting on, and I said, 'Horrendous.' I saw someone there who I now know to be a psychiatrist, who kept asking me about my father; and I couldn't see what he had to do with it, and I stopped going. I had a terrible nervous break-down, and I went to a major London hospital which is supposed to be very good. The nurses were superb, but not the doctors: I saw a different one every week, and they asked me the same bloody questions.

In hospital, what was really bothering me – that my mother had sexually abused me – didn't have a chance to come through. The doctors were all trainees, different each week – ridiculous. I saw the consultant once a month. They drugged me up so much I could hardly stand up, but it made no difference to my feelings. I was in seven months in all.

The hospital was very well known and it was worse than useless: just drugs and more drugs. And in those days the threat of lobotomy. I knew the ultimate was shock treatment, and if that didn't work I'd be walking around with a bandage. I had six months on drugs and a month of shock treatment and no therapy. The doctor who admitted me I could have talked to, but I had no chance to. And I do think the use of drugs in that way is terribly dangerous.

The second time I had to go into hospital I was so desperate not to that I tried to commit suicide, and I very nearly succeeded. I was on a medical ward for about four weeks. Then I was moved to a psychiatric hospital. It was a dreadful place. The nurses were appalling. The sister kept saying, 'I don't know what someone like you is doing in here – you've got so much.' The nurses just sat in their glass office. The psychiatrist there was lovely, but you only got a few minutes and there were usually others around. I needed therapy, but the system can't afford it. They just kept me on drugs until I felt a bit better, and then of course I'd push it all down again.

The psychiatrist recommended therapy: he said I must have that. I couldn't have managed without therapy. My therapist started out as god, and has ended up as the painful truth. Without therapy I think I would have spent the rest of my life being scared of being ill again. I was in a constant state of anxiety. I knew I could not have lived through another breakdown. I just don't know what would have happened to me. It's been extraordinarily painful but absolutely essential: a painful necessity. The truth about my mother emerged. All this time in therapy has finally shown me that the four most important people in my life were not what I thought they were.

If I'd had therapy when I was first in hospital I'm sure that would have helped. As it was, it was a waste of time. That was a dreadful time. Just these bloody drugs. I was so desperate. I was really ready then – I knew I had to make choices, to look at things. I was saying so. I was desperate for help, and it wasn't there. Nobody wanted to know.

RESOURCE IMPLICATIONS

Many more adults than we know, who have survived all forms of childhood abuse, desperately need help. They do not want to be labelled as mentally ill. Clearly, many of those I spoke to see traditional psychiatric care as damaging and unhelpful. But they still want help to resolve the terrible legacy of abuse. Help needs to be empowering, and it needs to be accessible. It needs to be widely available, and free of charge. Some of those I have quoted received help through the NHS or through other free counselling services. Others had to pay considerable sums for private counselling and therapy. The inability to pay is often given as a reason for not receiving help. The availability of a free, high-quality service is frequently dependent on geographical location rather than on need. Some areas of the country have very little provision of the kind that consumers want and feel to be useful.

Vital questions are also raised about children in care, and about how their experience affects them in adulthood. In recent years the abuse of children living in care has been widely documented. Official inquiries abound. Almost daily, more scandals come to light. The quality of care given to our children can be seen as the most crucial element for the future well-being of society. Children are our future. And yet care of the most vulnerable of them is not prioritized. Residential care workers are underpaid and overworked, and they frequently complain that they are not valued, respected or sufficiently consulted. Good-quality care has resource implications which have not yet been sufficiently recognized or followed up.

The question of service provision for both children and adults is crucial. Nowadays, ever increasing numbers of children are being identified as abuse victims. They need and they should have the best help available. That requires adequate funding, and highly trained and motivated staff who are supported and well supervised. Sadly, these are so often not available. Our care system is woefully inadequate. The National Association for Young People in Care (NAYPIC) is struggling for wider awareness of these issues, and has done so for some time. Far more serious attention must be given to the issues NAYPIC is spotlighting. Children in care, who have fequently already been abused, face a risk of further abuse. The unacceptability of this is indisputable. Horrific relevations occur almost daily: such as the scandal of 'pin-down' in Staffordshire children's homes, the years of ongoing abuse by Frank Beck on children in Leicestershire children's homes, and the abuse of adolescent girls in the Melanie Klein House in Greenwich. Reports of these types of abuse are increasingly commonplace. Many who work in the field of residential social work are not surprised: there is an ominous feeling that these cases are the tip of a very alarming and extensive iceberg.

It is now known that it is not unusual for children to be physically, psychologically and sexually abused. It is one of the most serious social problems of our time. Increasingly, it is given greater attention and more serious acknowledgement. But this marks only a tiny beginning in an area which needs flooding with resources if the picture is to change. If effective interventions are to be made, money must be spent on staffing and training. The availability of sufficient funding has been sadly lacking in recent decades. Whether this will change in the future remains an open question. Charities such as Childline are a significant innovation, offering a confidential service that ensures that children who contact them are at least heard. Far more must be done to extend their valuable and unique role.

Abused children grow into surviving adults, but the problem does not disappear with maturity, because the effects are ongoing. As with services for children, services for the adult survivor are insufficient. Those that do exist are under enormous pressure as more and more adult survivors present. The question of which services are the most effective, and what kind of services survivors actually want, needs to be addressed. With a few notable exceptions, psychiatric provision was dismissed by those I met as being unhelpful. If this is reflection of wider experience, it may indicate that existing resources need to be rethought and redistributed. Psychiatry is one of the most expensive resources, and it is reasonable to ask psychiatrists to examine their effectiveness rigorously. It is clear that the demand for more help is likely to grow, and yet there are few indications that adult services will be better resourced to cope with the demand. If this problem is to be taken seriously, finance is needed. Expressions of horror, political and public outrage and sympathy are mere cant unless accompanied by real action and actual investment.

SIX

THE DEVELOPMENT OF MULTIPLE PERSONALITY DISORDER

The development of Multiple Personality Disorder is an extreme response to equally extreme multiple abuse. Although it has been regarded with scepticism by many clinicians, and totally denied by others, there is now wider acceptance of its existence. Denial is of course endemic in abuse. The very nature of denial is that it is not open either to reasoned argument or to accepting evidence: denial is often a successful means of transcending sensible debate. In cases of abuse, there is a constant challenge to reason, since we would prefer to think of some of the facts of abuse as being impossible. This is even more so with multiple personality. Since it occurs in situations where abuse is almost unbelievable in its variety of horrors, the denial of the phenomenon of multiple personality could be interpreted as a denial of these horrors. Over the years many practitioners have had to recognize that their earlier beliefs and formulations regarding abuse have been erroneous, but there are many more who have yet to acknowledge this area as one where grave mistakes in diagnosis have been made, and where some forms of treatment have been inappropriately given. Goodwin (1985:2) writes:

> Most present-day psychiatrists were confidently taught, and tried to believe just as confidently, that multiple personality did not occur, but might be mentioned at times by female patients who were malingering or attention-getting... and

that intrafamilial childhood sexual abuse did not actually occur, but might be mentioned at times by female patients who
mistook their Oedipal longings and fantasies for realities.

Friedrich (1990:241), in his work with sexually abused children,
argues that:

> Diagnosis of dissociative disorders invites muddy thinking.
> At times when I have raised a skeptical voice about the fre-
> quency with which I hear some clinicians diagnosing them,
> I have felt unheard by them and somehow disloyal to the
> field of victim therapy. Yet I am aware of the marked sugges-
> tibility of people with dissociative disorders and question
> whether our interventions, on occasion can be iatrogenic.

Other writers suggest that the development of multiple personalities is a highly creative method of surviving and coping with
extremes of abuse. In my interviews with survivors in whom this
disorder had developed, the abuse they had experienced was so
severe that developing multiple personalities seemed an unconscious life-saving strategy. I was left with the question of whether
they would have survived without it. Clearly, it is important
to ask why it is that some severely abused children respond in
this way and others do not. Similarly, patterns of dissociation and
isolating of pain differ between individuals who have suffered
similar levels of abuse. There is no single answer: for some the
natural ability to dissociate appears greater. Multiple personality
should be understood as part of the continuum of dissociation.
Yet it is generally not accepted or understood as such. Whereas
dissociation is widely acknowledged, discussed and frequently
referred to in the literature, multiple personality is often notable by
its absence.

However, the work of some psychoanalytic theorists lends
weight to the possibility of multiple personality, as well as assisting in understanding its origins. Melanie Klein's work on splitting
and projective identification is particularly relevant (1975:144):

> I have maintained... that the fear of annihilation by the de-
> structive forces within us is the deepest fear of all. Splitting as
> a primal defence against this fear is effective to the extent that
> it brings about a dispersal of anxiety and a cutting off of
> emotions. But it fails in another sense because it results in a
> feeling akin to death – that is what that accompanying dis-
> integration and feelings of chaos amount to.

If similarly *external* destructive forces such as severe abuse cause similar fears of annihilation, splitting becomes not only a defence against fear but a life-preserving measure, as I demonstrate below. Klein continues (1975:166):

> A patient's feeling that parts of his self are no longer available, are far away, or have altogether gone is of course a phantasy that underlies splitting processes. But such phantasies have far-reaching consequences and vitally influence the structure of the ego. They have the effect that those parts of his self from which he feels estranged, often including his emotions, are not at the time accessible either to the analyst or to the patient.

Sandor Ferenczi was told about sexual trauma in childhood by his patients. He recognized the severe damage this caused, and in 1932 he presented a paper on his findings, in which he said (1955:162):

> When the child recovers from such an attack, he feels enormously confused, in fact, split – innocent and culpable at the same time – and his confidence in the testimony of his own senses is broken.

And (1955:165):

> If the shock increases in number during the development of the child, the number and the various kinds of splits in the personality increase too, and soon it becomes extremely difficult to maintain contact without confusion with all the fragments, each of which behaves as a separate personality yet does not know even of the existence of the others.

Ferenczi's words are extraordinarily near to the modern description of multiple personality, which is marked by the existence within the person of two or more personalities, each with its own memories, its own sense of self, and its own ways of acting, thinking and behaving. Several types of personality can exist within the host, including child personalities, who can hold traumatic memories; or persecutors, who can be involved in self-harm; or helpers, who can assist or advise in ways that are not open to the host personality. The personalities are frequently referred to as the 'family', as if they are intimately attached to the host, although they also exist independently. When the 'host' is referred to, this indicates the person within whom the personas are collected.

The stories that follow illustrate the complexity of multiple personalities in the survivor, and the situations that gave rise to this extreme form of splitting and dissociation.

CAROL

Although I have quoted some of Carol's interview in places in earlier chapters, what she told me about the phenomenon of multiple personality merits a more detailed account. She developed multiple personalities as a consequence of extreme sexual abuse by her father and physical abuse by her mother. By the time I spoke with her, her personalities had become integrated, although this has been a slow and difficult task. She had been in therapy for many years – an experience she viewed very positively. The different personalities, who can be identified by other names, are characters whom she actually became; in other words they had their own external lives and reality. This is true of all those whose stories are used in this chapter.

> I didn't know until well into therapy that I had been abused – it was all repressed. I was abused sexually by my father from when I was about four. And my mother physically abused me very badly. It was a whole game in the family: my father didn't know what mother was doing, and mother didn't know what father was doing. By remembering everything, and by my personalities joining me, I realized that my father knew and my mother knew. I thought most of the sexual abuse was done in love, because the first memories were of him calling me his beautiful daughter, and being very gentle and very caring. But it wasn't: there was an awful lot of pain. I started to relive other memories. His abuse turned violent if he was bad-tempered or angry. I only remembered that quite recently. When it was loving it was vaginal intercourse, and when it was angry it would be anal. They were never mixed – it depended on how he felt.
>
> My youngest personality was two. The abuse started at four. And then I had personalities join me all through my life to cope with everything. So they were all different ages – the oldest was seventy-six. The last of the personalities have

now joined me, and that was quite horrific because of the memories they held – that my parents knew, and that my father abused me anally. I am OK now, although I still get a few flashbacks. There are another three child personalities who will never join me. They never come out. They live in my childhood home and stay away. They need to be left alone. The rest of the 'family' have said they must stay there, they mustn't grow up and join us.

When I was sixteen I left home and I got into trouble. One of my personalities, Kate, became a prostitute, got pregnant, had an abortion. She had a pimp, escaped that, and took me back to my parents when I was eighteen. Carol got very depressed, and mother took her to the doctor. Antidepressants didn't work and I was referred to the psychiatrist. There was no help at all there. She saw my mother for an hour first, so none of my 'family' would say anything – the confidentiality was with my mother. Carol went in and the psychiatrist said, 'I know all about your past from your mum. She's told me you've been spoilt, that you're a daddy's girl, and that you need to grow up.' Carol didn't say a word, and it was suggested I go to the day hospital, and that a social worker visit once a week. That was useless: my parents were there too. I had a gap of a week when Kate, one of the others, ran away and then reappeared. I was threatened that if I disappeared again I'd be put on the wards. The 'family' were fed up, and wanted me to leave the day hospital; so Babs, one of my personalities, went to the hospital, saw the psychiatrist and said I'd got a job, that I realized I had to grow up, and asked to be discharged. I was told that was great, and that I could go.

I saw a behavioural psychologist for a while, which was a complete waste of time: the 'family' ran circles around him. Then I was sent to my current psychotherapist, and I've seen him for twelve years. When Carol first went she would say nothing. What kept the 'family' seeing him was that he said he didn't care about all the letters and reports, but he wanted to hear my story. That's how it all began. But it was a number of years before he found out I was multiple personality. It took four years before any of the 'family' came out. Kate was the first one. He said, 'Are you Carol?' and she stood up and said, 'No. I'm Kate.' And that was it. He said 'Hello, Kate,' and was so relaxed.

He recognized what was happening to me, and explained about the other personalities. They would talk to him, but I as Carol wouldn't know that. At first I didn't believe him, and I had to listen to a tape before I was convinced. To me it was normal, and I had nothing to compare it with. I had always been like that, and I just thought everyone was the same. Although I didn't know they existed, I was aware that all through my life I'd been called different names in the street, and I'd said, 'You must mean someone else; that's not me.' I was continually called a liar when I insisted I hadn't done something, because as far as I was concerned I hadn't: one of the others would have done it. I soon learned that if I told the truth and said I didn't remember I got punished. If I lied and said I did, I didn't get punished – and that applied even to the psychiatrist. She would accuse me of lying. So I'd just say, 'Yes, it was me.' But I just thought everyone had weeks they didn't remember: that you went to bed on a Monday, and woke up two weeks later in the living-room. You learn to con, but I thought everyone did. I didn't know I had a 'family' at all. And when you're abused you don't trust anyone anyway, so you don't exactly go around chatting to everyone – especially about things like that. So I had no awareness at all, and when I finally did accept it things were very difficult.

My therapist was very honest. He said it was the first time he'd worked with multiple personality. That made me feel even more of a freak; but he said, 'Let's work together, and perhaps the "family" will help us know what to do.' And it was literally like that. We muddled through. It was totally new territory for both of us, and we made mistakes along the way. There was no rule-book, but someone just accepting your experience is so important. To so many psychiatrists it doesn't exist, so you get pushed into hospitals and labelled as something else.

I had to give everyone in the 'family' time: the children had to have time to play; Maureen needed time with her girlfriend and so on. I would leave a tape recorder out, and they'd leave messages on the tape recorder. If I did that I didn't have any problems. I could be around when I needed to be, my life was balanced out. It was like a week's rota. There were about twenty personalities in all: different needs, different ages, different sexes. I had three boys, lesbians, heterosexuals, a lot of people. As more and more introduced themselves to my therapist, he had to make sure he gave them each time. One hour a week with a multiple personality is not enough. And it's very difficult to stay in the office. The little ones need to play, to go to the park. Some have never played in their lives, and they like to go to the park and feed the ducks and so on. There was Jane who was four, Lynne (five), Sean (seven), Debby was about eight, and Tim was about two.

They're in me now, so I talk about them with some distance. They are in their right places. I have to be careful, because all through my life I have to remember and respect them. Because it's not that they have joined me and no longer exist: they exist in me. My therapist had to be very careful as each one joined to say something to them, to show he still remembered them. Otherwise they split again, because they weren't getting the attention they need. So it's hard work for both the therapist and the client.

To help them join they had to be seen, and heard, and to know they weren't going to disappear but were to be a part of me. And I had to accept their past; to like them, whatever they've done; to take on board all of them.

I had to go through all the flashbacks. That took quite a while, because there was so much to cope with. Once you have a personality join you, you have no control. You can't do it bit by bit, so you take on all the memories. It isn't like an action replay. It's not like the flashbacks of people who've been abused, because then there is some familiarity. They are in them, and they recognize themselves. When it happens to me, I'm not me, I am that personality. So I not only take on the memory, but the feelings I've never felt, the body I've never felt. So when someone joins me I can feel smaller or taller: everything is distorted. The voice is different, and I'll use phrases I've never used before. It's odd until it blends into me. It's like it's not my experience at all.

When I go back to my therapist he seems very different, because he's talking to (say) Carol *and* Jean, not just to Carol. Of course the way you relate to one person is very different from relating to another. And for a few weeks there is a distance: I don't know him and he doesn't know me. It's like establishing a new way of relating, because it's a different person, so it can't be the same relationship. It's very difficult, but it is worth it, particularly if you're young. It is worth the pain because of all those years ahead. But it's hell, and you've got to be bloody strong. Self-help groups are really important, because they can call on each other's strengths.

Looking back, I wonder what other people made of it all. I know I was a wonderful photographic model, because I could switch from one way of being to another. And teachers used to see it as lack of concentration: that I'd be intelligent if only I would concentrate. One teacher always used to know by the look of me whether I was going to work, be withdrawn or be disruptive. What he was saying, without knowing it, was that it depended on who was coming to the lessons. Later, while Kate was a prostitute and a heroin addict, Babs was going to night school and got three A-levels; but I can't use them because they're in her name! So while she tried to help me she actually didn't. My memories of that time are of a real haze with amazing extremes of memory on the same day.

The last personalities to join were very difficult. Jean was blind. And when she joined there were times when I was blind. Jean was the one who used to be sexually abused by my father. One night after my parents had a row he had anal sex with her. It was terribly painful. He made her have oral sex too, and it made her vomit. Afterwards mother came in and told her she was a slut. She had put towels on the bed so the sheets weren't messed up, so she did know. Jean became blind because the 'family' said you were there to help Carol, but you didn't break any rules: and the rule was not to attack parents. But Jean got sick of it after that night, and tried to strangle my mother. She threw salt in her eyes, and Jean didn't see again. I had to take all that on board, as well as remembering that I'd tried to kill my mother.

Sally, one of the little ones, was put in a broom cupboard in the dark all day. Sometimes her ankles would be tied. So, when she first came to see the therapist all the blinds had to be drawn. She had to be in a darkened room, and gradually she became used to daylight. She couldn't stand it at first, because she'd never seen it. So they sat in the dark. When she first joined me, not only did I have to deal with the memories of being locked in, which was frightening, but my legs hurt and I couldn't stand. I'd try to, and the pain would be horrific.

Lynne wasn't abused: she was my fantasy. She'd come when I got really frightened. She had different parents, who were really kind to her. She had a completely different life. I took her on really well. But Debby had awful things to face. Jane had no abuse: she came when I was four. She came when mother actually bought me a doll – she would never buy me anything. I named the doll Jane, and I was over the moon. I got lost, and when she found me she lost her temper, dragged me out, and threw my doll in the bin. I only had her a few minutes, but Jane came and took that memory on. They came to hold on to good things as well. Her memory was that she'd lost her doll; and when she came she was very sad because of that, so we went out and bought her one. That was all she wanted. Her needs were easier to meet.

Kate was a prostitute. Carol was looking for love and was easily conned. She got pregnant and daren't tell anybody, so she met someone who could arrange an abortion. Kate took over and had it for her; but he had been a pimp, and she became a prostitute for him. Then there was Julie, who got into another relationship: that was in a cult. Julie would sit in my therapist's office and see the master behind him. She wouldn't talk, and tried to destroy the therapist. She was still acting out in a trance with the master. It was very difficult to break with the occult, and very difficult for Julie to leave it. My memory of that is still very hazy, even when she joined me. I do have a memory of Julie being very much regarded as a high priestess. She was on hallucinatory drugs.

They all had to come off their addictions before they joined me, otherwise I would have got addicted. I had an alcoholic personality too, on two bottles of vodka a day. What my body has taken I just don't know. But Carol wasn't affected at all. Kate had to go through cold turkey before she joined me.

Nobody had recognized before that I was multiple. My first husband said he'd married someone entirely unpredictable and moody, never the same from one day to the next. So I suppose people did pick something up. That marriage ended when I told him I'd been abused, and that I was multiple personality. He turned it into a game; he couldn't cope. He'd say things like, 'Can I choose who I sleep with, then?' I met my present partner four years ago, and most of me had joined by then. I'm getting married soon. I wouldn't until I was joined, as I didn't want to miss my own wedding!

My father is still alive and we don't get on at all. I hate him. Taking on board that Mum knew was an awful jump to make. Now she's dead. It was very tough. My father refuses to understand: says it's absolute pure fantasy. My mother when she was alive just said, 'Don't talk about it.' I have no idea why my parents did it. My father appeared totally respectable and was very well respected. He was physically abused, but not my mother as far as I know. You're left with this inner dream, that one day you'll have a mum and dad. It doesn't go away. It's left me wanting a lot, although I know I'll never have it all now.

I tell people now. I don't hide it. I know I won't get locked up now, so I feel safe. I've got the strength of completeness now. My partner knows and has known all of them, although he can get quite bemused at times. He sees that I'm OK and moving on and doing well. If I hadn't become multiple personality I'm sure I'd have been dead by now, or totally insane – whatever that is. I'd be in a ward now. I don't think I could have survived the pain otherwise. The abuse was so ongoing and relentless. I don't think the body or my mind could have stood it if I hadn't been multiple. It's like all that horror together would be intolerable. It would have been too much. So it got split into bits and given to different personalities. But there is a negative said to that. If I hadn't been multiple perhaps it would have been picked up, because my body wouldn't have stood it. [In my case] if one personality had been abused badly, and couldn't walk, or was in so much pain that they couldn't move, someone else would come in who didn't feel the pain. You see my personalities did collapse, but another would take over. It is a means of survival.

Once you join there is a great sense of loss around. I've been in mourning for about twelve months. A bit of me would really like to be multiple again, although I'm not going to be. Like any big changes, there are losses too. I've had to say goodbye to some security. I've got to face everything now. I've gained confidence in some ways, and lost it in others. There is a huge bond between those with multiple personality when they're together, and sometimes I feel a bit out of it now. It's a bit like belonging to an exclusive club.

Sometimes I wish I was part of it again. But I really do know I wouldn't have it any other way.

I have to face pain and loss now. I get ill, and have to cancel things like everyone else. The biggest gain is that I know I will go to bed tonight and wake up tomorrow morning – knowing that I'll still be there. It won't be a month later and I'll have missed my wedding, for example, because someone else will have gone. I think developing multiple personality has been the only sane way of dealing with a totally insane world. All those with multiple personality that I've met have suffered terrible abuse. It's like they dissociate to the most extreme degree.

MARIE

Marie is also multiple personality. She was also physically and sexually abused. Unlike Carol, not all her personalities had yet joined her. In the middle of my interview with her, I began to feel concerned that telling her story was proving too distressing. But just at that point the interview changed course: I did not need to intervene, as another of Marie's personalities came to the rescue. This new personality was confident, communicative and at ease, and coped well with the rest of our time together. I have included this in my record of Marie's reflections:

I'm multiple personality, and I only found that out about four years ago. I was at college doing a course, and we did something on child abuse. We watched a video, and suddenly it wasn't a child on the screen: it was me. I couldn't get away from it. I realized there was something wrong, although it was quite a while before I went for help. Although I'm in my fifties now, I hadn't realized before that I'd been abused. It was another eight months before I went for help. Bits and pieces kept coming back at me, and I couldn't make sense of it. It was very disjointed. I only had parts of memories, very little snatches.

Now I'm in the process of therapy and getting all the pieces together, and getting all the other personalities together. I still haven't got all the memories. All my life, as long as I remember, as a child and in girlhood, I've lost time. I always seemed to be in trouble without quite realizing what was happening. My mother died when I was four, and an aunt adopted me. My aunt was physically very violent. It was a strange and muddled family. I was never really sure who was who in the family – who was a sister and who was a cousin. At home I was always called different names anyway, so it was very confusing.

I was sexually abused by a man who used to babysit for me. He was actually my uncle, but I didn't known that then – he was my mother's brother. The abuse was pretty bad: it wasn't just straightforward abuse, and I'm still collecting bits and pieces of it. I think it was so bad that I had to split it up and put it in pieces – here, there and everywhere. I know I don't seem to have the same emotions as anyone else. I seem to smile a lot when I suppose I should be crying. I never seem to cry at anything at all in life. I think it got beyond crying about. I also seem never to get angry: I'm terrified of anger, but I was on the receiving end of an awful lot when I was a child.

Really I'm terrified of the whole world. I got married, but I don't remember my marriage – that disappeared as well. Someone was there, but it wasn't me. I have six children, and I think I remember their childhood but, even so, when they are together and talking there is so much I don't remember. I have lost an awful lot of time. I feel I've got to this age in my life and I've lost half of it. As far as I'm concerned, everyone seems to know more about me than I do, because when the other personalities come through it's the therapist they're talking to. I know nothing about it. The therapist has to tell me what has been said. I've no idea. It's very odd and very embarrassing.

Some of them do come out at other times, and some are very friendly to my daughters. I've tried to explain to my younger daughters, and they're fine. I've had a lot of problems with my elder daughter, who didn't want to accept it. We'll sit down and talk about it, and they'll remember a lot of occasions when I seemed to be acting out of character. They had a word for it: 'Mummy has this head on' or 'Mummy has that head on.' They had no idea how right they were! My husband died years ago, before it all started to come out, so he knew nothing about it. But strangely enough he always complained that if he knew me for a hundred years he would never know me, so he knew there was something wrong but had no idea what. He knew there was a real unpredictability about me: that he never knew from one day to the next how I would be.

The different personalities can be quite reliable, but there are complications. Like I've been keeping a journal, and I was getting quite annoyed because I'd be making an appointment and someone else would make an appointment somewhere else. I would like to join. I'm tired, and I'd just like to find out who I am. It didn't dawn on me that anything was wrong – I thought everybody was the same. When I lost time, I just thought that was what life was about. There are difficulties – in my last job one of the 'family' just turned against it and I just couldn't get to work, and that was that. A lot of the time it was someone else who actually went to work. And then it was decided we didn't like it any more. That was when my memory started coming back.

I worked in an old people's home, and a resident had been rushed into the home and was put into my unit. He'd been abusing children near another home. I was expected to look after him, and I was remembering my own abuse. It was pretty hard. If I had to go down to his bedroom I really was terrified, and it got to the stage where each day I dreaded going into work. Finally, although I tried, I had to leave and go to another home. But I think the damage was already done, and everyone in the 'family' viewed all men with suspicion. No one was safe any more. Also, I have quite a few child personalities, and they didn't like working. There was a lift in the home, and every so often you'd find yourself going up and down in the lift. The children liked the lift so suddenly you were in the lift – they wanted to play. It's very difficult to explain.

I'm not sure how many personalities there are yet. I would really like to get them all together now. Last weekend for the first time they started to use the tape recorder. Lorraine wants to talk most: she is in charge more, she's the social one. Everyone came for their own reasons, and most of them came to help with the abuse when things got very, very bad. One of two went on to help at work, and I've relied upon Lorraine quite a lot without realizing it. I think I'm a bit shy really, but she is very good in company, so she takes over and looks after me.

It seems they did a lot of rescuing of me when I was little.

My mother was my adoptive mother, and I have a lot of
memories of getting beaten up pretty badly, having a lot of
black eyes. I couldn't have told anyone – there was no one to
tell. Anyway, I would have been too scared that it would
backfire on to me. It might have got worse. I was afraid of
my mother. She was a terrifying person. I think the abuse
went on throughout my childhood. She never missed an
opportunity to tell me she didn't want me.

Other things are still very, very disjointed. As the memories come back, they are so painful. That's one of the very,
very, scary things as they come and join me. I'm afraid of the
memories that I'm going to get that I haven't got yet. I don't
know them at first hand yet, although I've been told they're
there.

Going into therapy was a case of necessity when I first
started. Because always, all through my life from being a
child, suicide was very high on my list. When I was about
eleven I was cutting my wrists and all sorts of things. Then it
seemed to be very high on the list again. All my life in one
way and another I've tried to hurt myself, time and time
again – cutting myself in particular. If I didn't do it, I'd find
it was done anyway. It was very strange at times. Recently,
one of the child personalities was having some very bad
memories, and didn't much care for them. She had the idea
of killing herself, but didn't really know how to, so she put
her hand through a piece of glass and cut herself. Some of the
children are very, very, young; and only today someone else
has come through. It's like getting confirmation of all the
things that have happened.

I now know that my family had known about the abuse. It
went on until I was about fourteen. Another cousin had been
living in the house, and my uncle had tried to interfere with
her too. It had been going on for years. My adoptive mother
didn't abuse anyone else, just me. When the memories first
started coming back, I felt I was going insane. When I first
started therapy I really didn't know what was happening. It
was very confusing for both of us. I did have a counsellor
before, and I think she was really very pleased to hand me
over because I don't think she could handle it.

It all started coming out in therapy; and when it was
explained to me I wasn't surprised, because by this time I
was losing a lot time. It had got worse, and I felt worse.

When you lose time, you don't always lose time in a block. One hour you're OK, and then you lose an hour, and then you come back. You get used to it. You get used to coming back in and picking up threads of conversations. You get fairly skilled when you realize that you can't remember. You say things like, 'It's just absent-mindedness' or 'I didn't quite catch what you were saying.' It's more difficult to cover up blocks of time. It's more embarrassing when you meet some-body in town whom you don't know, and they know you fairly well. It always has happened, and I thought I just looked like somebody else.

Since my husband died I think the other personalities have come through more, and have more or less set up a life of their own. I think that's where the problems are going to begin, trying to get them back in. One of the personalities won't talk to the therapist any more. She's keeping out of it, making a protest about something.

It's been a bit of a problem recently. I've been spending many hours trying to take it all on myself. There's always a battle going on inside me. The only way I can describe my life is that it's been like living in an empty shell: like there was nothing there, nothing on the inside. And if anyone took a fancy to me I could never understand why, because there was nothing there. I never felt there was any personality there. The personality had gone out with the beatings. I was just left with an empty feeling. So putting all the others in, or getting them in, is going to be like filling the empty shell: like having all the pieces and needing to put them into place – except some may not want to come in.

At this point Marie became very distressed. It all felt too painful for her. Her voice was faltering. It was at this point that another personality started to come in, although she didn't intro-duce herself immediately. What she went on to say came from the more confident personality, Lorraine. Then Marie was able to speak again, but from then on interchanged with Lorraine if talking became difficult. To show how multiple personality can show itself, I have attempted to distinguish the alter from the host in this account, and indeed the alter Lorraine eventually made it clear to me herself:

Lorraine: As far as some of them are concerned they are individuals in their own right, and they do not want to join.

So it's going to be quite hard to persuade them. Part of therapy is conducting a dialogue between them and her, like diplomatic negotiations. It's going to have to be very diplomatic because I'm sure one or two of them will take off. One of the other personalities, Deirdre, who was really more married than anyone, and who did a lot of caring for the children, is pretty lonely and I think she'd like to join.

Marie: There are a lot of children, and I don't seem to come to the end of those. I wonder how many more. I'm not sure if there are boys as well as girls, but they're all ages. They scare me quite a bit, because they carry the worst memories; and they're very frightening. They all came to protect me, and what I now realize is that I wouldn't be here without them; I wouldn't have survived. I did try to commit suicide many times, and I don't think we thought we would live anyway – there was that much going on.

There was the uncle, as well as my mother, and the sexual abuse from him was pretty bad. Mother seemed partly unbalanced at times. She'd fly into a fury and hit out, and if you were there you got it. And I was usually there. Very often you wouldn't know what it was for. Everything was for survival, for protection. I wonder when it started. Did it start with that baby? Someone seems to have the memory of that. Mothers frighten the life out of me.

Lorraine: None of us like mothers. Or adults in general. But particularly mothers.

Marie: Because there were times when the uncle could put his arm around you, and show you some affection; but it never came from anywhere else. There are no memories of nice touching. It's very scary. You're never sure, don't know who is going to come, or where it's going to take you.

Lorraine: The tape recorder helps. Lots of us will use that now.

Marie: I leave it in one place, and I go to bed and it's there on the pillow. I listened and there was an answer to a question I didn't know. I didn't recognize her. I'd never heard the voice before – like hearing a strange voice on my tape recorder. But no more strange than the journal: we have that going. You put something in that, and someone else answers it. The tapes are very important, but it would be nice to have everything first hand, not second hand, and not rely on other people to tell you what is going on.

My therapist tells me what has been said, and that can be very embarrassing and very strange, because somewhere this has all come out of the same person. It's very scary at times. But when you've lived your life like this, and suddenly someone tells you that you only have one mind, and that there is a problem with having all these different people, you think, 'Only *one* of you to deal with all the problems? No wonder there are so many of you in mental homes.' It's just unbelievable: how can anyone cope with all that? I sometimes think maybe we have it right and everyone else has it wrong. But the empty shell isn't so nice. There is always someone around to fill up the shell. It makes sense to join. But some of the others are very reluctant, because in many ways it feels a sensible way to cope.

Lorraine: You've been talking to two of us for a while. You were talking to Marie first, and I'm Lorraine. I'm more confident and more able to deal with people than Marie. Before we finish, I want to say that I don't want to join. There's a few of us don't want to, including me. I think this is a better way. It may need refining, but it is a better way. We didn't know Marie. It's only lately we've got to know her. To us that was the body and we were the people. There were jobs to be done and we did them, and we got on with our own life for a while. We got on with working with the old people. I wasn't very good at looking after children, so someone else did that.

Marie was just a body to us, but there was a reason for that. When she was about eleven or twelve, the abuse got very, very bad; and we had to push it away from us. There were about five of us dealing with it at the time. It was decided, though I don't know who exactly decided, that it was the body that was taking the abuse, and taking the pain, and it was a way to survive. It wasn't a conscious decision. It's not us. Each one of us could always self-hypnotize, by watching a spot within ourselves. We've all done that: it was just something natural that happened. Just taking yourself out of it. Marie can do it too, but she seems to hang on for a bit longer. It's a way of getting yourself out of the pain.

JUDY

I have referred to Judy's story in earlier chapters. She was involved from a young age in a child prostitution and pornography
ring. Many of the people she named as her abusers held senior
and responsible positions in the health service, in social services
and in the police force. This was the part of her story that was
relevant to multiple personality:

As you've gathered, I'm multiple personality, and I've
known for about five years. Before that I had no idea. I'd
worked out for myself that I'd been sexually abused, and I
was referred to my current therapist after various overdoses
and seeing psychiatrists, social workers and so on. The process of psychiatry was absolutely useless – I couldn't give
them a true picture, because I didn't have it myself. I knew I
had gaps, but tell a psychiatrist you have gaps and it's ECT,
drugs, up on the wards and you never get out.

I know now that I've been sexually abused, virtually since
birth, by my dad and then by my stepdad, and also physically and sexually abused by my mother; and that I was sold in
a ring. I've dealt with most of that, and I feel OK about
myself. The most important thing is that I know it wasn't
my fault. But also I now know why I had these gaps: that I
wasn't going totally insane, that I wouldn't end up in Broad-
moor. That has been very empowering, because I have an
explanation. It makes sense.

I discovered I was multiple after seeing my therapist for
a couple of years. I worked out that there were quite a few
times when I knew I hadn't been to see him but he hadn't
said anything about it. He had obviously begun to realize
something was going on. The way he handled things made
me feel that here was someone I could be honest to. I'd told
him I had gaps, and he didn't rush me to hospital, or to the
police station. He was saying, 'Hang on. We'll sort it out.'
That was so reassuring. He played me one of my 'family'
who had talked on his tape when I hadn't been one week,
and I listened to it. My initial reaction was to wonder what
on earth was going on. Yet there was a certain familiarity
about the voice – mine and not mine. Under hypnosis I met
one of the other personalities. I felt safe with my therapist
and I trusted him. Now about nineteen have joined; and each

time someone joins I feel different, and have to deal with new memories. And that's hell.

Paula, who is one of those who has joined, has been a drug addict and a prostitute. And it was horrifying to find that I had been virtually sold by my mum and dad to people who I knew. The drug addiction was very frightening at first. There are people around who I thought were nice ordinary people, who I've had sex with or been raped by. My therapist has talked to some of the personalities, so I've had some of the knowledge beforehand. But it's different when I come to experience it myself.

I avoid relationships now. Although I think I'm heterosexual, I'm frightened of relating. At present that feels right, although it might change in the future. Now I can plan when someone joins me. I know that Lorna, who hasn't joined yet, had a partner and a child who died in a car crash. It's very difficult to think that my body has had a baby and not to really know it. So when she joins I think it's going to be very, very painful.

I feel I no longer hide. I'm not ashamed of having been sexually abused. It shouldn't be kept hidden like a dark secret. I wonder about the films and photographs of me. I know a lot of them were for European and American export, and I don't know if they're still around or not: I wonder if the child me is still being abused. I do now know certainly that from as young as possible until I was sixteen or seventeen I was abused, in terms of being sold; and after that by working as a prostitute, working for pimps, because that was all I was useful for. But I'm still not sure how far out the web went. There was still contact, there was still control until a few years ago. I'd allow all forms of abuse. I was totally subjugated.

I still live with my mum, because a lot of the little ones still want to be there; and that is a big conflict. The only way I can deal with that is to be at home. She'll watch programmes on the telly on abuse, and say 'Isn't that awful? How can people do that?' It's virtually impossible to sit through that. She totally denies. There is no acknowledgement beyond her saying that I've had a lot of problems in my life.

I had to fail at everything. I went on a return-to-learn scheme. I was asked to go to London on a course and I was terrified – that's where I'd been a prostitute. And I was bound to fail. I'd been called mentally ill, schizophrenic,

mentally retarded, educationally subnormal. And they're all
written down – I've got letters saying that. It was a real
turning-point when my therapist said its OK to try and to
fail. Those words are imprinted on my brain now. That
was a real turning-point. It said, you're OK too: you're not
deranged; you've been abused and misused, but you're not
mad.

I've seen multiple personality and my 'family' as quite
creative and protective. If it hadn't been for that, there's no
doubt I'd be dead, or in a mental hospital somewhere. I
would have disintegrated if they hadn't taken it to parts for
me. Now I have an agreement with my 'family' that I deal
with everything. It's quite daunting – and frustrating, because Lorna has very impressive qualifications and I've had to
struggle to get O-levels and access courses. But those bits of
paper belong to someone else: they're not mine.

I know the only way is to remember things, although even
then I think there are some things that won't change. I can't
button my shirts up, because I can't take anything tight
around my neck – so often I had ropes and things around my
neck. And I can't wear bracelets for the same reason – too
many memories. No one ever knew as a child, although I did
tell them; but I wasn't believed. It was always, 'That can't be
true.' The first person I told was a ballet teacher, and she
said, 'No, it's none of my business.'

I told a teacher about the abuse, but he was an abuser, and
that brought about even more abuse from home: if I'd told
him, who else was I telling? Then I told a dentist, but both
he and his partner and his nurse were abusers. A lot of the
films used to be made in the dental surgery. One of my
'family' took an overdose and tried to get run over – this was
a seven-year-old – but it was put down to being an obnox-
ious child. And then I gave up. It just wasn't worth it. That
was it. It was quite a big ring. There was no way out.

As an adult, I got to the point where I wouldn't trust
anyone. And when I got referred to a different mental health
team I did almost trust a couple of the workers. They didn't
know I was like this – I was just a problem person. As I
began to get closer, the family started telling loads of lies.
The purpose was to get me thrown out. They just told
stories. They accused people of all sorts of things. But if I'd
told the helpers what was really going on I would have had

to explain that I didn't know what they were talking about – these people weren't really me. You have to understand that they're already telling me I'm disturbed, and it would just have confirmed it. And then I was referred to a psychiatrist and she was OK and referred me to my therapist. He was tried and tested so much – with overdoses, with accusations and so on. But he's understood and been able to take it. I gave him a pretty rough ride. I've seen him for seven years now.

If I hadn't been referred to my therapist, I think I'd be surviving – just an automaton, just existing; never actually getting anywhere; in and out of jobs – until I'd have come to the attention of the police or a psychiatrist. And I might have been lucky, but I might not have been. As it is, I've gone back to study, and that can be tricky because some of the others in the 'family' don't like it. And if I lose a lot of time I miss deadlines. I have to fit everything into a four-day week because the 'family' have to have the rest. We negotiate: one has to have disco time; Lorna has her classes; the children need time to play. Some people notice I have a lot of mood changes, and my tutors think I'm very peculiar. Some of my subjects relate to politics, and I hate that because of my dad's involvement with politics.

I now know I'll never sort it all out, that I'll never be able to confront all the abusers, although I used to dream about doing that. I have to live with what there is now and to work with that. It's all I can do. In the future I think I want to be integrated, but I'm not quite sure. I want to get a degree; I want to work in the field of sexual abuse. In terms of permanent relationships and children, I'm not sure; I don't know. I like being with other people's children, and I may have to be happy with that. I have some very special friends now, which is wonderful.

I would like to say that if people seem to be lying then explore if they are losing time. That can be why. And to explore why people overdose and cut themselves – particularly children. It's always about something, or trying to say something. Don't distance people if they lie: they might be hiding the truth that can't be spoken. And on a practical basis, for anyone working with sexual abuse victims, and particularly multiple personality, always offer a few appointments ahead, so if that person can't make it, or aren't around, and they're frightened of phoning, they know when they're coming again. And appointment cards are important, because you can forget. It's practical, but very important.

WORKING WITH MULTIPLE PERSONALITY: THERAPEUTIC IMPLICATIONS

Those of us who specialize in abuse work are aware of a few references in the literature to working with multiple personality. For instance, Kluft (1985:9) recognizes and distinguishes a number of issues in the psychotherapy of Multiple Personality Disorder, such as:

> developing trust, making and sharing the diagnosis, communicating with each personality state, contracting, gathering history, working with each personality state's problems, undertaking special procedures, developing interpersonality communication, achieving resolution or integration, developing new behaviours and coping skills, networking and using social support systems, solidifying gains and following up.

However, most clinicians have not encountered this phenomenon directly. There must be many therapists who have had clients with multiple personality in their own clinical practice but did not have the experience to recognize the fact. Fortunately I was able to draw upon the first-hand knowledge of two therapists with expertise in this field. It is mostly their words that I record in this section.

The importance of accurately recognizing and of identifying the existence of multiple personality is clearly basic to any therapeutic work. As was clear from the personal accounts above, misdiagnosis is common. One therapist described the difficulty of recognition:

> It's different for me now to my first very early experience. In that instance it was very simple, because an alter personality spoke and introduced herself to me. I don't think I was surprised or shocked, because I'd been very aware of how differently she could present: for instance, some of the switching that would occur made me think at one time that this was a marvellous example of someone who was borderline. Now I would think the other way: if someone is such a good example of borderline syndrome they maybe multiple.

Some indicators come from referral information, and, as in other cases of sexual abuse, greater familiarity leads to earlier and more accurate diagnosis. Indicators especially include amnesic periods – inability to remember periods of time or life events. For example, a client may have a very turbulent psychiatric history, but has suddenly recovered, but with no memory of that earlier period of time. This could suggest another personality taking control. Other indicators include people with considerable doubts about what is real and not real; symptomatic presentations such as frequent headaches (alongside other indicators); and people who have extreme concerns about confidentiality. Although none of these are indicators in themselves, they invite further enquiry. Here-and-now, face-to-face indications are also significant, such as people momentarily going blank and 'switching' from one personality to another in the way Marie/Lorraine did in the example above. The therapist explained further:

> You get to recognize switching when it occurs, and the coming back and being different, and covering up. You get people who are multiples who are extremely accomplished at concealing that they don't know what has just been happening. If you're sensitized to that, it becomes clear and you can check it out.

There are often chaotic, turbulent types of experience, conflicting stories about the same events, people claiming that both this and that happened; or the client reports, or is reported as, lying about their behaviour. People who are multiples are constantly accused of being liars, and there is often considerable confusion about events surrounding them. An experienced therapist may even be aware of the possibility of multiplicity before the client:

> In one case the client herself gave me a hint when she said she didn't remember some particularly awful material that had emerged in the previous session. That led me to ask her if that was a frequent experience of hers, and we got at it that way. If I'm reasonably convinced, and I notice switching, I might just ask who I am talking to, and the other personality may introduce him or herself. With another client it was such an obvious switch that I thought I would try it out, because I couldn't really make good sense of her behaviour. The referral suggested she might be schizophrenic or be having schizophrenic episodes. The picture was very, very confused.

It's been hard for that person to accept it. But once you start talking about missed time it can be quite a relief for the person to have it acknowledged, and to be able to talk about it.

How might a client respond to the unexpected question 'Who am I talking to?' Clearly the client has made considerable effort, albeit unconscious, to develop this complicated strategy, and discovery could be threatening. Might such an intervention be received with hostility, anxiety or relief? Might the alter want to deny, or cover up their presence?

This seems to vary with the alter: some want to meet the therapist, others do not. The host personality, who is unaware of what happens in the gaps, is the one most likely to cover up. An alter can come in and take over while the therapist is talking to the host, and then go away. If the therapist then refers to something said by the alter, the host knows nothing about this; and as a result it is not surprising if she or he covers up. So there is a problem for the host personality, who is amnesic and unaware of the existence of other personalities. This can be very confusing and frightening, leaving them unable to understand other people's responses. Nothing makes sense. Introducing ideas about possible meanings is clearly a problem, a difficult task for the therapist who has some sense of what the presentation is about while the client does not. Furthermore, the client has had to hide their experiences for a long time. Handling this with care and sensitivity is essential:

The first thing is for the person to be able to acknowledge the experience: to feel they no longer have to cover it up. Once that has happened, all kinds of things are likely to follow. It's hard for other people to understand that in one sense the experiences are normal, because for the client life is as it's always been. But it's not accepted as such by others, so the client has learned very early to hide what is happening to them. Once the person has acknowledged what happens to them, you can be reassuring: that they're not mad; that there are very sensible reasons for the way they experience things; that it doesn't mean anything dreadful is going to happen; that it doesn't mean they're beyond reach, and so forth – those things need to be said before you can move on. Unfortunately, of course, such things are often portrayed as signs of madness – schizophrenia is a frequent diagnosis – so the importance of reassurance is obvious.

I discuss presentations with very few or fragmented memories in the next chapter. Amnesia suggests repressed trauma, but it can also indicate multiplicity. Despite the amnesia, there are other indicators: the client may have contacts with alter personalities through dreams, or may have other experiences they do not readily reveal. Although memories are not accessible, the experience has not gone away – it remains somewhere inside the client. At a particular time remembering may be too painful; but the memories may be partially expressed, although not summoned up consciously.

Those with multiple personality have to learn about very difficult events. In many ways the alter personalities make considerable sense as a healthy way for a young person to cope with and survive trauma. There are no other escape routes. But the ordeal of discovering the abuse they have survived may be tremendous, and especially traumatic for the host personality, who may have no recollection of anything but a loving and secure background. Whilst the biggest problem is for the host personality, the other personalities, or many of them, are aware of some of the abuse, and they need a place and a space to tell their own stories.

The concept of multiplicity is not an easy one to grasp, and the question of communication between alters is a significant issue. Initially the host is unaware of the alters, although there is also a question about how the alters are organized and whether they are aware of one another, which would point to an unconscious element in the host's ego. There are different levels of awareness, and forms of organization vary greatly from one person to another. It is very complex, and personalities may relate to one another in complex ways. Some personalities can be very isolated within the internal organization, whereas others can be closely involved with other personalities. There may be hierarchical arrangements, so that some personalities can only be accessed through others. Sometimes, when an alter is dealing with a trauma that becomes too much or too severe, a second-level alter is called up to rescue the first-level alter. One of the therapists I spoke with described this:

I was given an example of trauma getting more and more severe. It was trial and error to find the best way of dealing with it. Someone was created and they went to the wall because the attempt wasn't successful. It was too much for them, so things had to be split up in different ways. Some bits of an experience were taken by one, and other bits by another, so as not to be together in the same body at the same time. It is an extraordinary survival mechanism. In fact it can be hard to reconstitute the experience, because it's been shared by quite a number of different personalities. To get it back together you have to access the pieces held by each different person. You have somehow to gather the alters together to see the complete picture.

Acting as a facilitator to assist communication between the alters is a potentially important role for the therapist, although it is no easy task. Alters may already have their own system, an internal network for communicating. The therapist can invite the host to join this communication and can foster it, directly or indirectly: for example, once the host understands the existence of multiplicity, the host can be invited to keep a diary for their family of personalities. If the family want to convey things to the host, they can do so in writing, because there is no other direct way of doing it. A tape recorder can be used at a later point, although this may be too frightening in the early stages.

The therapist almost becomes a go-between, although this can create further complications. In most therapeutic situations a client can tell a therapist something one week and it can be referred to the next, even if it has been painful. But if an alter who is unknown to the host talks with the therapist and reveals details that are also unknown, this cannot always be safely talked about with the host. Issues of confidentiality, of alliances within the client, and of remembering not only the material but also which personality imparted the information are real and complex. It has the flavour of the most complicated form of family therapy, in which the parameters of the family are unknown or as yet only dimly understood. How does a therapist cope with such problems?

> There are a lot of interesting issues, and the one to do with information given by an alter can occur within a session, not just between sessions. You may have some idea yourself of who has access to particular information at a particular point in time. And generally, while the host may be amnesic, other personalities will have access to the host's experience. So you don't need necessarily to tell *them* about communications, because they have been listening in and observing – silent witnesses to what has taken place. The other issue it raises is whether you're going to allow alter personalities to share

information with you in confidence: for example, if they don't want the host informed, will you accept that? Or will you insist that you won't have any such contracts within the network? Do you want to be free to repeat anything that's told you?

There is no single answer, but confidentiality for each alter can become unmanageable. Personalities can and do share information, and in any case a therapist may not know just who is listening in. But if and when a therapist feels it necessary to communicate what has been said, there are difficulties:

The material can be so horrific that it's hard to cope with hearing it yourself. You may need to wait until you feel the host can cope. The host isn't always ready to receive information. You may have to be prepared not to share things with the host if they're not ready. And it can be that alters need therapeutic work for traumas *they* have dealt with.

There is, however, some degree of in-built protection: if a therapist tries to share information with a host who is not ready to receive it, they will either exit, or will not hear it, or will deny it. The general objective is to promote communication across the boundaries and to break down the segregation.

I have already made it clear that those who develop multiple personalities have suffered enormously. They have devised a strategy that protects them at a deep level and is possibly life-saving. Giving this strategy up in order to become integrated marks a huge change in the structure of their lives. In the accounts recorded above, both Marie and Judy regarded the prospect of joining with ambivalence. Carol talked of a sense of loss as well as of gains. Having accepted their multiplicity, how do such people view the prospect of integration? The therapist who specialized in this work explained:

It can be frightening, and accompanied by tremendous feelings of loneliness. And it can be very burdensome to know you've always got to be present to yourself. Being aware of what is going on inside and outside at the same time can feel particularly difficult. And there's an enormous sense of loss for alters. They go through a dying process when they're involved in becoming one, because they give up their identity and their relationships: these can't be preserved if the alters no longer exist.

We need to remember that the basic rationale for multiplicity – and one reason that makes joining very difficult – is that the affects carried within different personalities have been clearly polarized. It is consequently very hard for them to coexist within an integrated person. For example, one personality might be very attached to the abuser, while another feels totally murderous. It makes sense to have such opposite feelings expressed through separate personalities. Inevitably, this involves many conflicts. Similarly, alters can have different sexual orientations – a difficult issue to resolve if they become joined. As in any family network, there are many other conflictual issues, alliances, coalitions, enmities and jealousies. A further complication is that some alters have not experienced the early abuse but have 'arrived' on the scene later; they may not want to take on the memory of the pain. The difficulties are considerable:

> The process of giving up multiplicity is so painful you can see why someone might prefer not to do it, if life is manageable. Obviously, the necessity for that solution is not so urgent once the abusive situation is no longer ongoing. But it's very difficult to give up dealing with things by dissociation. It is a very open question whether integration is better than collaborative multiplicity.

Carol was one of those who preferred integration, even if the process of achieving it was long, painful and difficult. It has to be remembered that essentially there is only one person, even if the alters see themselves as separate and unconnected. The therapist needs to be able to make an alliance with each of the different personalities; and at some point sufficient consensus is needed within the system that integration is desirable. The personalities need to be persuaded of the value of integration, and to that end their different needs have to be worked through. Some alters may stay partially integrated, while others may stay out; but the system has to be reasonably collaborative. There has to be a common agreement that they will not sabotage integration, even if they do not all join.

But, remarkably, the therapist can also be helped from *within* the system:

> There can be alters who are wonderful therapists, who advise and help the therapist, and who can be extremely supportive. It's like having personalities working as co-therapists and

offering very useful guidance. Some of the American literature describes the 'inner self-helper'. It can be affectless – almost a pure bit of mind, rather than another personality – but cognitive of all the organization; an overseer, knowing everything that goes on, both part of it and not part of it. The system may need someone like that, who never took part, who never experienced or helped deal with the abuse, but who can be an internal organizer and controller.

Joining is hard because it involves the host taking on all the knowledge and all the detail of the abuse. The material may come to them raw. Each time this happens is potentially a fresh trauma, because they are experiencing something they have not consciously known. It is not just knowledge that is taken on – abuse is actually *experienced* for the first time. This can be extremely hard for the therapist too, who may need to be very accessible to the client:

> Ideally the therapist should be available by phone, and see them three times a week or more. But without other back-up that is difficult to do, and you feel yourself sinking under the pressure. It's very, very difficult work, and it can feel very punishing. Really what is needed is a therapeutic team for those clients who need a lot of resources, with a primary therapist within that. An hour a week isn't enough. There is a real problem in terms of therapeutic resources. It's very demanding on the client, and quite a severe challenge to the therapist.

Persecutor personalities can pose particular difficulties. These personalities may wish to harm the host, to interrupt therapeutic work, or to act out in other inappropriate ways. Gaining access to and communicating with these alters is therefore most important. Eliana Gil (1988:155) suggests that:

> in dealing with them you must set firm and consistent limits; if they test the limits, tell them their behaviour is unacceptable and will be stopped. External controls may need to be set. At the same time, these alters can be given an opportunity to explain why they want to hurt the client, and give them tools to express their hostility harmlessly. In addition, you must convene the helper personalities and encourage them to form a protective coalition.

Therapy with Multiple Personality Disorder is possible and it can be effective. It is also extremely demanding, painful and exhausting. It requires a high level of knowledge, care and expertise. It is most important that all those working with abuse survivors know of the existence of multiple personality and are alert to possible indications, particularly given the likelihood that presentations of this kind can be misunderstood. Therapy should perhaps only be offered by those who have sufficient skills and resources. Putman, however, argues against an 'expert' stance (1989:134):

> Although some therapists become 'instant experts' on seeing their first case, most feel they do not have the skills necessary to treat these patients. Usually this is not true. The most important qualification for doing good work with MPD patients is the ability to do good psychotherapy. Most of the dynamics and resistances are similar to those found in neurotic or borderline patients. The differences lie in the personification of these dynamics by the alter personalities. In many ways, this personification makes it easier to work directly with these dynamics.

When appropriate therapy is available, there is little doubt that it can lead to dramatic changes, as Carol's story vividly depicts. It is obvious that short-term therapy is unlikely to be helpful, and that a long-term commitment is vital. If the therapist is able to offer this, it is not only productive and valuable: it also opens up possibilities for understanding the internal complexities of the personality, which of course has repercussions for all therapeutic work.

SEVEN

STAGES IN THE PROCESS OF COUNSELLING AND THERAPY

The initial contact which any new client makes with a counsellor or therapist is always significant. For clients who have been abused, the decision to seek help is in itself a major step. I have shown in earlier chapters how threats are often used to prevent an abused child from telling anyone, and that the attempts of both children and adults to speak are often met with denial, disbelief or rejection. Experience of trustworthy relationships is often limited or non-existent, and relating well to another person in any depth or for any length of time may be an unknown experience. Just by coming for counselling or therapy, such clients put themselves in a situation that reflects their particular difficulties: they have to trust someone sufficiently to talk about what has previously been a forbidden and forbidding subject. They have to hope that this will not lead to further betrayal.

Although the process in any therapeutic work does not fall neatly into definite stages, it is valuable to acknowledge key features that have particular significance at different times. For the sake of clarity I refer to these as the initial, middle and final stages of therapy and counselling. It needs to be remembered that the features in any of these stages are not inevitable, and the points I discuss are not intended as hard and fast rules. Individual therapists and counsellors have to find their own style; and, while it is important to integrate anything that is useful, it is also necessary to discard anything that is not. There is no single way and no blueprint for this type of work.

COMMON FEATURES OF THE INITIAL STAGE

1. The impact of previous help and first-time clients

Some clients have seen many helpers. In Chapter 5 these experiences were described as positively damaging, useless but relatively
harmless, and more positive and helpful. Previous experiences of
help have repercussions which inevitably affect the new contact
for therapy. These need to be acknowledged. The client may
come with high hopes – especially if the new therapist has been
recommended – or it may feel like a last desperate hope, or there
may be no hope at all. For example, Susie had seen psychiatrists
and counsellors previously. She was scathing about the psychiatrists, neutral about one counsellor and positive about a second,
whom she had not wanted to leave:

> I'm telling you: you're my last hope. I've just had a birthday,
> and if I'm not feeling better by the next one, that's it – I'm
> ending it all.

Depending on the nature of these earlier encounters, a wide
spectrum of feelings is evident. One man had been told by his
previous counsellor that he needed to see someone who was more
experienced. However true and appropriate this was, this confirmed his fears: not only that he could not cope with the abuse
and its effects, but that no one else could either. A woman was
referred by her doctor, who genuinely felt she had neither sufficient time nor the necessary skills to help. Both referrals were
appropriate, and both those making the referrals tried to be honest and helpful. However, both clients were left feeling rejected,
and fearful that they were overwhelming. Until this was acknowledged by the new therapist, and assurances were given that
they would not be deserted again, therapeutic work could not
begin.

A new client can come with good previous experiences that
have been prematurely curtailed by their therapist. However well
handled, the client has not been able to control the ending. This is
a particular problem for those who have had so little control over
much in their life. Responses to this vary, but they commonly
include an underlying sense of abandonment.

Liz was sexually abused in childhood. Her therapist left to have
a baby:

I didn't believe she could go and leave me, but I couldn't say so. She didn't look very well. But I just kept thinking, 'What about me? After all I've told you, how could you? I need you!'

Paul had been physically abused, and he found it hard to acknowledge that he cared about his therapist leaving to take up a new post:

It didn't bother me. After all, you all do the same job. I expect your qualifications are about the same, and it doesn't really matter. It's only a job. You can't blame him for moving on. It was promotion.

Both these people had difficulty in making the transition. It was hard for Paul to say he was angry, disappointed and sad: as a child, expressing such feelings had led to punishment. But for both, the acceptance of their loss and anger was essential if the new therapeutic relationship was to develop. Accepting these feelings and taking them seriously was an indication that other aspects of their lives would also be accepted and taken seriously.

Other clients arrive without having seen helpers previously. They may themselves have decided to come, or it may have been suggested to them. For this group it can be the first time they have ever told anyone their story. They may be both desperate to speak and also wary of doing so. In a first session, Kim, who had suffered severe physical abuse, became extremely distressed recalling some of the details. She had never told them to anyone before. It was evident that she had said more than she had intended, and this left her feeling both vulnerable and anxious. At the end of the session, with her hand on the door handle, she said:

I don't know how you can do this job. I don't know how you can stand hearing such awful things. I don't think you'll cope with me, because nobody ever can; and I can't believe you'll be any different.

At this point, with another client waiting, a response had to be brief. However, it was important to acknowledge what she had said and to offer some reassurance. In the next session the therapist started by recalling these words. She made it clear that she would take care of herself, and that the client could say anything she wanted, but only when she was ready to. However, she wondered if Kim's departing words also reflected her own anxieties: perhaps she was worried about whether she could stand talking about it, or whether she would be able to cope.

2. Setting boundaries

Whether or not a client has been seen previously, they are now in a new, different situation with a new helper. As the accounts in Chapter 3 showed, abuse invades the boundaries of the body and the self. Making clear the boundaries can help to make therapy a safer place. Knowing that they will be seen regularly, and how long a session lasts, gives the client some security and predictability. Neither caring nor predictable behaviour has been part of the abused person's experience, and it is important that the therapist establishes both within the therapeutic framework.

Abuse faces the helper with aspects of human behaviour that are indeed appalling. The effects of this work are examined in Chapter 9. The horror of some stories is such that counsellors may feel they will do anything to rescue the victim. If the abuse also touches on unresolved pain in the helper, such feelings can be very intense. However, it is not helpful to assuage these by promising or offering anything that cannot in reality be consistently given. Helpers need to be clear about their own boundaries and to communicate these to clients. Inviting clients to contact them between sessions, or giving a home telephone number, should be done only with due care: it should not be a way of coping with the helper's anxieties. The implications of such actions must always be very carefully considered. For instance, offering contact between sessions, especially in the early stages, may reinforce in clients anxieties that neither they nor the therapist can cope.

Many of those who have been abused experience a morass of feelings that are chaotic and overwhelming. External boundaries that are safe, that do not collapse when challenged and that are clearly understood on both sides begin to act as a counterbalance to the chaos, as well as reflecting an alternative model of behaviour.

3. Controlling the process

Control inevitably lies with the therapist when it comes to decisions about frequency of meetings and length of sessions. Clients must know that, although they had no control over the abuse, they can take charge of the use, progress and content of the time offered to them.

The client needs assurance that they can proceed at a pace that is comfortable, and that there will be no pressure to disclose anything that cannot yet be tolerated. Frequently in early sessions painful details are only referred to briefly. It is as if casual references at this stage are the only safe way of disclosing distressing memories. These can be mentioned but not dwelt upon.

The counsellor needs to listen carefully, to acknowledge what they have heard, and to indicate that they have taken serious notice of what has been heard. A constant dilemma in working with abuse survivors is how to avoid becoming yet another person who invades, like the abuser, while also not ignoring or denying the realities of the abuse, as many others have done. The therapist's acknowledging that they have heard, and inviting the client to say more, but only when ready to do so, helps to overcome this dilemma. The abuse of children is the abuse of power, and it is crucial that this is in no way reflected in the therapeutic process.

4. The development of trust

This is an issue throughout the therapy, and trust is tried and tested many times. The development of trust is not simple, yet it is central to the process. In many ways the ability to trust is the cornerstone of being a person, essential for the satisfactory development of close relationships, the foundations of which should be laid in childhood. For those who have been abused, this is not the case. They have grown up in a world that has proved itself extremely untrustworthy. In any case, trusting a stranger is not easy. At the beginning of therapy, the new client will be very aware of the therapist:

> The first face-to-face contact is very important. You – the therapist – represent both the (longed-for) nurturing and the (feared) rejecting, abusive parent. Your client will be struggling desperately to feel safe, monitoring everything you say or do.
>
> (Gil 1988:67–8)

In addition to the establishing of clear and safe boundaries, there are other aspects of the initial stages that need to be considered if trust is to be encouraged. The guarantee of confidentiality is important, particularly if previous experience of other agencies has been that shared information has not been safeguarded. Abuse has meant the complete disregard of privacy in a most exploitative and invasive manner. All clients have a right to confidentiality, but it is a particular issue for those whose basic rights have been so disregarded.

If trust is to develop, clients need to feel they are taken seriously, and that what they say is accepted and believed. They need to know that their counsellor is not going to be damaged, overwhelmed, shocked or frightened by what they say and recall. Careful, empathic listening and a calm, supportive presence are vital. Such clients, even more than most, probably feel ambivalent about their therapist and therapy. They may in part be very committed, but in part in a state of great doubt. Therapy is a painful process, and it needs to be openly recognized as such. Mixed feelings are almost inevitable: they need to be identified and accepted. At the same time, therapists need to check that their particular style and presence do not pose their own problems.

Other factors are also important. Therapists need to be aware that sitting with their back to a door makes many abuse survivors feel intolerably anxious. Clients may need to choose where they sit, and be given the opportunity to move the chair. It is not sufficient to expect someone who has been abused to be assertive enough to ask for such changes, especially in early sessions. Being abused and being assertive do not go together. Abuse survivors have had their most basic rights smashed. Since their self-esteem is likely to be very low, therapists need to be especially sensitive to the issues that arise in this way.

Similarly, during the early stages of therapy it is not wise to allow long silences. These can also be deeply threatening – abuse often takes place in silence, and a silent therapist can be experienced as abusive, as well as unfriendly and uninterested. If a client is having difficulty in speaking, they clearly need encouragement. It is not surprising that abused clients find it difficult to speak freely – they have had little previous encouragement to do so – so it is important to identify, understand and validate their difficulty. This helps them to begin gaining confidence in expressing themselves. But this will not be a smooth path – hesitations and doubts will inevitably arise.

The importance of the therapist's manner should be obvious. However, one woman who had waited eighteen months to be seen by a psychotherapist, and who had been sexually abused by her father as a child, described what happened:

> I wanted to see a woman anyway, and I didn't know who it would be before I went. Just getting there was the most enormous effort, and I felt terrified. I didn't know where to start or how to start. He just sat there. I couldn't believe anyone could be so passive. He didn't make me feel welcome. He just waited for me to start. I couldn't. It's hard to say the words even. I tell you honestly that there was a silence that went on half an hour. I went three times and it got no better. I wrote and complained, and the letter I got back told me to discuss it with my therapist, and really suggested it was simply part of my problem. That may be true, but I thought his job was to help me with it; and discussing it was just what I couldn't do. So I never went back. I'll never see anyone again. It was dreadful.

Her therapist knew from an earlier assessment interview that she had been sexually abused, and that she was very anxious about seeking help. His style and his attachment to a particular stance outweighed any real consideration of its effectiveness or, in this instance, of its abusive nature. It is an example of what Racker refers to as the 'vengefulness of silence' (1968). The denial of the implications of gender issues is also apparent. If trust is to develop, a therapist must pay attention to her or his style and must take responsibility if either this or other factors hinder the therapeutic work.

If sessions are interrupted by telephone calls, or if there are other disruptions – change of appointment times, cancellation of a session owing to illness, even a change of room – this can be difficult, especially in the first few weeks. The therapist needs to be sensitive to this. For a client who has suffered invasions of personal boundaries and unpredictable behaviour in childhood, such changes can be unsettling. A new client is likely to be extremely cautious, and will be on the lookout for signs of untrustworthiness.

5. Telling the therapist about the abuse

Over the first few weeks, clients begin to tell their stories. Some initially underplay the seriousness of events. They do this in several ways, such as the throwaway line:

A friend of mine suggested I came because I've been a bit depressed. I don't know why really. Mind you, work's been a bit difficult – lots of changes of staff and so on. My friend says it was because of what happened to me when I was a kid, but that's a long time ago. That's all in the past. And the kids have been playing up a bit, but it's just their age. And my husband's really good and we live in a nice house, so I don't know what's wrong.

This client continued in similar vein for a while. The reference to childhood could easily have been missed or dismissed as something she was not ready to talk about. This was true, but her therapist noted her words and assured her that she had heard but that she need not say more if she felt unable to. A few months later the client said:

Somewhere in me I knew it had been really bad, and only my friend knew. I realized how much it got to me, but talking about it was so hard. If I thought you hadn't taken any notice of what I'd said, I wouldn't have come back. And if you'd jumped on it I wouldn't have done either. But you just accepted it and you were very gentle. I believed you when you said I could tell you more whenever I felt ready to. It meant so much.

In other clients the burden of carrying so much for so long expresses itself differently. It is as if defences are suddenly breached, and memories come rushing in. Both client and therapist can feel overwhelmed by this outpouring. Such a presentation may reflect the whole experience of abuse: it is uncontrollable and terrifying. Therapy should not be an endurance test, and it should not be abusive. The client can be reminded that there is plenty of time.

Some describe the abuse as if it happened to another person, or as if it was of no consequence. They attempt to deal with the abuse by rationalizing it away:

Really, when you think what happened to other people, it was nothing at all. Other people have absolutely awful things done to them. I've really nothing to complain about. It was a long time ago. He didn't rape me or anything really bad like that. He just used to lie on top of me and squeeze my breasts until I cried. He used to hit me, too – but he used to hit all the kids.

One way of dealing with such events is to convince yourself that they were not really distressing, or did not really happen to you. Care has to be taken to assure the client both that they had a right not to be treated in that way then and that they have a right to feelings about it now. But this should not be done by bulldozing down their defences. Denial is often a necessary and functional defence. It needs careful, gentle handling while not colluding with the statement that 'It was nothing.' Hall and Lloyd, discussing the disclosure of sexual abuse, suggest (1989:99):

> She should be encouraged, rather than pressurized, to disclose and reminded that only by breaking the silence about her memories will they lose some of their pain. Where she has already disclosed memories, it is useful to remind her of the benefits of that process, and she will need to be constantly reassurred that it is safe to tell, and that she will be believed.

6. The duration of therapy

A frequent question asked by new clients is how long it will take: 'How long will I need to come?' It is impossible to give an accurate answer, but it is generally agreed that offering a short-term, time-limited contract is unlikely to be appropriate, and that it is more helpful to work in other ways. Again, it is important for a therapist to be clear about what is offered, and only to offer what s/he knows can be given. If an open-ended contract is offered, i.e. one that does not yet specify a date for ending, check how the client feels about this. Some reassurance may be necessary that, although it cannot be forever, therapy will not be withdrawn suddenly or unilaterally, and that as far as possible an ending will be negotiated.

In the first stage, the foundations of all later work are being laid. Considerable trouble has to be taken to provide a structure for therapeutic work that is safe, understood and predictable, and where the boundaries are clear and honestly stated. Clients need to be absolutely sure that the therapist will take them seriously, will listen with the greatest of care and will not be personally overwhelmed. Clients need to know that they are firmly in control of what is said in the sessions, that confidentiality will not be broken and that they can proceed at their own pace. Only when these basic points have been established will a client be able to move on. In essence, what is formed is the beginning of a therapeutic relationship and a working alliance, without which nothing else can be done.

COMMON FEATURES OF THE MIDDLE STAGE

1. Facing the abuse

As trust in the therapist develops, more details of the abuse are likely to be remembered and reported. It is common for adults abused in childhood initially to have only a few, vague memories. As more and more is recalled, the client is faced with an increasingly alarming scenario. If memories have been repressed, their return can induce powerful, conflicting and unpredictable feelings. As previously missing pieces are reproduced, fitting them together is not a comfortable process. They do not fit together with ease, and the resulting picture is unlikely to be a pleasant one. Some memories occur as flashbacks which are terrifying in their immediacy: it is as if the client is transported back through time with no control over the journey. I discuss the management of flashbacks in Chapter 8. At such times, when pain is so much in evidence, clients like Kim may have mixed feelings both about their therapist and about therapy:

> Sometimes I wish I'd never come to see you. All this is too painful. I'm not sure I can stand remembering. It always seems to happen when I'm alone, and it just paralyzes me. And you're not there then. It's like going through it all over again. I just don't know what to do with it all. I've got no control at all.

Kim's feelings of helplessness and lack of control were combined with a sense that her therapist was partly to blame for uncovering all this. Her therapist might easily feel that she was not doing enough, and that she was not there when her client really needed her. However, it is crucial that the therapist does not fall into the same pit of despair as the client. When clients feel no hope, and feel that they are drowning in a sea of pain, the therapist must stay afloat. It is hard for a therapist to carry hope for someone who feels none, at a time when the therapist's own sense of hope is under challenge. Carrying hope for both is further complicated by the parallel necessity to help carry the pain and the agony. It is not straightforward balancing these two requirements. Clients can worry that they are dragging their therapist down with them.

Martin, who had been sexually abused, had the following dream:

> I dreamed I was sitting on a rock with you by the sea. I dived into the water, and just went down and down. I felt I was drowning. You had dived in after me and were trying to pull me out. You kept trying, but I was caught up in weeds. Eventually you managed to free me and you helped me up to the surface. We were both gasping for breath, and it felt very touch and go.

His therapist thought this dream very much reflected her own feeling of the struggle of working with Martin. She also remembered thinking, in a previous session, that he was jumping in too quickly. She had wished that he would 'paddle around the edge'.

Facing the extent of abuse often means shocks for the client, as was the case for Maggie:

> I'm having to face that she's never been there for me, never been a mother, never put me first, never really cared. She put her own family and her husband in front of me. Whatever he did to me, she would never leave him.

Maggie was finally driven from home because her father's physical abuse became life-threatening. She faced many horrors in remembering his violence. Further recognition of her mother's role meant that the pain of her betrayal was considerable, and difficult to describe:

> She was fascinated by him. It's as if she was under a spell. I know she was badly hurt herself, but I find it unbelievable that she never intervened, never stopped him, let him nearly kill me, would not leave him. I was a sacrificial lamb. If I think of her as my mother, it fucks me up. If I try to see her as a friend, it distances her a bit and I can just about tolerate her. But a mother – never. I haven't had one.

The client's agony at these times, and the complexity of their feelings, has to be addressed. The reader may well ask: how this can be done? Unfortunately there is no one answer, but the following guidelines may be useful.

If a client states that they can't cope and that it is all too much, this should be taken seriously, although the response should be calm and containing. If the client is feeling scared by unmanageable feelings, the response should not reflect alarm and fear. It is important that the therapist *can* cope with what is happening. It is supportive and helpful to acknowledge the client's feelings and that they are entirely appropriate. To have one's experiences, albeit such difficult ones, validated, especially when previously these have been denied, is empowering. It is reassuring for clients to know that their experiences, however powerful, are a normal response to dealing with abuse. Many feel that they are 'going mad'. They are not. But they are having to deal with events and memories that often make little sense, and that induce powerful and seemingly unmanageable feelings.

Again, clients can be reminded to take time, not to talk about anything until they feel ready, that the time is theirs and that they can control the pace. If this is a problem for a client, it may be a reflection and replay of their total lack of control over the abuse itself. Exploring this can be useful, and recognizing the repetition can enable the client to begin to assert the control in the present that was so ruthlessly denied to them in the past.

There are times when a client really cannot cope. The strategies suggested in Section 2 below may be sufficient to handle this; however, when they are not, the therapist can be faced with the problem of lack of suitable alternative resources. Some clients will not contemplate psychiatric admission, especially if they have had previous and negative experiences of it. It is essential to have knowledge of good local resources, and helpful to have made prior contact with a psychiatrist in the area – especially one who is sympathetic both to abuse survivors and to these particular dilemmas. If hospital places are available for use as a real place of refuge, this can be invaluable.

Susie had been sexually abused by several family members at a very young age. She was admitted to a therapeutic community. She had to wait several months for admission. Shortly before she moved there she said:

> What was so important at the time was that I felt I was really screaming out that I could *not* go on any longer, that this time I would just kill myself. What really made the difference was that you heard; and I think it was the first time anyone had really taken notice and listened to me. You took me entirely seriously; and that meant I could hang on, because I knew without any doubt that you were doing everything

you could to find somewhere. It's been hard waiting, but I knew I could because something was happening.

Clients may ask what they can do to help themselves. Looking at coping strategies is useful if done with care. They need to be planned *with* the client, not *for* them. What helps one person does not help another, and the therapist should not assume that he or she knows best. The person with most knowledge of what is helpful is the client. Possibilities should be explored, not imposed. The role of the therapist is to facilitate exploration and to empower, not to dictate. The following extract from a session illustrates this, with the therapist acknowledging that:

It really sounds as if you feel you've been to hell and back this week, and I guess when you think of what we've been talking about that's really not surprising. You've been having to face some terribly painful things. Am I getting it right that the really scary times are evenings and early mornings?

When the client confirmed this, she went on:

I'm not sure if this will be helpful, but would it be an idea to try and work out together to see if anything might make those times a bit more tolerable?

With the client's agreement it was possible to work out a plan. Put into action, it made those hours more tolerable. It did not wipe out the pain, and the plan was realistically undertaken with no false promise that it would do so. It was not a total solution but a helpful palliative. In this case it involved arranging for friends to ring her early in the morning, for her to get out of bed and for her to stay up when they rang. In the evenings she either arranged 'treats' for herself or made contact with others. One treat was to allow herself to enjoy a long, hot bath. She had previously banned these: as a young girl, she had constantly bathed to try to 'wash away the dirt of the abuse'. Allowing herself to enjoy baths, and to luxuriate in them, was an important step forward for her. She was recapturing for herself something that the abuse had stolen.

There is a struggle at such a time to understand what is happening. This client, like many others, began to recognize that remembering her childhood reproduced in the present the same helplessness and lack of control that had characterized her childhood. She began to recognize that her adult self could exercise control. Making sense of the present by making sense of the past is both empowering and liberating. It confirms the validity of present experience, while offering hope that it need not always be so. A client who had been physically and sexually abused said:

> I was on the phone to my mother, and all the old feelings just flooded back. I felt I was ten again, not knowing what was happening or what she was going to do. I suddenly felt so sorry for me when I was little, having to feel that all the time. And then a bit of me thought, 'Sod her! She's not going to go on ruining everything all the time.' I remembered what you and I had agreed, and I told her I had to ring off, that I'd ring her back. I did, but only when I was ready to. It was on my terms, not hers.

This client had suffered enormously at the hands of her mother. One area of work had been aimed at preventing her mother's continuing domination over her. Although taking charge of a telephone call may sound trivial, it was a major move forward. In the midst of her pain she felt able to begin to develop some control over her life. A crucial step was to recognize that her powerless, frightened feelings were those of the hurt and frightened little girl who had been truly helpless. Connecting current feelings to past experiences enabled her to make choices as an adult that had been denied to her as a child. This was a hard and painful time for her. Changes are not easily made. Each one is a battle hard fought, with setbacks along the way. When such enormous barriers have to be overcome, progress is inevitably not smooth. Again, it can be helpful to say this to clients, explaining this as part of the process of overcoming abuse.

Clients who are dealing with recollections of events that most people would prefer to deny feel a whirlpool of emotions swirling around them. Their inner world can be chaotic and disturbing, while they live in an external world that is usually unaware of their inner struggle. They have to meet the demands of daily life. No wonder there can be a feeling of going mad. They are trying to make sense of senseless behaviour towards them.

A student who had been psychologically abused by both parents described how:

> I'm sitting in my room trying to write an essay, and all the time I'm thinking, 'How could they have screwed me up like that? Did they really just hate me that much?' Words they

used to hurl at me suddenly come back to me. It's as if they're in the room with me. Is this what madness is? I feel so terrified, sometimes I think I must look it. I want to scream out, 'Please don't say these things,' but they're not really there. I could never tell anyone what's going on. They'd really think I was mad.

The extreme loneliness of his position is vividly expressed. He was unable to share either his thoughts or his experiences. He felt alienated from his peer group, as he always had been, having been denied contact with others throughout childhood. Additionally, while desperately trying to continue his studies, he feared he was going mad. It is important to assure clients that they are not: these feelings, although frightening and extremely unpleasant, arise from facing terrifying events. The feelings cannot be taken from the client, but the fear of madness can.

2. Issues of dependency

Working with an adult survivor of abuse involves both the adult in the present, who is remembering, and the child of the past. Abuse denies the child the safety and secure dependency that are ultimately the springboard for independence and separateness. Dependency on the therapist can give the client enough of what was earlier denied them to enable the movement towards a genuinely more autonomous position.

Clients are most likely to have difficulties moving from dependency to independence if they have a therapist who has difficulty in encouraging autonomy or in dealing with endings. Alternatively, there are difficulties if a therapist is overdirective or is uncomfortable about allowing dependency. Generally, clients move towards greater autonomy when they are ready to do so, and when they have been allowed a safe experience of dependency on the therapist. Clients need to know that their therapist has confidence in them.

However, difficulties can arise. When clients are coping with dreadful memories and are struggling to survive each day, it is not surprising that one hour with the therapist each week – frequently the maximum that can be given – does not seem enough, especially if there is no other support. They may well feel that their therapist is not giving them sufficient time. The therapist can feel inadequate and helpless too, especially in the context of such extreme levels of despair and neediness.

It can be extremely helpful to see a client more frequently if the time is available, although sometimes this is impossible. But offering more time needs to be done with care and discussion; it should be a joint decision. It should be made clear whether more time is offered for an unspecified period or for a certain number of weeks while a particularly difficult patch is traversed. It is unhelpful to promise availability at other times unless there is absolute certainty that the promise can be fulfilled and that the therapist can comfortably tolerate the possible consequences. If extra time is given, it is important to be certain that it is for the benefit of the client and not simply to reduce the therapist's anxiety or guilt.

However, extra time may not be appropriate. A client may be trying to say how angry they are, that nothing is sufficient to take away the pain. And that is correct: no therapist can take it all away. It is inevitable that much of what a client suffers has to be suffered alone. It is important to acknowledge the magnitude of the suffering: it cannot be wiped out by an extra hour or two, or by giving a home telephone number. The client needs help to cope with the pain, rather than false assurances about a therapist's power to remove it. All this suggests a cardinal rule: take what a client says seriously, discuss what it means and look together at how best to begin to deal with it.

The stage of dependency on the therapist has to shift at some point to a greater degree of independence and to appropriate levels of dependence on others in the client's own world. This initially feels very unsafe to someone who has experienced early betrayal. Additionally, many who have survived abuse have developed a coping persona that effectively disguises their vulnerability: moving away from such a front has dangers. These should be acknowledged and discussed: they cannot be dismissed. Becoming more real carries its own risks.

As clients gradually begin to rely more on themselves and on those around them, encouragement can be given. It is helpful to explore safe ways of making these changes. Relationships with others can be tried and tested carefully, so that risks are minimized. At first minor setbacks feel like huge obstacles, and confidence grows only with time. Clients should not be rushed in this process. It is helpful to recognize that a setback is a setback, but not a disaster. A young woman who had been physically and sexually abused over many years described how:

I felt things were really getting better for me when I could see that someone making a mistake, or doing something like being late, or being irritable, wasn't betraying me. They weren't out to get me. They were just being human. That was great.

3. Loss, depression and anger

Recognizing the extent of abuse and its effects is also a time for acknowledging the profound losses that have resulted. I have shown in Chapter 4 how these extend to all aspects of life: relationships, career, employment and educational opportunities. A major loss is that of a real sense of self and of self-esteem. Various clients have expressed other losses:

Never remembering what it's like to be a virgin.

I never played in a park, never went on a slide or the swings.

I can't remember having a cuddle from anyone; sitting on my father's lap, he'd touch me up.

No laughter, no fun, no lightness, no nothing.

My father separated me from my mother. He was waiting for me to grow old enough. So I lost her too. And she allowed it.

I can't chat with other women about my family. I can't even have an ordinary moan like other people do. There's no shared experience.

My mother knew. All along she must have known. And I think others knew too.

No good memories. I'd hoped to find some. There aren't any.

I could never look forward to anything; realizing as I got older that other people did – something I'd never known.

Realizing simply that I had no childhood, and that you can't have another go. Bits you can fill in, but I can't really go back and do it all again differently. That's what I'd really like. Accepting it all is hard.

This catalogue could be even longer, but the message is already clear. There are many losses, and much that cannot be replaced. There is never sufficient compensation for a destroyed childhood. To move on and develop as a person involves facing, grieving and accepting the losses.

> You must grieve for the loss of your feelings. You must grieve for your abandonment. You must grieve for the past, and grieve for the present, for the damage you now have to heal, for the time it takes, for the money it costs, for the relationships ruined, the pleasure missed.
>
> (Bass and Davis 1988:118)

In this discomforting process, both anger and depression are likely to result. Annette summed up the struggle:

> I honestly felt quite murderous towards my flatmate at the time. She was going on and on about feeling she'd never get over her boyfriend finishing with her. I knew she would, and she did; and in a few weeks she had another one. I remember thinking, 'It's all very well. I can't get another mother. You can't replace that. It's like a one-off: there's only one chance.' I so much wanted it to be different with my mother. But I couldn't rewrite history: I had to come to terms with it. And a bit of me did realize that if I didn't it was going to stop me having friends and boyfriends and so on, and I'd lose that too. But I really had to struggle. It felt the most appalling loss to think she really was like that, she really did those awful things – I just sank at that time. But a bit of me was also saying, 'Somehow you've got to move on, or she'll ruin the rest of your life as well.'

There is a powerful combination of factors: anger with her friend for distress that would relatively easily go; anger at her friend for having 'normal' difficulties of life while she was struggling with so much; anger with her mother for what she had done to her. Facing her losses was a huge task: at times she felt deeply depressed and desperately sad. Yet another part of her was determined she should not have any more losses imposed on her, and there was a real struggle between these different aspects of her experience. This type of struggle manifests itself in many ways.

Trying to make sense of the abuse, of why it occurred, inevitably evokes feelings of anger and depression. As I have already indicated, children who are abused are frequently blamed for it. In some ways it is easier for a child to accept that blame than to hold the aggressor responsible, especially when that person is a close family member. By believing it was their own fault, the victim has sense of having had some control – thinking, for example, 'If only I'd have decided to behave differently, it wouldn't have happened.' It is also less painful to hold oneself responsible than to recognize such a degree of betrayal by someone who was trusted.

There is no definitive answer to why abuse happens, but it is essential to stress that abuse is never the child's fault. It is always the responsibility of the abuser. To describe a child as 'seductive' or as 'asking for it' is an unacceptable avoidance of, and denial of, reality. Responsibility must be put clearly where it belongs. Some abuse victims have a clear sense of what went wrong in their family. For others it is not so obvious, and they are left trying to puzzle it out. Solving such riddles can become unproductive, and clients may need encouragement to leave these questions unanswered. For others it is less important anyway, as if they know it was not their fault and that is sufficient.

I suggested above that the client may ask what they can do to help and that it may be useful to look at strategies. Further on in the process, having faced so much already, clients can be both depressed that there is still more to deal with and angry that their therapist does not have the solution. The therapist can be experienced as being another bad or non-protective person, either adding to their suffering, like the abuser, or not intervening sufficiently, just as others previously have let them down. The therapist must be continually alive to the possibility of their own practice of therapy as being in some way abusive, but if they are genuinely convinced this is not the case this negative transference can be usefully worked through, as the following example illustrates.

Betty had been in therapy for nine months. Her childhood had been marred by terrible levels of neglect and psychological abuse. She had described her childhood as one of 'grinding poverty', although her parents were not financially poor – her father was well known locally, and in a responsible job. She had become increasingly depressed as she faced more and more the harsh realities of her childhood. She felt very despondent. The possibility of resolution seemed distant.

In one session she remained silent for twenty minutes. Any attempt by her therapist to understand the silence met with no

response. In her notes, the therapist recorded that Betty seemed
full of smouldering rage. After twenty minutes had elapsed, the
therapist commented that she felt Betty was 'full of rage', albeit
unable to say so. At last Betty responded:

> If you really want to know then I'll tell you. I'm pissed off
> with you just sitting there while I have to deal with all of
> this. You just go away and forget about it, when I have to
> live with it. Well, it doesn't all go away. You're just like my
> mum and dad. They didn't care; they just went away and got
> on with their lives, and didn't take any notice.

She continued in this vein for some time, while her therapist
struggled not to feel offended and defensive, knowing that she
had worked very hard for and with this client. She was able to
look at the following areas with Betty. Firstly, she acknowledged
that Betty was carrying a very heavy burden, but she wondered if
there were now people who might share this; but perhaps something was preventing that happening. Secondly, she realized that
she was unable to help as much as Betty would like – she could
not take all her suffering away: that might indeed make her seem
to be like Betty's parents. However, it was important to say she
was also *not* like them: she would listen and take Betty seriously,
and she would not reject her, no matter what she did or said. It
was then time to conclude the session, the therapist noting that
there was more to say but that it could be said the next time they
met.

The next session started with Betty saying that she was surprised that her therapist was still there. She went on to describe
that, as a young teenager, the only occasion she had shouted
at her father had resulted in her being thrown out of the house.
She began to identify for herself how she created self-fulfilling
prophecies in relationships: she would behave in a way that made
failure likely, and this then confirmed her belief that no one was
trustworthy. Similarly, she knew she could ask a friend for support, and that this friend was happy to give it, but putting this
into practice was hard when she was most in need. Allowing
positive experiences was still a problem – a part of her still sabo-
taged good things. Her fear that they would be spoiled sometimes
outweighed a more hopeful perspective. At this stage in therapy,
Betty gradually improved as her depression became more manageable. She started to accept her angry feelings, to understand
their source and to express them less self-destructively.

4. Challenging boundaries

Although boundaries have been established in the early stages of therapy, it is not surprising that clients who have experienced such extensive invasion of their own boundaries should also challenge those that have been established in therapy. While boundaries exist to hold the client psychologically, and to provide predictable containment for their confusing experience, it is equally important to be aware of the appropriateness of moving or changing a boundary:

> This is not to say that the counsellor should turn into a passive recipient when boundaries are challenged by the client. Such reactions can be discussed, and the reasons for them understood. This is very different from an authoritarian approach; boundaries exist to provide a safe but gentle holding. They should not become a strangulation.
>
> (Walker 1990:151)

Challenges to boundaries need to be explored and understood, not simply acceded to. Unless this happens, a client can be plunged into even greater confusion and chaos while the real issues get lost.

A woman in her fifties, both sexually and physically abused in childhood, was seen in therapy by a young woman therapist. The therapist had seen her client for six months when, in supervision, she described how:

> Sometimes she comes, sometimes she doesn't. Sometimes she'll come ten minutes before the end of the session; and if I try to finish on time she'll get very abusive, or she'll storm out threatening suicide. She rings for different appointment times, and the secretary doesn't know what to do, and so she nearly always rings through to me; and another client's sessions get disrupted. She's always contacting her doctor's surgery and demanding emergency visits. Basically she's causing chaos, and I'm afraid I feel heartily sorry I ever took her on.

It was obvious that the client's behaviour was proving intolerable. The therapist felt as if 'I've got my back to the wall and she's throwing things at me.' She was feeling abused by her client, and unable to contain or prevent what was happening to her – doubtless a reflection of the client's experience of her childhood abuse.

In beginning to unravel this, the therapist first had to decide whether or not to continue working with the client; then, if she did not continue, how to terminate. She decided to carry on, and her decision to do so partly arose from recognizing that she was feeling abused by the client. When she next met her client, who was again late, the therapist started the session. She described the situation in therapy as she saw it, and suggested that it was not helpful. She restated her own boundaries: that the client had an appointment for an hour each week at an agreed time. Even if the client did not attend on occasion, the space would be kept open for her; but if she was late the time would not be extended. She also stressed that she would not take calls when she was with someone, but suggested a time in the week when she would be prepared to talk on the phone, if they both thought it would be helpful.

During this time she was aware that she was talking more than usual and acknowledged this with her client, asking her to bear with her as it was important. She described her client as initially 'quiet and rather surprised', though 'coming back to the attack later'. She continued by suggesting that perhaps her client's way of presenting herself could be understood in other ways: it prevented others helping, and this perhaps reflected her difficulty in trusting and accepting help. Part of her undoubtedly wanted help, while another part rejected it. In turn, this reinforced her view that the world and everyone in it were untrustworthy and bad. It also felt as if she was attacking others as she herself had been attacked, and that possibly reflected and demonstrated how badly she herself had been hurt.

As the session progressed, the client again became more attacking. However, her therapist continued to understand what this was saying. She did not feel trapped as she had before, and she was able to feel more empathy. She was able to work with her client once more, no longer feeling she had to defend herself. Therapy with this client continued to be difficult and demanding, but it began to settle.

In retrospect, the therapist's recognition of her client's abusiveness towards her was central in enabling her to continue. She saw that this abusiveness was both unacceptable to herself and unhelpful to her client, although it also pointed to her failure to recognize a crucial aspect. This was that the client saw people as divided into two categories – those who abuse and those who are their victims. Having been a victim for so long, she was determined not to be one again. This became a valuable focus in later sessions.

Beginning to understand that other ways of relating were possible, and ultimately far more satisfying, played a central role in the client's therapy. The therapeutic relationship became a living example of the possibility of relating differently. In such situations a therapist needs to be very careful. When under attack, it is easy to attack back and to be forced into the role of yet another abuser. This therapist's intervention also modelled the possibility of saying, 'No. I'm not going to be treated that way,' said assertively but not aggressively. Learning to say 'No', and believing in the right to do so, is central to recovery for anyone who has been abused.

5. Working with the child in the adult

Whenever we work with an adult who has been abused as a child, we also work with the frightened and hurt child they once were, and who is still hiding within. As Alice Miller says (1991:189):

> The goal of therapy is to allow the silenced child in us to speak and feel. Gradually the banishment of our knowledge is revoked, and in the course of this process, as the erstwhile torments and the still-existent prisons become evident, we also discover our history, ourself and our buried capacity for love.

The child can manifest themselves in many ways, but when they make an appearance they need to be noticed, listened to and treated with the greatest care and respect.

Cathy had only vague memories of her childhood, and did not welcome the intrusion of her little-girl self:

> I can see this little girl over there in the corner. She's sitting all hunched up, and she's crying. It's me when I was about seven or eight, and I don't want her here. I don't want to know. I want her to go away and leave me alone.

Cathy's fear was that the sad little girl, whom she knew to be herself, carried memories of events she could not yet face. It was too soon for her to incorporate these, so the image of the child disturbed her greatly. Cathy and her therapist agreed that she was not ready to allow the child nearer and that for now the child would be told to wait. (Notice the similarity here with working with multiple personality). Later in therapy, Cathy was able to draw nearer to her child self: she could describe how she looked and felt, and what was happening to her. But this process was slow and painful. The child held the key to much of what had been repressed, and led to the uncovering of extensive abuse. During this later phase, Cathy became the child, speaking and feeling like an eight-year-old.

When any kind of regression occurs, the therapist has a responsibility to exercise the greatest care. Pressure should never be placed on a client to enter their child self, and any such development should arise only from the client's needs, not from the therapist's ambition nor from any pet theories such as regression therapy. Great sensitivity needs to be shown during regression, not to act in any way that is abusive or invasive, that may later embarrass the client, or that may make it difficult for the client to return for future sessions. Although physically holding a client may seem appropriate at such a time, a therapist must be entirely clear about the motivation for doing so. Male therapists working with women clients should take particular care. If there is any doubt at all about its appropriateness, therapists should not use physical contact.

Clients normally have to leave a therapy session to return to everyday life, and many have responsibilities to fulfil. They need to recover their adult self before they leave the room, and the therapist has a responsibility to help this happen. During one session, Cathy, as her eight-year-old self, was recalling a particularly unpleasant incident. With fifteen minutes to go, her therapist was concerned to bring her back to the present:

> Cathy, I know at the moment you're feeling like the very little girl who was so hurt; but I want to remind you now that grown-up Cathy is here as well, and that she's going to have to go in a while. I wonder if we can start to say goodbye to little Cathy for today. We can promise her we'll talk to her again next week. Can we do that, do you think?

Cathy responded favourably, and agreed that she could say goodbye to the little girl for now. Her therapist suggested that she (the therapist) should look after the little girl and keep her safe until they met the following week. Cathy spent the last few minutes of the session telling her therapist of her plans for the forthcoming week, thereby reintroducing herself to the external world. Following previous discussions, Cathy and her therapist had agreed that this was a helpful way to conclude, enabling Cathy to recover her adult self sufficiently.

Jacqueline Spring vividly expresses the importance of this process (1987:79–80):

> This was the discipline within which we worked, the discipline of reality. I was a wife and a mother. This was the present day, and at the end of it I had to go home and make the tea... She could speak to the child in me, reaching right through the wife and mother, through the adult I had become, through the adolescent, with all its questions, to the child, transfixed with fear... And at the end of it, she had to bring me up through all those levels again, and send me home a functioning adult. I never left her without her using my formal name once, setting me back on my feet.

6. Facing the abusers

As different losses are faced and worked through, one question that frequently arises is whether the victim should confront the abuser(s). For some the decision has already been pre-empted, since the abuser is dead. But others face a real dilemma. The decision varies from person to person. What is important is that clients recognize that they have both the right and the power to decide their own course of action. The therapist's role is to assist the process: possible implications need to be discussed and examined, and clients need to be encouraged to consider whether they feel strong enough to deal with possible consequences.

The outcome of confrontation can vary greatly. Nineteen-year-old John decided to involve the police. He knew his abuser, a well-respected member of the community, was still abusing young boys. His abuser was ultimately prosecuted and imprisoned. Kevin, at the same age experienced a different outcome, he thought his younger brother was at risk from those who had abused him – his father and stepmother – and he involved social workers. He felt betrayed when they did not act, and then he was banned from the house by his parents and prevented from having any contact with his brother. In this case the losses he had already suffered were compounded. Susie decided to confront her family. The response was a partial acknowledgement that abuse had occurred, although they were not prepared to confirm its extent or that they had known about it at the time. However, Susie, who had anticipated total denial, was quite satisfied:

I had reached the point where I was prepared for anything. I was prepared to have no more contact with them if necessary. I was prepared for total denial. I knew that, come what may, I was going to tell them what I'd been through and what it's done to me, and how much I've suffered because of them. It actually didn't matter too much any more what they said or didn't say, so in a way I got a better response than I expected. The main thing was that I needed to say it. I am very different with them now, much more grown-up, and I won't take any nonsense from them. It's much better. It'll never be what I want, but something is better than nothing.

Annette, after much thought and agonizing, decided not to confront her mother directly:

She's old, and it's just not worth it. It won't achieve anything. She'd just have hysterics. It would all be my fault. I'd just get pulled in, and I want to keep my distance. That's my aim. I just don't want heavy scenes.

She felt empowered by this decision, and found that making it did not preclude her from telling her mother very firmly not to 'talk nonsense' when she reminisced about Annette's happy childhood. Her decision enabled her to say 'No' more firmly to her mother, and to be less influenced and distressed by her mother's difficult and demanding behaviour. Although she had not directly faced her mother, she had faced the issues relating to her, both within herself and with her therapist, and as a result she gained a greater sense of separateness, autonomy and self-worth.

COMMON FEATURES OF THE FINAL STAGE

1. Who decides the ending?

Whenever possible, the timing of termination should be decided with the client. It should not be imposed, but agreed. Some will know for themselves and will say when they are ready to leave. Susie was like this: her new-found confidence enabled her to tell her therapist that she felt ready to conclude therapy. Both felt this should not be done precipitately, so they set a date two months ahead. Susie wanted to be able to return and see her therapist in six months:

It can't be sooner, because I need to know we've finished, and I need time to manage alone. But I really want to see you, just to tell you how I've been getting on. You know me so well, it doesn't make sense never to see you again.

She came back after six months, and both she and her therapist enjoyed the meeting. Susie was doing well: life was not perfect, but she was able to cope with its difficulties and she felt she was progressing.

Others are unable to make such a decisive move on their own and need help to do so. Careful discussion is necessary. There should not be any pressure to finish quickly. As with all other features of this type of work, it is important to take time over decisions. There will inevitably be occasions when a mutually agreed ending is not possible. The therapist may fall ill, leave the area or change job. It is sometimes appropriate for clients to see another therapist, but they still have to leave the original therapist. Transferring should certainly not be a way of avoiding an ending. Clients who are left against their wishes will find this hard enough: they need time and encouragement to express their feelings. Both therapist and client may be tempted to fall into rationalizations or platitudes, but these are not helpful since they merely avoid the issue.

2. Knowing when to end

Various factors can be taken into account by the therapist and client in deciding a date to finish. The client's level of self-esteem is important: do they feel a sense of self-value? Can they accept things that are good, and feel a right to them? Have the losses and pain of the past been sufficiently mourned? The past will not go away, but it can be stopped from getting in the way. It is unrealistic to expect depression to disappear entirely, but it should be manageable – as should be the levels of pain that might still be experienced. It is also important that a client make use of opportunities to allow relationships with others, without being compelled to sabotage them. Reasonable autonomy needs to have been established, and preferably the client should have some ability to be appropriately dependent on others. But the client is striving towards a sufficient resolution, not a perfect solution.

Susie, for example, felt good about herself in a way she had never known before. She changed her job and began to see that she had skills that were valuable. At times she would still feel depressed, but she did not fall into unmanageable despair. She could cope with her depression, which no longer scared her. By being assertive with her mother, she no longer felt repressed by her. Dealing with her mother gave her the confidence to begin to develop friendships.

3. Uncertainties and doubts

Sometimes the decision to finish therapy can throw a client into doubt and confusion. This is more likely to happen if the client has not been party to the decision. However, anxieties can surface even when the ending has been mutually agreed. Occasionally this is a sign of a wrong decision, and in that case it is essential to allow flexibility over ending. Generally, however, it is more productive to work with the client to help them cope with the anxiety. To respond simply by extending therapy can be very undermining: it suggests or reinforces the idea that the client cannot cope without the therapist. It is more helpful to confirm that ending is a major step and that anxiety is both understandable and acceptable. Again this is a good modelling, because difficulties in life will continue to exist and anxiety will inevitably be felt: all this can be acknowledged and explored, and overcome.

Betty had been pleased when she decided that she could now cope alone. But the nearer the final session came, the more her anxieties increased. She required reassurance and encouragement. In her last session she felt triumphant at having reached such a point, although she was sad to say goodbye.

The possibility of uncertainties in the final stages reinforces the importance of not rushing endings. Time is needed to explore doubts, and to look at any new material that emerges because the end is on the agenda. There is still much work to be done in the final stages. The prospect of ending often helps both the client and the therapist to focus on outstanding issues.

Should the client's circumstances change considerably, the original decision might become inappropriate. Six weeks before she was due to leave, Annette experienced two major life events: a close relative died suddenly, and another family member revealed that he too had been abused. She and her therapist decided to continue, and therapy was finally concluded six months after the original date.

4. Clients who leave unexpectedly

This can happen in many ways and for many reasons. Kevin, for example, was so angry and disappointed at the failure of social services to protect his little brother that he terminated therapy abruptly. In the last session he made it clear that he intended to do this, in a mixture of despair and self-destructiveness: 'What's the point of all this for me, if the same thing's happening to my brother?' His rage extended to anyone in a helping profession. At one point he said to the therapist, 'I know it's not your fault; it's not fair on you,' but he added that he felt his therapist had betrayed him. Although he recognized that this was irrational, it did not help. He could not be persuaded to stay, although he was invited to come back at a later stage if he wished to. But he did not return to that particular therapist.

Cathy had to leave to take up a job in another area. If she had chosen to stay in therapy, she would have remained out of work. This was not an easy choice for her, and she had only four sessions before she had to move. She wanted further therapy and she discussed the possibility with her therapist, but this was painful for her, because time was very short. It was important to help her with her feelings about leaving therapy and the area, and with her anxieties about starting a new job, while at the same time looking at the practical issue of finding a new therapist. Both Cathy and her therapist felt rushed. Neither felt they had sufficient time to deal adequately with this charged and unexpected situation. Both had to accept the reality of the situation, although they were able to share their disappointment at a hurried ending.

Beryl also had to leave before she was ready to. Her situation was further complicated by her having to move for the sake of her partner's job. This triggered many issues relating to equality in their relationship. She did not want to live away from her partner; neither did she want to lose her therapy. It was too far to travel for her sessions, so finally she asked if she could have a longer appointment monthly. The therapist agreed, but the arrangement did not work well. Beryl reluctantly and angrily stopped coming. It was a most unsatisfactory ending: the therapist felt great concern for Beryl and her relationship but was unable to offer any effective help in the circumstances.

Most of those who work with victims of abuse have clients who come for only a few sessions and then do not reappear. This may be because they find it too painful to cope with feelings that emerge too strongly and too soon. While it is important that they do not feel harried, neither should they be ignored. It can be reassuring, but not invasive, to receive a letter acknowledging that it can be difficult to come and inviting them back at a future date if they so wish. Some clients respond immediately to this. Others do not, but it may make their eventual return easier.

One client who responded positively had missed two appointments, following a break in sessions for her holiday. She was sent a letter offering her another appointment, saying that her therapist would be pleased to see her if she would like to come. When she returned, she told her therapist that if she had not received the letter she could not have come. She needed welcoming back: she wanted her therapist to reach out to her, and she could not bring herself to ask.

5. Reviewing the course of therapy

Most clients will have entered therapy with considerable ambivalence. Leaving it will produce similar mixed feelings, although for different reasons. The client and the therapist have travelled far together on a journey that will not have been altogether smooth. The client has shared and explored feelings and events that were previously untouchable and unspeakable. It is hard to leave someone who knows you so well. Reviewing the course of the journey is important. Clients who are helped to say goodbye gain an overall perspective of the work they have undertaken; they recognize that risks have been taken, that obstacles have been overcome, and that mistakes have been made, but that they have survived. This is a valuable model for other relationships.

As at the start of therapy, such mixed feelings should not be ignored. Recognizing that conflicting emotions are legitimate and sometimes inevitable is an important lesson. The client both wanted to begin therapy, and did not want to. Now they want to leave, but do not want to. Coming into therapy meant starting to trust and facing unknown agonies. Leaving it means accepting that progress has been made, but leaving the person who has shared in all of this. It also means acknowledging that not everything has been dealt with as the client might have wished. There are inevitably disappointments along the way and at the end, as well as successes. The client needs time and space to accept the disappointments and to celebrate the successes. It is important that both negatives and positives are freely expressed, reinforcing that negative aspects do not have to be destructive and that positive aspects can be enjoyed.

6. Styles of ending

It is better for the therapist and client to decide together whether to end once and for all or whether to arrange an opportunity for a later review session. There are no hard and fast rules. Some clients, like some therapists, prefer to make a clean break. Others prefer gradually to reduce the frequency of meetings, with a final session after a few months. If this latter option is chosen, the therapist and the client need to be clear about what is being offered, and about any conditions attached to it. There can be a difficulty, for example, if the therapist believes sessions have concluded whereas the client thinks they can go on having regular sessions on request after the final review.

Whatever the decision, it should not obscure the reality of ending, which must be clearly stated and understood. The ending, like the whole process of therapy, needs to be approached honestly, carefully and supportively. This means offering real negotiation over the style of ending as well as its timing, and encouraging the client to say how they feel – expressing equally what feels good and what feels bad. This process should not be diluted by the therapist denying, or by the therapist colluding with a client's denial of the reality of ending. Whatever the practical arrangements, a successful conclusion to the work is vital to the overall process.

EIGHT

PARTICULAR ISSUES
IN THE PROCESS OF
THERAPY

Whereas the previous chapter examined the overall therapeutic process, in this chapter I identify particular issues that arise and explore specific aspects of therapeutic method. Therapy with each individual follows its own unique path. Different therapists and counsellors have their own favoured methods and theories, but effective counselling and therapy with abuse survivors essentially requires flexibility. Those who adhere rigidly to a particular model, and who are unable to incorporate and integrate other ways of thinking, may not be best suited to work in this field. There is a continual need to think about what is happening at any time and to consider what might best help. This requires a therapist to be open to the validity and value of a wide range of theoretical stances, and to have sufficient knowledge of their potential clinical application. Clinicians who are comfortably rooted in one therapeutic model should not become so securely settled in it that they are unable or unwilling to consider what others have to offer.

PRESENTATIONS OF ABUSE

My main emphasis has been on working with men and women who present as at least consciously aware of the fact of their abuse, although the details and feelings may remain buried. There are, however, other ways in which abuse may be presented, even though it is not clearly stated. Some abuse victims are unable to acknowledge the abuse to themselves, let alone to a stranger. Instead they give signals that might indicate to the therapist the possibility of abuse. As always, it is important to listen carefully so that these are not missed or ignored. Such signals include references to a forgotten or missed childhood (similar to presentations of Multiple Personality Disorder):

I never was a child.

My first ten years are a mystery to me.

My memories are very patchy – some years just aren't there.

All these remarks were made by clients in an early session, and subsequently abuse was disclosed, although it had initially been repressed. Of course abuse cannot be assumed. Other childhood traumas cause similar repression: for example, the death of a close family member, or a serious accident. Nevertheless, a therapist notes the possibility of abuse as a factor. Working with the client to recover lost years and events has to be undertaken sensitively. There is good reason for repressing some events. Defences are erected only when there are real threats; dismantling them must be on the client's initiative and at the client's pace.

If a client wishes to fill in the gaps in their life history a useful starting-point is to locate the years where memories are lost and to work towards building a picture of their world at that time. Key people and places might be described and explored in the imagination, allowing feelings and details to emerge over a period of time. Some clients like to visit places where they lived, or look at photos, or talk to other family members and friends. Discovering their childhood can be traumatic, and memories can be unwelcome. It is not an automatic passport to recovery or happiness, and it does not bring instant relief. Clients who set out on the journey into childhood need to be aware of that. Remembering is only the start of the process: it is not sufficient in itself.

Sheila knew she had been sexually abused by her father but believed her mother was kind and supportive. She initially had little recall of her first eight years; but when her memories returned they were of her mother violently physically assaulting her:

It almost feels worse to remember all that. I feel shocked and betrayed. How could she inflict such pain on such a little girl?

I always dreaded finding out what happened in those years. I needed to know, but never thought it was all this. Part of me wishes it had all stayed hidden.

Another signal of abuse is the therapist's awareness that what is being presented does not make sense. Abuse may be the missing link. Various symptoms can be presented – commonly, anxiety states, depression, relationship and sexual problems, eating disorders, or drug or alcohol misuse – but there is still a mismatch. The client's explanations may not match the severity of the symptoms. The therapist feels as if there are missing pieces of the picture that are nowhere to be seen but that could be crucial to further understanding. Such confusion, and such feelings of something important and significant but also unattainable, may reflect the inner world of the client:

It's like something is missing: there is a part of me that has been taken away from me; something of me has gone. I've lost part of myself.

Again, this does not mean that every client who presents a confusing picture has been abused: it is just that the possibility exists. George described himself in a first session as severely depressed, and frightened by his suicidal and violent fantasies. Although he had been depressed intermittently since early adolescence, he felt he had no reason to be depressed other than some difficult recent experiences which he himself recognized as not sufficiently serious to explain his level of depression. He therefore concluded that he was mad. The therapist suggested that his depression might have deeper roots, even if these might be difficult to uncover; that he was not mad, although he was certainly very unhappy. In the third session, George started to speak about his childhood. Neither parent had given him any affection or attention. In his words:

I never had a hug, a cuddle or a kiss – ever. I was hit a lot – hard – and I think my mother enjoyed that. As I got older they ignored me completely. I began to feel I didn't exist.

Without gentle encouragement to explore further, it is unlikely that George would have linked these earlier events to his present depression.

Eating difficulties are now known to be frequently linked to abuse in childhood (Oppenheimer *et al.* 1985; Palmer *et al.* 1990).

Certainly the language used to describe eating difficulties sometimes vividly recalls abusive behaviour. A bulimic client, sexually
abused by her father, described how:

> I just force food in when I don't want it. I can't stop myself.
> It's almost being done to me. I can't control it. I just stuff it
> in, and I can almost be vomiting, but I carry on. Then, when
> I make myself sick I can feel enormous relief just to get rid of
> it.

When a client presents with an eating disorder, care is needed in
the initial sessions. Diagnosing according to the initial presentation might suggest (to some therapists) a very specific treatment programme. This is often the case with anorexia. Once
the problem has been defined, redefinition is more difficult, and
inappropriate interventions might be made. A particular risk in
cases of abuse is that incorrect early diagnosis often reinforces
secretiveness and the client's belief that they must not tell. The
therapist needs to try to avoid being identified as another adult
who cannot see or who does not want to hear the reality, and
who apparently all too readily accepts an obvious but incorrect
explanation.

Many of the patients who end up in psychiatric hospitals have
been abused. I have recounted some of the mistakes made in their
treatment in Chapters 2 and 5. Abuse frequently remains uniden-
tified as a major causal factor in their distress: those who work in
psychiatric hospitals need much more awareness of this possibility. There is research that verifies the personal experience of many
of those I spoke with: firstly that there *is* a connection between
childhood abuse and later admission to psychiatric hospital
(Metcalfe *et al.* 1990; Mullen *et al.* 1988; Bryer *et al.* 1987); and
secondly that psychiatrists miss this crucial factor. The majority
of psychiatrists questioned in the study by Haegar and Dalton
(1988) claimed they had never knowingly come across an adult
who had been sexually abused as a child.

Although it is a less common occurrence, clients who present
with fits, which may or may not have been diagnosed as epileptic,
sometimes have a history of childhood abuse. The onset of the
first fit can be triggered by the abuse, and further abuse maintains
the fits. This was Amy's experience:

> I'm not epileptic, but I was diagnosed as such and put on
> very powerful drugs as a result, without anyone really know-

ing what it was about. I didn't black out completely, I just couldn't talk. I remember when it first happened. I was trying to find a way out of the abuse, I suppose. When I was first in psychiatric hospital, when I was nineteen, it was the first thing they latched on to, that perhaps I was epileptic, and they stuck me back on phenobarbitone.

Abused children develop many strategies to remove themselves from abusive situations, including fits (Goodwin *et al.* 1979; Gross 1982). These can continue right into adult life. There is some evidence that therapy can reduce or remove these particular symptoms. Describing her work, Jean Goodwin reports:

All six patients experienced relief from their hysterical seizures when psychotherapy began to explore the incest experience. All six had histories of running away from home; all had either threatened or attempted suicide. Four were promiscuous, one was non-orgasmic, and the sixth was homosexual. All presented psychiatrically in their teenage years. Prior incest should be suspected in hysterical epilepsy which presents in this way, since psychotherapy is rapidly effective in such cases.

(Goodwin *et al.* 1979)

DEALING WITH FLASHBACKS

Flashbacks are commonly experienced by abuse survivors. They are suddenly and unpredictably taken back into an abusive incident in childhood. Peter described the power of a flashback:

Last year I was just sitting on the bed, and all of a sudden it was like an explosion took place. It was like my brain became a videotape and someone put it on to play without my permission. It was like he was in my room. I was hysterical, hiding under the bed. I was completely gone. I was an eight-year-old being very, very badly beaten by my father; and then being thrown on the bed and him raping me. The terror – I was there, it was me, the child who couldn't do anything and was completely and utterly helpless. There are hardly words to describe it, in the same way that I didn't have the words for it when I was a child. I was completely terrorized. It was very weird. It went on for a couple of hours.

This incident was the beginning of Peter's recovery of memory, that precipitated him into seeking help and finding a counsellor. Before the flashback he had been unaware of the abuse.

Others experience flashbacks triggered by watching films or TV programmes, particularly when abuse is discussed; or by entering a new relationship and attempting sexual contact; or by children reaching an age that was significant for the abused parent; or by numerous other incidents: a smell, a word, a room, or the dress, hairstyle or mannerisms of another person.

Talking with a therapist is another trigger. Sheila first recalled her mother's abuse in the middle of a session. She was talking about something else, and was suddenly transported back into childhood. She relived in the room an incident of appalling brutality. In her next session she described what had happened to her:

> It was so peculiar. It's never happened before. It's as though I was there. It was another me talking. Like me with another head, that I had no control over. I didn't know what I was going to say. It was like me as I was then that was talking. Until that time I had completely forgotten what had happened. I completely put it away. I wonder what else there is to remember. How much more. I went away and could do nothing. I just felt awful.

Flashbacks *are* frightening. They appear as if from nowhere. They are not easily controllable, and they are an unwelcome intrusion – just as the original abuse was. As Peter and Sheila so vividly describe, the adult becomes the abused child. He or she speaks and feels as if the past has become present, and horrors and pain already survived once have to be undergone yet again. Being with a client who has a flashback can be as alarming for the therapist as it is for the client, especially when it is a new and unfamiliar experience for the therapist too.

At the time of the flashback it is impossible to examine or discuss its content: the client's level of fear and anxiety is too great. It is possible, however, to introduce the idea that the client is reliving an old experience. However terrifying and real it seems at the moment, it can be stressed that it happened in the past, that it will not happen to them again now, and that they cannot now be hurt in the same way. This attempt to reassure should not deny the power and reality of the present experience, or that the client feels unable to cope. It is important that the client is encouraged to say as much as they wish about what is happening to them. But the reassurance is an expression of the fact that it is different now.

A client may need some help to return to the present and to the adult self. How this might be done can be seen in one of the examples used in Chapter 7 (page 166). After a flashback, clients are likely to feel physically and psychologically shaky. They often fear they must be going mad. It helps survivors to know that these experiences are very common among adults who have been abused as children. The flashback does not mean that the client is going mad, but it does show that there is much still to deal with that is as yet unresolved. Clients can be told that one of the goals of therapy is not to obliterate past events but to allow exploration of them and to encourage familiarity with them; because only then will these events start to settle rather than to interfere with the client's present life. Also at these times, when clients are recovering from a flashback, they can be encouraged to be self-nurturing. Liz Hall and Siobahn Lloyd suggest this for women incest survivors (1989:125), but it is valuable whatever the gender of the client and whatever the form of abuse:

> After experiencing a flashback and discussing it with her helper, a woman should be encouraged to look after herself as if she has had a recent injury. This could involve going to bed, having a warm bath, taking mild pain-killers but most of all giving herself permission to comfort and take care of herself. For many incest survivors, this is a totally new experience and can lead to better self-care.

When flashbacks are reported by the client, or after they occur in sessions, it is valuable to encourage open discussion and disclosure of their content. As the unspeakable is spoken, and as appalling events are acknowledged and examined, the pain and the horror slowly begin to dissipate. The terrifying secrets that are often recalled in flashbacks start to lose their power when the private is made public. Recurring flashbacks can also be helped by using imagery techniques to change the ending of the original incident or to redistribute power in the original relationship.

Susie had been sexually abused by her brother. She found sex with her partner difficult. She very much wanted to be free to enjoy it, but was constantly troubled by a flashback of her brother entering the room naked, about to abuse her. This scenario was explored many times. Susie agreed, with the help of her partner, to try to alter the scene. She enjoyed playing with this idea and with different endings in her therapy sessions. She was able to decrease the frequency of this flashback, and later to prevent it altogether. The scenario she rehearsed involved telling her brother to get out, telling him that he was not spoiling anything else ever, showing him the door, and shutting it firmly after him. As an adult, she was able to claim back the control denied to her as a child.

Although the flashbacks ceased, Susie's sexual difficulties remained. Although valuable in themselves, imagery techniques are not always sufficient. In Susie's case it was important to acknowledge the underlying dynamics – a good example of the need for a flexible approach. Two other factors were at work that were powerful in preventing further progress.

The first was that the therapist was being identified with Susie's mother: Susie was angry with her mother, and consequently with her therapist. She felt her mother had not suffered as she had, and neither had her therapist. Her mother was always making helpful suggestions, just as the therapist had done. Susie was not prepared to get better to suit them. She was angry. Until that factor was addressed, she unconsciously blocked further progress.

The second factor was that many of her feelings relating to her brother had not been sufficiently resolved. She was still unable to deal with him firmly in the real world, and she felt that her mother catered for his every whim. She could not effectively say 'No' to her brother and have that undermined by her mother's inability to say 'No' to him. She could only say 'No' to her partner. One side of her wanted to enjoy a sexual relationship, as she had with a previous though less important boyfriend; another side of her felt she would lose too much. This denial of sex with her partner was an important unconscious communication to her mother, her brother and the therapist. It also gave Susie some power, even though she also lost out. It was important for her shaky sense of self-esteem to say 'No' firmly to someone like her partner, who would accept it from her. Until the unconscious wish was rendered conscious and all these complexities were addressed, dealing with her flashbacks by imagery techniques was no more than a mildly helpful palliative.

Whatever techniques are used to control or limit flashbacks, they are as useful as the client will allow them to be. Care has to be taken in their use. An over-enthusiastic approach can intimidate the client. Abused clients do not find it easy to say 'No' to any-one, including enthusiastic therapists. Furthermore, a therapist must always consider whether the use of some techniques adds to the twin collusive dangers of avoiding pain and creating distance through *doing to* rather than *being with* the client.

DISSOCIATION

During abuse in childhood, dissociation is an effective method for minimizing the effects of trauma and for coping with pain and humiliation. Children cannot physically remove themselves, but they can remove themselves psychologically. It is as if the body has to take what comes but the inner self moves somewhere safer. This is not a conscious manœuvre, but it is none the less a deeply protective strategy for the child. Clients describe it in different ways:

> When I was small it got so bad that I just didn't feel the pain any more. I'd just cut off. Nothing could touch me. I don't know where I'd go – just nowhere – but I wouldn't feel.

> I'd see my father coming towards me, and I'd know what was going to happen. I'd just switch off, as if I wasn't there. Sometimes I'd get the sense of looking down on my own body as my father abused me. I could see me, but I wasn't part of me.

> I'd hear my mother screaming. I'd be trying to comfort my brothers and sisters. I'd be so distressed. And then it was as if I weren't there – like being on automatic pilot. I would be there – I think I'd carry on looking after them – but I wouldn't feel anything. I cut off. I'd do the same if I was being beaten – just sort of go away.

Adult survivors sometimes do the same. It feels as if they have left the room and disappeared to somewhere unreachable. Some-times they sit in silence; at other times they continue to talk, but there is no sense of contact or connection with them. What they are saying appears to have nothing to do with them – it seems to belong to another person, in another place, at another time. In this way a perfectly sensible discussion can take place devoid of any real meaning or impact, as one client explained:

As you've noticed, I can talk about most things quite happily and at length. I can even talk about the abuse, but only as if it is nothing to do with me. It's like it's right out there, some-where in the world, but nowhere near me – like an interest-ing subject but absolutely distant.

In such a situation the client feels lost to the therapist, and in one sense they are. It can be disconcerting if the therapist is unaware of what has happened but knows that something has changed, or when the therapist is aware that something is missing in the first place. It is essential to recognize dissociative behaviour in therapy. The client is generally not aware of it: it is as if an internal switch has been pulled, but not by conscious intention on their part. The client quoted above could only acknowledge what was happening after her therapist pointed out that she seemed to talk about the abuse as if it was nothing to do with her. She agreed with this, and linked what happened in therapy with her response to the abuse in childhood. She would 'remove myself from the scene'. By increasing the client's level of awareness, the unconscious process starts to become conscious: the capacity to gain access to inner experience increases, and the potential for understanding, gaining control and changing patterns of be-haviour develops.

Dissociation is not unusual, especially when the abuse has been severe or prolonged. But, although it was functional for the child, it can be dysfunctional for the adult:

The ability to dissociate is a life-saving, pain-sparing survival strategy. However, useful as dissociation is during trauma, it can later interfere with conscious participation in reality. Dis-sociation is also a frequent precursor to amnesia, which can be disturbing to adult survivors and keep them confused about current reactions or life situations which might be more easily understood if more information about early ex-periences is available.

(Gil 1988:149)

It often helps to explore with the client what triggers the withdrawal. It might be a painful memory, a difficult and uncom-fortable feeling, particular words or other significant details that no one else would be aware of. One client could not tolerate one of the pictures in her therapist's room: it was similar to one in the room in which she was abused. It is also useful to invite her/him to explain what happens when they enter a state of dissociation. Various responses are described: the body may go completely numb; there may be a sensation of frozen but distant awareness – 'looking down on the self'. Some people fix their eyes on a certain spot and block out everything else.

It can assist further exploration to ask a client if they are willing and able to return to the trigger, whatever form it takes. There must not be any pressure to do this if they are at all hesitant, although the reasons for their hesitancy can be acknowledged. If the client is able to return to the experience, the therapist needs to offer reassurance that, although s/he may feel awful, nothing awful will happen and the therapist will not leave them to go through the experience alone. Encouragement to stay with the experience, rather than escape it, can be also given – though again only if it feels safe enough.

James was a particular concern to his therapist because he injured his body badly during periods of dissociation, which were triggered at times when he felt ridiculed or ignored by others. He would disappear psychologically, and would reappear sometimes with severe injuries. It was excessively painful for James to stay with his feelings. Present-day triggers brought back powerful and extremely unpleasant memories of his father's abuse of him, of cruel ridicule by his brother and of his mother's denial of the abuse, although she was aware of it. At those times he had learned to dissociate: he could not have otherwise tolerated the pain, humiliation and betrayal. In his childhood he did not hurt himself but others did, and as a child he returned to self awareness to find his body injured. In adulthood the same would happen but this time he had inflicted the injuries himself.

Working with James focused on several different areas simultaneously in an attempt to enable him to control his self destructive behaviour; to give him space and time to uncover and share his dreadful memories, and to help him understand his present difficulties in terms of past experiences. In this way considerable time was spent with him as he went through the painful details that he had previously avoided. He started to see the effects of these earlier experiences on his current self-image and his relationships. He was also encouraged to become more aware of trigger times, and to attempt different responses. This was a slow process, full of problems. Gradually the periods of dissociation started to lessen, although his desire to hurt himself remained for a long while, but now at a more conscious and therefore potentially controllable level. It became possible for him to monitor what went on inside him at those times, by asking himself questions such as, 'Why am I feeling like this?' 'What function will it serve to hurt myself?' and (most importantly) 'How else can I deal with this?' This was a painstaking process. There were many setbacks and disappointments, but he gradually began to gain more control over his thoughts and actions. It was agonizing for him, but for the first time in his life he began to feel that he had some power.

Once the triggers have been identified, the process of understanding and exploration starts: what the dissociation means, how it began, the purpose it served – all these can be unravelled. At such a point it becomes possible to work *with* the phenomenon, rather than have it working *against* the therapist. Of course dissociation also works ultimately against the client too, because it not only creates potentially or actually dangerous and risky situations but also excludes many of the healing processes of therapy.

SEXUAL DIFFICULTIES

In this chapter and in Chapter 4, I have included a number of references to the adverse affects that abuse has had on many survivors' sexual relationships: Peter experienced his sexuality as 'all over the place'; Susie could not enjoy a sexual relationship with her partner; Rachel could not bear to be touched. Difficulties range from anxiety about specific physical activities to absolute inability to have any sexual contact. One example of such extreme difficulty was a woman who was unable to look at herself in a mirror: she could not tolerate the sight of her own naked body. Any form of physical contact was impossible for her, and sexual contact was inconceivable.

Many studies have examined the effects of sexual abuse on adult sexuality. Meiselman (1978) found an extremely high correlation between incest and difficulties with sexual adjustment: 87 per cent of her sample were described as having serious problems. Courtois (1979) gives a similarly high figure: 80 per cent of former incest survivors in her sample reported either an inability to relax and enjoy sex, or abstinence from sex, or a compulsive desire for sex. Others such as Herman (1981) suggest a lower proportion, but nevertheless confirm this as a serious problem that is frequently presented. The relationship between sexual

abuse and later difficulties is clearly documented and is supported
by the clinical experience of many therapists. However, there is
also a link between physical and psychological abuse and sexual
problems. This may seem less obvious, and it may not occur so
frequently, but it is still a severe problem for many who have
been abused in these ways.

One man, who was psychologically abused, told me:

> The thought of a sexual relationship is beyond my imagina-
> tion. I feel so nothing, so worthless, that I can't imagine
> anyone wanting me near them. And I can't see I'll ever feel
> good enough about myself for that to be different.

Samantha, who was physically abused and also severely neglected, said:

> It's a huge achievement for me to even be able to talk to
> anyone beyond just superficial chat, and I'm not very good at
> that. Being really intimate is an utter impossibility. All the
> time I'm really just keeping back from people, just getting
> by. Any more than that would be too much.

Another woman was sexually abused on a single occasion when
she was fourteen. Nothing like it ever happened again, but her
trust in her father, whom she had so loved and liked, and who
had always been her protector, was shattered by this one incident.
At the age of twenty-five, she entered a relationship and found
she had great difficulties sexually:

> I always have to be totally in control, in charge of everything
> that happens. There are some things he just must not do to
> me. I can't relax and let go at all. I can only describe it by
> saying it's like a performance, with me in charge of all the
> moves. My boyfriend is incredibly supportive, but it's not
> how I want to be; and I can't see a way forward, to make it
> different.

Finkelhor (1986:188) concludes that:

> With adult victims of sexual abuse, sexual problems have
> been among those effects that have been most researched
> and best established. Clinicians report that victimized clients
> often have an aversion to sex, flashbacks to the molestation
> experience, difficulty with arousal and orgasm, vaginismus,
> as well as negative attitudes towards their sexuality and their
> bodies.

If we add to this the numbers affected in similar ways by other forms of abuse, we are clearly identifying a major difficulty, which therapists inevitably encounter in their work.

The origins of sexual difficulties are complex, relating to a variety of responses to the abuse. It is helpful to unravel with the client the responses which are particular to their experience. For instance, a common response to abuse is to feel both guilty and ashamed. These feelings have often been reinforced by negative or unhelpful responses from people who have been told. Neither guilt nor shame is conducive to a satisfactory sexual relationship.

Alternatively, there may have been aspects of the sexual abuse that were enjoyable or satisfying. Sheila was finally able to acknowledge what she felt. With tears streaming down her face, she said to her therapist:

> I've never told anyone this, and it sounds so awful when I've been telling you how terrible it all was. But I did enjoy some of it. It was the only time I felt special, or noticed, or cared about. It was the only time I felt anyone loved me, or was nice to me. My mother terrified me. There were no cuddles or hugs or kisses from her. My father would hold me and cuddle me and I liked that. I miss that. And – this sounds even worse – it felt like a way of getting back at my mother, like winning in some way. I feel so bad about that.

The complexity of the experience of abuse is obvious: a mixture of guilt, pleasure, anger, shame and retaliation. Not surprisingly, as a young adult, Sheila found herself unable to allow intimate contact with her boyfriend.

In other cases, the inability to enjoy sexual relationships can be a way of saying 'No', of at last being able to assert one's rights and one's power. This was clearly true of Susie, described above. I have also shown, in the interviews recorded in Chapter 4, that low self-esteem, feelings of being different and isolation are common in survivors. A sense of deep betrayal is often evident, with consequent feelings of disillusion and disenchantment with the world in general and with close relationships in particular.

The association of sexuality with pain, humiliation, fear and lack of control is a particular issue for those who have been sexually abused. But physical abuse also gives rise to problems with how survivors relate to their body. The association with pain and humiliation are carried around still in a body that remains both the cause and the source of pain and difficulty, rather than of pleasure and enjoyment. Angry and hostile feelings can be very strong. An additional factor is that intercourse can be physically painful. Making a close relationship and allowing intimacy to develop requires trust, optimism, hope and belief in oneself and in the other person. It is these very qualities that are so often absent in the abuse survivor.

If therapists are to be helpful to the survivors of abuse, they must be at ease with their own sexuality. They need to be able to discuss sexual matters openly and in a relaxed manner. It is likely that sexuality will be a dangerous area for the survivor, full of problems and connotations. If the therapist can be matter-of-fact about sex, this helps make it normal and opens it up as a subject that can be talked about. Conversely, if a therapist feels ill at ease with sexuality, this reinforces the view that it is a forbidding and forbidden subject, and one that it is not safe to talk about.

It can be reassuring to acknowledge that a sexual difficulty is a likely result of the abuse, and that the client is not to blame. Where a survivor experienced some pleasure during the abuse, it is also helpful to say that this does not mean they are bad or depraved or immoral, or even (as some people may have suggested) that they invited the abuse. It only means that the body, when it is touched or stimulated in particular ways, finds it difficult to respond any differently. It may, as in Sheila's case, have been the attention that was pleasurable, not the abuse itself. In any event, the abuser, not the victim, remains responsible for what occurred.

If the client has a partner who already knows about the abuse, then s/he might be encouraged to discuss any difficulties with him or her. If the partner does not know, issues arise about telling the partner, and these need careful thought and thorough discussion. The client might become very anxious about how to say something and about the implications of doing so, although crossing such a barrier is often a relief in itself and may even lessen the sexual pressures on the client. Many partners are anxious to help, although they themselves frequently need help to do so. Sometimes it is appropriate to work with the couple together, but only if this is a genuine wish on the part of the original client. It is essential, as at any other point of decision, that the client is in charge of what happens. Clients often prefer to work individually on their difficulties, and to take their discussions with the therapist back into their relationship.

By locating the exact nature of their difficulties, and by inviting clients to explain what happens to them, what they think and how they feel during sexual contact, the therapist and client can decide together what interventions will be most useful with the client's partner. It is often helpful to encourage honest communication of their experience of sexual contact with their partner. If s/he is unable to do this, it might indicate that there are other aspects of the relationship that need exploring. Bass and Davis stress the value of communicating in this way for women that have been sexually abused (1988:248–9), but their comments have wider application:

> Often there are some sexual acts that feel okay but others that don't; some places you're comfortable being touched and some that you're not. Tell your lover. Just because you say yes to one thing doesn't mean you're saying yes to everything possible. And just because you say yes once doesn't mean you have to say yes every time. Don't keep going through the motions while you are disconnected from your feelings. Even though you may be scared, awkward or embarrassed, come back. Give yourself – and your lover – the respect of honest communication.

The nature of abuse is that it is secretive, furtive and denied. Facilitating open discussion of sexual difficulties and reinforcing a client's right as an adult to choose what they will accept and to say 'No' when they wish to are in themselves very empowering. To discover that a partner is supportive, and willing to help, can be equally encouraging. Some types of contact might best be avoided, particularly if they carry too many reminders of the original abuse. Other types of contact can be challenged and overcome. Just as in dealing with flashbacks, imagery techniques can help, although the underlying, unconscious dynamics also need to be addressed.

Clients who report physical pain may have a physical problem that needs medical assessment. Some abuse is so severe that permanent damage results. It should not be assumed that pain is always psychological in origin. If it is, once physical causes have been checked, extreme tension and anxiety may be the problem. This indicates that some aspects of the abuse need to be given more time and attention. Not surprisingly, unresolved issues or memories commonly surface at intimate times in relationships. Tension can also be helped by relaxation techniques, which give the client greater control over the body. Once it has been learned, relaxation can be used almost whenever it is needed, and this too gives a client a greater sense of control.

Those who have suffered abuse do not easily enjoy or like their bodies. They may have very distorted information about sex and about their own body. Encouragement can be given to explore, understand, enjoy the body. If accurate information is needed, either it can be given or the client can be directed to where it is available. The essential message is: your body is yours; you can reclaim it; you have a right to enjoy it, and in ways that are acceptable to you; you have an absolute right to say 'No' to anything you do not want, without feeling guilty as a result; and you can proceed at your own pace.

When clients are struggling to overcome sexual difficulties, they need to recognize that a setback is not a disaster. They can be helped to be realistic: sex can be wonderful, but it can also be a neutral experience, and sometimes it is distinctly uninspiring. The most sexually contented people sometimes wish they had not bothered. Sometimes reading a book and having a cup of tea is just as attractive an alternative.

Nevertheless, despite such realism, it is undoubtedly true that clients who overcome sexual difficulties experience a sense of recovery of self that is truly therapeutic. One client, Lawrence, was physically abused by his father and witnessed his father's horrific sexual attacks on his mother. He remembered watching his father rape his mother when he was very young. His mother had attempted suicide as a result. Lawrence was in his late twenties and was sexually impotent. His marriage had not been consummated and had ended in divorce. Sex terrified him. He strongly associated the expression of male sexuality with violence against women. After a year in therapy, he started a new relationship. For the first time ever he told his partner about his family history and about his difficulties with sex. She was sympathetic, relaxed and helpful. When finally he was able to participate fully in a sexual relationship, he told his therapist:

> It's like I've lived in a black–and–white world all my life. And now it's become glorious technicolor. Everything used to be cold. And now I feel I'm basking in glorious sunshine.

BLOCKS TO RECOVERY

Recovering from abuse is painful and often slow, but there are points when it seems as if no further progress is possible. Such blocks have many sources. A first step in tracing these is to acknowledge the lack of progress with the client: by doing this, the therapist opens the door to discussion of the difficulty and invites cooperation in understanding possible reasons. It may be that unresolved aspects of the abuse, that need more attention, are surfacing. The nature of abuse is that memories cannot be neatly parcelled away but continue to surface for years. Even aspects that once seemed resolved can reappear, because their resolution was ultimately insufficient. Partial resolution was the most that could be achieved at the time, but it is not always easy for clients to acknowledge this:

> I thought I'd dealt with all that ages ago. I couldn't bring myself to tell you about it. I thought you might be really fed up. We worked so hard to sort that one out. And I didn't really want to face it myself. I've really had enough of all this. I just want it all to go away.

This person was fed up with herself and disappointed with her therapist, although she found it hard to say so. Her therapist responded:

> This may not be right, but I wonder if you're a bit fed up with me. You could be feeling that this wouldn't have happened if I'd helped you more. I know how hard it is for you to say that you feel let down by people, but I guess that applies to me too.

In this instance the client's block had two components: firstly unresolved issues, and secondly anger with the therapist that was difficult to express. Once these were made explicit, discussed and worked with, progress again became possible and the therapeutic alliance was further strengthened in the process.

Getting better also means losing the therapist. Another client commented on the unusual nature of the therapeutic relationship:

> This must be the only relationship that means when you feel all right you lose the person who has been so important to you. Most times, that's when relationships get better. This one disappears.

It is very important that clients are able to leave their therapist and take what they have gained into a wider world, but it is not easy to leave the person with whom they have shared so much. It might be thought that successfully dealing with the abuse enables a welcome entry into a more satisfying and enlarged way of living. But it is not that simple.

Susie, whose therapy I drew upon above in connection with a block over sexual enjoyment, was able to resolve that problem after considerable unravelling of the reasons for it. Some weeks later, when progress once again seemed to grind to a halt, Susie said to her therapist:

> I'm not at all sure about getting better. I've been thinking about all the things I'll lose out on. For one thing I won't be able to come here any more. And I'll never get the same attention from people if I'm just ordinary and normal. There's all sorts of things I'll be expected to do. And I'm not sure I want my mum to think I'm OK.

Her honest statement contains many different aspects. Losing her therapist was only one of them. There were gains in remaining troubled, and therefore in need of help and care. In her childhood years, Susie had received little love and attention. Her brother, who was the one who had abused her, was identified as the difficult and needy one; and her sister had developed severe depression leading to hospitalization at the age of fifteen. Her mother struggled to leave a violent marriage and was also very depressed. Susie was therefore labelled as the one who would always cope, who would be no trouble, and who would care for her mother. During this time in therapy, her mother had acknowledged Susie's neediness and was spending considerable time with her. Her sister was greatly concerned and very supportive. Susie's partner was too. This seemed to Susie a lot to give up, and at this stage in her therapy it was indeed too soon to do so. Her therapist reaffirmed that the ending would be negotiated when Susie was ready. At the same time, the therapist was aware that Susie would continue to experience real conflict regarding 'getting better', and for an ending to take place at all this needed to be an ongoing focus of their work together.

Susie's words also hint at the reasons for another block to progress for some people: recovering from the abuse can be perceived as 'letting the abuser off the hook'. It is as if continuing to suffer makes a point to the abuser that cannot be made in any other way. It is not necessarily a very effective way of making the point, because the abuser is not likely to be aware of how the victim feels, but for the survivor it seems like an important statement. One survivor put it this way:

I will *not* give him the satisfaction of thinking that I'm fine. I want him to suffer. He has to know what he's done to me. If he thinks I'm all right, it will just add to his view that what he did was not that serious anyway. I want him to see that I'm not.

This particular client used to cut herself, partly as a visible statement to her abuser to show him how he had damaged her. Her self-mutilating action was explored in two ways: firstly by looking at the possibility of using different means to communicate the same message to her abuser; and secondly through reinforcing and validating the client, assuring her that she mattered, and suggesting to her that her own importance and her potential well-being might outweigh her desire for revenge. When she was faced with it, she could see that the person who was really being hurt was once again herself. The therapist appreciated the client's desire for revenge, but in reality the abuser carried on unperturbed, while the client went on suffering.

Progress can also be halted when clients set themselves unrealistic targets. For example, clients can encounter huge difficulties if they believe that true recovery has to involve 'forgiving' the abuser. There are some 'therapeutic' approaches that appear to advocate such forgiveness as an essential sign of the final stage of recovery. In my opinion such an outlook is gravely mistaken, since it induces guilt feelings in those who cannot forgive or do not wish to forgive. For many survivors (although not all), forgiveness is an entirely meaningless and erroneous concept. If it is useful for a victim to forgive, they will. If it is not, they need not. There is no single correct path to recovery, and each client will find their own way. Bass and Davis (1988:149) firmly state:

> The only necessity as far as healing is concerned is forgiving yourself. Developing compassion and forgiveness for your abuser, or for the members of your family who did not protect you, is *not* a required part of the healing process. It is not something to hope for or shoot for. It is not the final goal. You may never reach an attitude of forgiveness, and that's perfectly alright.

They develop this idea of self-forgiveness (1988:153):

> You must forgive yourself for having needed, for having been small. You must forgive yourself for coping the best you could. You must forgive yourself for needing time to

heal now, and you must give yourself, as generously as you can, all your compassion and understanding, so you can direct your attention and energy towards your own healing.

Aiming for the impossible impedes recovery. When abuse has occurred, it cannot be eradicated from the past, although it can be prevented from interfering so obviously with the present. History cannot be rewritten. It has to be integrated into the whole person in the most comfortable way possible. Clients have to accept that the abuse will never go away. It has happened: it is a part of them and a feature of their life history. There is, however, a huge difference between the abuse being one part that is incorporated into the whole and feeling that the abuse *is* the whole, with nothing else to put it into perspective.

As I have already made clear, making progress also necessitates the acceptance of many losses. Sometimes this feels too much, or acknowledging the extent of the losses is resisted. This is a particular problem for older adolescents and young adults. Final acceptance is often marked by psychological and physical separation from their abuser. If this was a parent or other close relative, separation is not straightforward. Separation is hard enough for many young people from caring backgrounds, who can both choose and look forward to a more independent lifestyle. But for young people who have been abused, home is not a safe spring-board into an adult world or a secure base to retreat to if difficulties arise: it is a place to escape from. Progress means recognizing the necessity of moving away from the family.

Furthermore, resources to support this particular age group are scandalously poor. When resources and support are practically non-existent, and locating the little that exists requires considerable tenacity and determination, the young person's dilemma is obvious – and all this exists on top of having faced appalling truths that may have exposed real vulnerability and may have given rise to low morale. Small wonder, then, that blocks to recovery occur.

NINE

ISSUES FOR THE HELPER

Therapists, counsellors and other helpers who work with abuse survivors regularly encounter a world of agony and despair. They hear details that the majority of people would prefer to avoid; they face realities that most people generally would not dream about. They also experience and share the joy and triumph that come with the lessening of pain and the healing of wounds as difficulties caused by the abuse become resolved. The journey from what seems like total despair to sufficient resolution is long and often arduous. Of course the client has many difficult obstacles to overcome, but neither is the process at all comfortable for the helper. Accompanying someone on such a tortuous journey is immensely worthwhile, but it is not a smooth ride. Issues and dilemmas abound. Just as abuse survivors often feel alone in their suffering, so helpers can feel isolated in their work. Yet there are common dilemmas for the therapist which can be shared by all those who work in this field.

EFFECTS ON THE HELPER'S OWN RELATIONSHIPS

The personal relationships in which the therapist is involved can be affected in many ways. It is a considerable bonus for a helper to be in a loving relationship which is supportive and understanding, but stresses can be imposed upon the strongest of relationships. Both partners should be aware of this possibility and should understand something of the cause of such stresses. Continually hearing details of abuse makes the most trustworthy relationship open to question and doubt: the helper begins to feel that nothing is ever what it seems. Sexual difficulties can arise, especially if the helper is working with clients disclosing the details of sexual abuse.

Working with such material can often distress the helper more than they can acknowledge to their partner, or to themselves. A partner who is not involved with this type of work may genuinely find it difficult to understand the stresses involved. If these are explained, many partners will offer support, but they cannot do so without some understanding of the process. The helper's 'secrets' about the personal effects of their work can be shared without breaking confidentiality about particular clients. Without explanations, tensions can be misinterpreted, causing further strain. Those who are able to ask their partners for support and reassurance are greatly helped when this is generously given.

Helpers' relationships with their own children can be also be affected. They realize through their work that the world is a far more dangerous place than they had thought. Helpers learn only too well about the nastier side of human nature, and that children are hurt and damaged. They know too that abuse is widespread and that there are abusers throughout society. They can become over-protective of their children in the same way as abuse survivors can be of theirs. Achieving the balance between reasonable precaution and appropriate protectiveness is not straightforward, and becoming over-anxious and unfairly restrictive of a child is sometimes difficult to avoid. Here again, the reassurance of a partner is invaluable. These dilemmas seem greatest for helpers who are single parents, although they also exist for others. It is perhaps inevitable that they will affect all those who work with abuse survivors to some degree.

HOLDING ON TO HOPE

Abuse work can be draining and exhausting. Feelings of inadequacy, hopelessness or even despair are commonly experienced by helpers, who then have to walk the tightrope of their own emotions while still needing to contain equally difficult emotions in their clients. A defensive armour that prevents such feelings from surfacing is unhelpful – even damaging. But neither is it useful to become an emotional sponge, soaking up all the client's negative, despairing feelings as well as holding in one's own. Looking after oneself as well as the client requires a delicate balance and is difficult when such degrees of pain are witnessed and shared. Helpers have to be self-protective, while remaining accessible and empathic. They have to try to find a position that represents the ideal interface between objective distance and personal involvement, if they are on the one hand to convince the client that they will be with them, will believe in them and will fight for them; and on the other are not to collapse with them.

Helpers therefore have to believe in the value of this type of work, so that they retain optimism even when they are caught up in the greatest bleakness. It is essential that, amid the pain and despair that are inevitably part of the therapeutic journey, the helper believes that the end is worthwhile and that progress and resolution are possible; there will be many times when the client cannot feel this. When the helper experiences despair and inadequacy, this is often a reflection of the client's feelings. Such emotions are powerful enough in themselves, but they are even more threatening to clients if they feel their helper has been similarly overwhelmed, damaged or hurt by them. The helper has to hold hope for both of them, and to demonstrate resilience on behalf of them both. This is a very valuable model for the client, but it is also central to the helper's own well-being.

GENDER ISSUES

Issues about gender, and the significance of the gender of the helper, need greater acknowledgement in caring work. This is a particular issue for abuse survivors. It is not unknown, for example, for children's homes to assign young male staff as key workers to adolescent girls who have been sexually abused by male relatives. While there may be occasions when this is appropriate and helpful, it should be done only in response to the girl's request; and even then only after very careful thought. It is essential that skilled supervision is readily and frequently available when gender issues are obviously so significant, and that supervisors recognize the potential difficulties of such cross-gender pairings. I suspect, however, there is as yet very little recognition of these issues.

Most women and girls abused by men prefer to see a woman, and they must be able to exercise that choice: provision needs to be such that their choices can be met. One therapist gave me her views on this:

I'm not absolutely against men working with abused women. I think the client should always be given a choice – that's most important. It's never right to force a man on a woman. It depends on what the man can model. He needs to be gentle, able to be a different sort of man. It can then be very helpful. I'm interested in why some women choose men, although most don't. Sometimes women will want to disclose to a man but not do any more. But that has been important. It may feel a big step if you can tell a man what another man has done to you.

To do this work, a man would need to be very aware of power issues – authority and power are always around with a therapist and a client, and are rarely addressed. This is particularly significant with a male therapist and a female client, as it reflects societal structures. So a male therapist in particular has to be very aware of how he uses his power and his authority.

The area of seductiveness is also important. I have a feeling that men, for reasons of their own, can sometimes set up relationships with women clients that have a seductive element. I'm not necessarily talking about actual seduction – though that can happen – there can be something more subtle, but quite harmful. That whole area has to be very well monitored and watched. And also I wonder if it can be quite voyeuristic. Sometimes that *can* be around for a woman too, but I think those areas need to be in the forefront of male minds, and again need to be carefully monitored. They assume too easily and blandly that they are OK and not like that, and that they are dealing with these issues really well. They may not be.

Men who are working with sexually abused women are usually working with clients who have been abused by men. Their own gender identity and their feelings about their own sexuality can be adversely effected. In supervision, one male therapist reported:

Hearing what this man had done sickened me. It made me so ashamed of being a man. And made me feel that I must never do anything to hurt this client, that I must be so careful. It's made me think: do I misuse women sexually? And it's made me realize how many men do, in so many ways. I don't know how to deal with all that.

There are issues for women too. A woman therapist in supervision said:

Hearing about her father abusing her and her brother was awful. I felt powerless and helpless, just as she did. It's horribly easy to identify, as one oppressed woman with another. When I heard about her mother abusing her too, I wanted to give up. I'm a mother. I thought: mothers *cannot* do those things. I didn't want to believe that. It was too much.

These are just a few examples of the significance of gender; there are many more factors that remain to be explored. It is essential to be aware of the various strands and the many layers of gender issues. It is also important to recognize that although men need to take special care, for the reasons already stated, inevitably men and women alike are by nature enmeshed in issues of gender which are especially important in abuse work.

BOUNDARIES AND LEVELS OF INVOLVEMENT

Abuse invades personal boundaries so totally that it is hardly surprising if helpers often encounter difficulties with their own boundaries. Yet, if the helper is not to become burnt-out, ineffective or overwhelmed in working with abused clients, limits need to be established and maintained. Such maintenance of personal boundaries has the added value of providing a clear model for clients, helping them to create limits for themselves in their own life and relationships. Abused clients have little experience of saying 'No' effectively. They often do not believe they can set limits without causing harm or giving rise to other negative repercussions. A helper who appropriately says 'No' to a client demonstrates that limits can be enforced without harming the relationship, and that the consequences need not be negative or destructive. Of course the consequences still have to be acknowledged and dealt with, but within an established safe boundary.

It is very easy to become overinvolved and to give more and more to the client. Every client is indeed important and should be given respect and care, but helpers have to learn to give the same attention to their own needs too. No one can take away all the client's pain. No one can fulfill all their needs. With some clients, any attempt to do so can feel like trying to fill a bottomless pit. I have already stressed in Chapters 7 and 8 that clients inevitably have to face losses in order to move towards resolution. These involve grief for their many unmet needs, including those in therapy. In order to help clients express this grief, helpers have to acknowledge what they cannot do, even though they continue to give generously of the skills and resources they have. It is very unhelpful for clients to feel they have damaged or depleted their helper, or that they have successfully broken through the helper's boundaries. There are sometimes battles over these issues; but if the client wins, it is usually an empty victory, reflecting and reinforcing their own experience of broken and abused boundaries. They have simply repeated old patterns rather than having been helped and encouraged to establish new ones.

FEELING ALONE AND ALIENATED

As I have shown throughout this book, abuse survivors frequently feel alone, alienated and different. Those who work with them can share these feelings. Therapists involved in this work enter a world that is beyond the experience and comprehension of most people. They thereby acquire access to special knowledge, unfamiliar to most other people – although, of course, all too familiar to those who are forced to dwell in the world of abuse. Once visited and seen, this other world cannot be denied or ignored. Previous perceptions of how the world is organized, and how people behave, may be starkly challenged. Other people in the helper's personal life either find it hard to comprehend this other world or may appear to live on a level that by comparison seems to have little relevance or significance and may even appear relatively superficial. A counsellor who was new to working with abuse survivors described how it felt:

I've not got many cases like this, and I suppose it's the first time I've heard that much detail. It was horrific: I just wanted to cry and cry for that hurt child. And I was shocked. I went home, and it felt really difficult and awkward. It's not that my partner isn't interested. He is, but he works in industry and it's a different world. We went out to dinner in the evening with friends. They're quite interested in my job, but you can hardly say, 'I spent this afternoon with a woman who was multiply abused. And what you're talking about seems utterly unimportant.' I started to feel as if I was on a different planet, and very angry – quite unreasonably. I remember thinking that if anyone mentions mortgages again, I'll scream. It gives you a different perspective, a different understanding, a different view of the world. It changes you. And it's lonely.

The sense of alienation is further intensified each time the helper is faced with new or different levels of abuse:

I'm just starting to hear about satanic abuse. And I think, 'Oh no! I don't want to hear about that. I don't want to have to work with that as well. It's too much!' I hear about ten- and eleven-year-olds and young teenagers being involved. It's such a vulnerable age that I can't see how they could survive that healthily. I don't seem to have the optimism in me to work with that. It's the callousness of those who are organizing it, and the exploitation – using other human beings as objects. There's not enough of me left to start dealing with that.

Entering the world of abuse can also create feelings of guilt in the helper, as if they have no right to enjoyment, to pleasure or to an easier life. This is further compounded by what is frequently reported, and is alluded to in the example above, as a sense of alienation from the mainstream of everyday life.

HELPING THE HELPER

The problems and difficulties that arise in counselling and therapy with abuse survivors must be realistically acknowledged, both by helpers and, where applicable, by their employing authorities. Those who manage helpers should ensure that unreasonable demands are not made. The size of a helper's case-load has to reflect the particular difficulties and demands of this work, and may need to be adjusted if the numbers of cases of abuse rise. Adequate time for reflection is not an optional extra, and training, consultation and skilled supervision are not self-indulgent whims. The validation of the counsellor's work and the recognition of its value by employing institutions is ultimately of crucial importance to the client.

Helpers need to be aware of their own limits, and to tell themselves and others that their own needs are equally important. It should be clear to helpers that they have the right to set limits not only to the client but also to an agency that demands too much. They should not take on any more work than is comfortable and reasonable. There is nothing to be gained from the exhaustion and disillusion that is created through being overloaded. It is simply counter-productive: worn-out helpers are not actually helpful.

One therapist, who was experienced in working with abused women, was able to recognize what she needed:

> I need the usual things like supervision and support; and I need colleagues around who will listen and give me a cuddle if I feel particularly affected. I think the most important thing I need is acknowledgement of the work that I'm actually doing. And that's what I find is usually not around. I need acknowledgement in all sorts of ways: that this is heavy work; and that it is being done, and done well. I'm not sure why it's so important, but it's partly to do with the nature and the content of the work. It's about women who have never been acknowledged and valued, and whose self-esteem is very low. It's very difficult not to reflect that, and not to collude: not to sink into being powerless and depressed women together. If you feel you are not acknowledge and your work is not valued, you can get sucked into that. Empowering women takes a huge amount of energy, and you need to be given some yourself.

Busy helpers need to ask themselves what they need to survive this kind of work without it becoming abusive to them, although under pressure it is a question they can easily forget. Priority must be given to the helper's personal responses to and feelings about the work. Helpers' own needs *are* important. It is essential that helpers have access to reliable, regular and trusted supervision which is supportive but also able to challenge creatively without being destructive. When a helper is undertaking a considerable amount of abuse work, the supervisor should have sufficient expertise and experience in this particular area. The helper needs to feel safe and comfortable with the supervisor. Supervision is a space in which to share anxieties, doubts and difficulties, while at the same time providing an opportunity to draw upon the skills of another practitioner. In addition, it can be tremendously reassuring and comforting to meet regularly with others involved in similar work, who often have the same feelings. This helps to relieve the possible or actual isolation or alienation about which I have written above.

It is especially valuable for the helper to recognize that, in the process of therapy and counselling, a helper's feelings may echo and reflect the experience of the client. Being aware of this prevents the helper from passively soaking up feelings, and often enables creative use to be made of much that the helper goes through, both in the sessions and afterwards. It is always a complex business to create and maintain real contact with a client while simultaneously trying to grasp the various levels of meaning in the therapeutic relationship. However, when this can be done, it helps prevent the slide into collusiveness or overidentification, both of which can be harmful to helper and client. When helpers can maintain a sense of clarity and direction, they are less likely to feel overwhelmed and are more able to protect and nurture themselves.

When the helper experiences anxieties and difficulties, it is important to recognize that she or he is not alone. Just as abuse survivors are reassured by learning that their feelings are a normal response to very abnormal treatment, so the helper needs reassurance that this demanding work does create stress. Stress is not in itself a sign that the individual helper is incompetent, ineffectual or lacking in strength. If helpers feel undermined by the difficulties, it is important to remember the positive messages that came through the retelling in Chapter 5 of the experiences of those who had received effective help. Disconsolate therapists, counsellors and helpers need to be reinforced in their conviction that they have a key role in helping survivors through the mire and misery created by abuse.

MOVING ON AND LETTING GO

In order to undertake this therapeutic work, a combination of knowledge, skill and energy is required. Underpinning all this, a therapist also has to have the ability, with necessary compassion and care, to make contact at a deep level with people in great pain, who themselves have little reason to trust the motives of those who offer help. On top of their compassion, many helpers also feel considerable passion: they are both very angry at and deeply saddened by what they see and hear. They experience many intense emotions in the therapeutic relationship and in the therapeutic process. As I have already suggested above, to be effective, helpers give of themselves while essentially retaining the core of an inner self.

The phrase used by one client of her therapist – 'a mother to thousands' – captures something of the quality of this relationship. Providing a model of good parenting is an essential element of such interactions. Another element is the ability to acknowledge disappointment: helpers can never become the parent that many clients wish for. An element in good parenting is meeting the child's needs sufficiently to facilitate self-confidence, so that they can become autonomous, with their own identity, able to separate successfully from their parents. Ultimately, clients have to leave their helper and, like a good parent, helpers have to make possible and to encourage such a separation. Clients' sadness will be acknowledged, but so will their success. Their journey has not ended, but they can now travel on alone. They have the resources to deal with the obstacles that are bound to arise, as they do in everyone's life.

Letting-go can be an anxious time for the client, and it is similar for the therapist. It is not helpful to communicate such feelings to the client, although their presence indicates that the therapeutic process has been significant to both the therapist and the client. Doubts invariably remain in the helper's mind: 'Have I done enough? Will the client be all right? What will happen if she or he isn't? Did I do my job well? Could someone else have done better? Or given more?' Such questions are important and reflect the significance of therapy for both those involved.

In researching and writing this book, I have been aware that many people entrusted to me their own journeys through the survival of their abuse. They were at different stages. Some were feeling triumphant at having arrived at a place that offered fulfilment. Others were continuing to struggle among the debris caused by their abuse. All of them gave of themselves so generously, and more bravely than many readers may appreciate, that allowing this book – in many ways their book – to end is hard.

Just as therapists, counsellors and other helpers have to let their clients go, knowing that final resolution and total healing are never attainable, so this book has to end with my knowing there is much more that could be said. I can only hope that I have said enough for those I interviewed to feel that they have been accurately and adequately represented, and for those who read it to appreciate the experience of abuse and the complexities of its ongoing consequences. I hope too, as did those who spoke with me, that all those who work in the caring professions can learn and benefit from the honest accounts of those whom I interviewed and that their learning will be reflected in improved quality of care for abused children and surviving adults. If that can happen in some measure, the shared secrets will be of even greater benefit.

REFERENCES

Bass, E. and Davis, L. (1988) *The Courage to Heal: A Guide for Women Survivors of Sexual Abuse.* New York, Harper & Row.

Bryer, J. B., Nelson, B. A., Miller, J. B. and Krol, P. A. (1987) Childhood sexual and physical abuse as factors in adult psychiatric illness, *American Journal of Psychiatry,* 144, 1426–30.

Courtois, C. (1979) The incest experience and its aftermath, *Victimology: An International Journal,* 4, 337–47.

Eaton, L. (1991) Ritual abuse: fantasy or reality?, *Social Work Today,* 26 September 1991.

Elton, Lord (1989) *Discipline in Schools.* Report of Committee of Enquiry into Discipline in Schools.

Ferenczi, S. (1955) Confusion of tongues between adults and the child. In *Final Contributions to the Problems and Methods of Psychoanalysis.* London, Hogarth Press.

Finkelhor, D. (1986) *A Sourcebook on Child Sexual Abuse.* London, Sage Publications.

Friedrich, W. N. (1990) *Psychotherapy of Sexually Abused Children and Their Families.* New York, Norton.

Gabarino, J. and Gilliam, G. (1980) *Understanding Abusive Families.* Toronto, Lexington Books.

Gil, E. (1988) *Treatment of Adult Survivors of Childhood Abuse.* Walnut Creek, Launch Press.

Goodwin, J. (1985) Credibility problems in multiple personality disorder patients and abused children. In R. P. Kluft (ed.) *Childhood Antecedents of Multiple Personality.* Washington DC, American Psychiatric Press.

Goodwin, J., Simms, M. and Bergman, R. (1979) Hysterical seizures: a sequel to incest, *American Journal of Orthopsychiatry*, 49, 698–702.

Gross, M. (1982) Incest and hysterical seizures, *Medical Hypnoanalysis*, 146–52.

Grubman-Black, S. (1990) *Broken Boys/Mending Men: Recovery From Childhood Sexual Abuse*. Blue Ridge Summit, PA: Tab Books.

Haegar B. and Dalton, J. (1988) Attitudes of general psychiatrists to child sexual abuse, *Bulletin of the Royal College of Psychiatrists*, 12, 271–2.

Hall, L. and Lloyd, S. (1989) *Surviving Child Sexual Abuse*. Lewes, The Falmer Press.

Herman, J. (1981) *Father–Daughter Incest*. Cambridge, MA, Harvard University Press.

Kempe, R. S. and Kempe, C. (1978) *Child Abuse*. London, Fontana.

Klein, M. (1975) *Envy and Gratitude and Other Works: 1946–1963*. London, Hogarth Press.

Kluft, R. P. (ed.) (1985) *Childhood antecedents of Multiple Personality*. Washington DC, American Psychiatric Press.

Lamb, S. (1986) Treating sexually abused children: issues of blame and responsibility, *American Journal of Orthopsychiatry*, 56(2), 303–6.

Meiselman, K. (1978) *Incest: A Psychological Study of Causes and Effects with Treatment Recommendations*. San Francisco, Jossey-Bass.

Metcalfe, M., Oppenheimer, R., Dignon, A. and Palmer, R. L. (1990) Childhood sexual experiences reported by male psychiatric patients, *Psychological Medicine*, 20, 925–9.

Miles, R. (1991) *The Rites of Man*. London, Grafton Books.

Miller, A. (1991) *Banished Knowledge*. London, Virago Press.

Mullen, P. E., Walton, V. A., Romans-Clarkson, S. E. and Herbison, G. (1988) Impact of sexual and physical abuse on women's mental health, *Lancet*, i, 841–5.

Newman, C. (1989) *Young Runaways: Findings from Britain's First Safe House*. London, The Children's Society.

Oppenheimer, R., Howells, K., Palmer, R. L. and Chaloner, D. A. (1985) Adverse sexual experiences in childhood and clinical eating disorders: a preliminary description, *Journal of Psychiatric Research*, 9, 357–61.

Palmer, R. L., Oppenheimer, R., Chaloner, D. A. and Howells, K. (1990) Childhood sexual experiences with adults reported by women with eating disorders: an extended series, *British Journal of Psychiatry*, 156, 699–703.

Putman, F. (1989) *Diagnosis and Treatment of Multiple Personality Disorder*. New York, The Guilford Press.

Racker, H. (1968) *Transference and Counter-transference*. London, Hogarth Press.

Spring, J. (1987) *Cry Hard and Swim*. London, Virago Press.

Walker, M. (1990) *Women in Therapy and Counselling*. Milton Keynes, Open University Press.

INDEX

abuse
  of boys, 2–3, 32
  in care, 29, 39, 100, 111; *see also*
    children in care
  extent of, 2, 4
  facing, 150–7
  frequency of, 2
  history of, 2
  by mothers, 3, 40, 68, 74, 83,
    85, 87, 88
  perpetrators of, 29–31
  presentations of, 174–8
  rings, 43–4
  and self-perception, 52–5
  telling about, 96–110
abusers, 41–6
  current relationship with, 84–8
  death of, 11, 86–7
  facing the, 167–8
  gender of, 31–2, 197–9
  imprisonment of, 21, 22
  prosecution of, 21
addictions, 121, 131
alcohol addiction, 121, 176
alter personality, 134, 136
amnesia, *see* loss of memory

anger, 65, 67, 159–62, 181, 187,
    188, 191, 204
anorexia, *see* eating disorders
assessment centres, 18, 39
'At Risk' register, 100

baby battering, 28
Bass, E. and Davis, L., 160, 189,
    193
Beck, F., 111
blocks to recovery, 190–4
borderline states, 134
boundaries, 146, 147, 151, 163–5,
    199–200
boys, abuse of, 2–3, 32
Bryer, J. B., 177
bulimia, *see* eating disorders
bullying, 29, 56–7

care, abuse in, 39, 42, 100, 111
careers, 72–4
caring professions, 102–3
child in the adult, 64, 116, 125,
    128, 165–7
child pornography, 42, 130, 131
child prostitution, 42, 130, 131

child psychiatry, 44
child-rearing patterns, 4
Childline, 104, 112
children in care, 17, 38–9, 45,
    49–50, 58, 71–2, 90, 102, 111
children's homes, 111
church, 30, 42, 45, 103
circle of abuse, 58–9
circumcision, 4
class, 4, 29, 31–2, 99, 102
collusion, 37, 101–2, 151, 182
confidentiality, 147–8, 151
confronting the abuser, *see* facing
    the abuser
controlling therapeutic process,
    146–7, 154
coping strategies, 152–4
coping with the past, 63–72
counselling, 84, 91, 105, 106
    107–8, 111; *see also* therapy
Courtois, C., 185
culture, 4
current relationships with abuser,
    84–8

Dalton, J., 177
death of abuser, 11, 15, 86–7
defences, 150, 151
denial, 2, 113, 122, 131, 151
dependency, 157–9
depression, 159–62, 169, 176
disclosure, 151
dissociation, 114, 116, 182–5
drug addiction, 121, 131, 176
duration of therapy, 151–2

eating disorders, 26, 27, 56–7, 72,
    176–7
Eaton, L., 3
education, 10, 16, 31, 55–9,
    72–4, 98, 100, 120
effects on sexuality, 67, 69, 77–8,
    81, 82, 83, 131, 180–1,
    185–90
effects on the helper, 195–204
Elton, Lord, 57

employment, 47, 48, 72–4
empowerment, 155, 156
ending therapy, 168–73, 191–2
epilepsy, 47, 177–8
everyday life, 46–50
experience of abuse for child,
    34–41

facing the abuse, 150–7
facing the abuser, 167–8
Ferenczi, S., 115
Finkelhor, D., 50, 186
flashbacks, 119, 152, 178–82
forgiveness, 193
foster care, 7, 17, 29, 101
Friedrich, W. N., 114
friendships, 50–2, 78–9
funding of services, 111, 112

Gabarino, J. and Gilliam, G., 1
gender issues, 166, 197–9
gender of abusers, 31–2
Gil, E., 50, 141, 147, 183
Goodwin, J., 113, 178
Gross, M., 178
Grubman-Black, S., 3
guardian *ad litem*, 21–2
guilt, 22, 25, 107, 187

Haegar, B., 177
Hall, L., 151, 180
health visitors, 98
helper's relationships, 195–6
helping the helper, 201–3
Herman, J., 185
history of abuse, 2
holding, 166
hope, 152–3, 196–7
host personality, 115, 136, 137

imagery techniques, 180, 181
imprisonment of abusers, 21, 22
institutional care, 8–9, 28

Kempe, C., 2
Kempe, R.S., 2

Klein, M., 114
Kluft, R., 134

Lamb, S., 45
Leicestershire children's homes, 111
Lloyd, S., 151, 180
loss, 61–2, 122, 123, 159–62, 194
loss of memory, 26, 35, 57, 119, 123, 135, 137, 152, 165, 175, 191

marriage guidance counselling, 105
medical profession, 12, 97–8, 105, 107, 130
Meiselman, K., 185
Melanie Klein House, Greenwich, 111
memory loss, *see* loss of memory
Mental Health Act (1959), 12
mental health workers, 132–3
messages, 88–91
Metcalfe, M., 177
Miller, A., 165
Miles, R., 57
mothers, abuse by, 3, 40, 88
Mullen, P., 177
Multiple Personality Disorder, 113–42
    therapy of, 134–42
mutilation, 83, 126, 133, 184–5, 193

National Association for the Prevention of Cruelty to Children (NSPCC), 11, 109
National Association for Young People in Care (NAYPIC), 111
neglect, 29, 161
Newman, C., 48

Oppenheimer, R., 176
organized abuse, 43–4
over-involvement, 199–200

Palmer, R., 176
perpetrators of abuse, 29–31

persona, 116
physical effects of abuse, 31, 72, 189
'pin-down', 111
place of safety orders, 38
police, 23, 44, 130
presentations of abuse, 174–8
projective identification, 114
prosecution of abusers, 21
psychiatric care, 8, 12–13, 45, 103–4, 109–10, 112, 117, 130, 177
    use of drugs in, 9, 13, 103, 104, 107–10
psychologists, 44, 108, 117
Putman, F., 142

Racker, H., 149
Rampton Hospital, 9
rationalization, 150
reassurance, 151, 154, 179, 180, 188
recovery, blocks to, 190–4
regression, 14, 166
relationships, survivors',
    with others, 14–15
    with own children, 74–8
    with partners, 80–4, 188–90
relaxation techniques, 189–90
resistance, 2
resources, 112
revealing abuse, 96–110
revenge, 36, 71, 86, 193
rigidity, therapeutic, 174
ritual abuse, 3, 121

satanic abuse, 3
secrets, 14, 35, 177, 180, 189
self-forgiveness, 193
self-help groups, 120
self-mutilation, 12, 83, 126, 133, 184–5, 193
sexuality, effect of abuse on, 67, 69, 77–8, 81, 82, 83, 131, 180–1, 185–90
silences in therapy, 148–9
social services, *see* social work

social work, 18–19, 21–2, 29, 44, 90, 100, 111, 117, 130, 171
splitting, 114–15, 116, 119, 122, 124
Spring, J., 167
Staffordshire children's homes, 111
strategies for dealing with abuse, 19, 37–8
substance abuse, 121, 131, 176
suicide attempts, 9, 14, 44, 68, 69, 110, 130
supervision, 202–3
support group, 14
switching, 135

telling about abuse, 96–110
therapeutic communities, 13–14, 154

therapeutic process, 146–7, 154
therapeutic rigidity, 174
therapy, 14, 77, 84, 91, 110, 111, 116, 118, 123, 127, 130, 132, 133
  duration, 151–2
  ending, 168–73, 191–2
  initial stages, 144–52
  touch, 166
time, losing, 127, 135
touch, use of, 166
triggers, 183–5
trust, 14, 23–4, 75, 78–9, 95, 108, 134, 143, 147–9, 152, 203

Walker, M., 163
world of a child, 93–6